REA

ACPL ITE ‖‖‖‖‖‖‖‖‖‖‖‖‖‖‖‖‖‖‖‖‖‖‖‖ P9-EDI-939

DISCARDED
361

(The) Self-help sourcebook

THE SELF-HELP SOURCEBOOK

Finding & Forming Mutual Aid Self-Help Groups

4th Edition

Compiled and edited by

Barbara J. White and Edward J. Madara

American Self-Help Clearinghouse
Saint Clares-Riverside Medical Center
25 Pocono Road
Denville, New Jersey 07834

201/625-7101
TDD: 201/625-9053
CompuServe 70275,1003

Made possible by an initial grant from

*Hoffmann La Roche, Inc.
Department of Community Affairs
Nutley, New Jersey*

Allen County Public Library
900 Webster Street
PO Box 2270
Fort Wayne, IN 46801-2270

THE SELF-HELP SOURCEBOOK:
FINDING AND FORMING MUTUAL AID SELF-HELP GROUPS

Library of Congress Card Catalog Number: 87-641482
ISBN: 0-9634322-0-6
ISSN: 8756.1425

Published by St. Clares-Riverside Medical Center

Copyright   1986, 1988, 1990, 1992. All rights reserved.
No part of this publication may be reproduced or transmitted in
any form or by any means, or stored in any information storage
and retrieval system, without prior written permission of St.
Clares-Riverside Medical Center, 25 Pocono Rd., Denville, New
Jersey 07834.

*The logo on the cover was specifically designed for our
Self-Help Clearinghouse in 1981 by Ben Ruiz*

Cover jacket design by Williams Design Group, Inc.

DEDICATION

To all the self-help group founders who have had the courage to take those first steps, as well as those group members who are ever giving of themselves. Very real heroes... ordinary people who so often do such extraordinary things. Helping to make self-help groups into the truly unique caring communities that they come to be. This work is dedicated to their spirit... those whose efforts may never be fully acknowledged, because in very selfless or anonymous ways, they placed group needs ahead of personal recognition. May their initiative, dedication, and tireless volunteer efforts be an inspiration to others.

ACKNOWLEDGMENTS

First, we wish to express our sincerest and continued appreciation to all the **mutual aid self-help group members** who contributed information on their work in order to make this resource possible.

We are grateful to those persons who over the years have consistently shared leads and information on new groups, especially **Lisa Saisselin** (Self-Help Clearinghouse of Greater Washington, DC), **Mellen Kennedy** (Self-Help Center, Champaign County, Illinois), **Sue Kollmeyer** & **Toni Young** (Michigan Self-Help Clearinghouse), **Julie Gordon** (Mothers United for Mutual Support), **Pat Green** (Florida), **Joal Fischer** (SupportWorks, North Carolina), and **Barbara Fox** (Self-Help Information Services, Nebraska).

We extend our heartfelt appreciation to each of our outstanding volunteers - **Marge Archer, Joanne Bessor, Elaine Bloom, Dolores Bruzzi, Jackie Burd, Aldona Dauciunas, Lois Fallat, Howard Feinman, Jean Hansen, Hopes Henes, Ruth Kaplowitz, Jeannette Lee, Howard Neu, Mary Parrish, Ron Rossi, Paul Thormann, Evelyn Weber**, and **Helen Weiss**. Special thanks to **Esther Foster** for time spent developing special sections. Without their hard work and consistent efforts, this edition of the Sourcebook truly would not have been published. Through their continued updating, data entry, handling of referrals, detective work in tracking down new groups, and related support efforts, they continue to give of themselves to help so many others. Thanks to those other Clearinghouse staff who worked hard on this effort - **Gail DeGirolamo**, **Dottie Koziol**, and **Wendy Rodenbaugh**.

Appreciation is also given to the **New Jersey State Division of Mental Health and Hospitals** for their funding of the first statewide self-help clearinghouse in the country and the development of our national database that has helped so many hundreds of New Jersey residents start new self-help groups.

Finally, we wish to thank **Hoffmann La Roche, Inc.** for their support which made the Self-Help Sourcebook a reality and an on-going resource to communities across the country - as well as their initial support over thirteen years ago that resulted in publishing the first Directory of Self-Help Groups in New Jersey.

FOREWORD
- Alfred H. Katz, DSW

The biennial publication of this Sourcebook has been an extremely useful service for many people with diverse interests - individuals who are looking for a group to meet their special needs, professionals seeking an appropriate referral point for a client, or information about a problem, academics and researchers who want local or national self-help group contacts and information, policy-makers at all levels of government, media people seeking personal reactions to recent crises.

But the significance and value of this publication exceeds the simple purpose of providing accurate information on the growth and ever-widening scope of the world of self-help, mutual aid groups. It marks the growing maturity and acceptance of a dynamic social movement that is increasingly seen as an integral part of the American culture, way of life and ethos, and as an important social resource. The values of cooperative self-organization, non-bureaucratic mutual helping methods exemplified by the hundreds of organizations listed in this Sourcebook have penetrated the general culture inescapably and irreversibly. Self-help is seen as a social resource so that people no longer have to suffer in isolation or feel despair that they can find no help in confronting and coping with their problems.

Self-help, mutual aid groups provide an accepting environment of social support that may not be available from other sources - family, neighbors, friends, work-mates and social institutions, such as religious, human service and educational organizations. Their help can have the intimacy and informality of the best family and neighborly assistance to those with short-term or longer needs. There is usually no financial barrier to joining them and using their services - need, and a wish to participate are the only criteria for membership.

They usually bring together accurate, up-to-date information on resources and methods for coping with the problem; they often include people at different stages of dealing with it, so that newcomers can learn from the more experienced.

Both the 12-step groups on the A.A. model and non-12-step groups provide philosophies and methodologies for personal growth and change, role models of people who successfully cope, recognition for personal effort and achievement, and opportunities to contribute to the well-being of others. Many groups also engage in education and actions and advocacy that have furthered and often led to change in government and private institutional policies and programs. A result of these varied activities and interactions in the self-help groups is a growth in self-confidence, self-esteem and psychological well-being for the individual member, and of confidence, cohesion and effectiveness of the group. In these ways, the self-help movement can be viewed as an important contributor to social development - the historic process of growth toward a positive, humane, people-oriented society. Self-help's philosophy is that of working with people in a mutually helping way, that is non-bureaucratic, holistic, open to change, and that recognizes and seeks to optimize the inherent strengths and capacities of individuals, families, community groups and institutions.

This is not to imply that self-help is a panacea for all problems-- material, environmental, political, of the society, or that self-help groups are without many difficulties--internal strains of growth, lack of resources, personality and program conflicts, leadership burnout, and so on. Like all human organizations, they are subject to human weaknesses, and do not always overcome them.

But as the vast variety and continuing dynamic growth of groups this Sourcebook illustrates, in late 20th century America (and elsewhere in the modern world), they are an indispensable human resource, a permanent and major social utility. ♦

Dr. Katz has served as Professor (Emeritus) in the U.C.L.A. departments of Medicine, Public Health, and Social Welfare. His ten books, and more than one hundred professional articles, have included Parents of the Handicapped (1961), The Strength in Us: Self-Help Groups in the Modern World (1976), Helping One Another: Self-Help Groups in a Changing World (1990), and Self-Help: Concepts and Applications (1992). In regards to promoting an increased recognition and understanding of self-help group efforts, he has been a consultant to the World Health Organization, the Ford Foundation, and many government and voluntary agencies.

TABLE OF CONTENTS

SELF-HELP GROUP LISTINGS

6

Health (cont'd)

Health (cont'd)

8

Health (cont'd)

Health (cont'd)

Mental Health

Parenting / Family

Physical / Emotional Abuse

Other Miscellaneous

OTHER RESOURCES

HOW TO USE THE SOURCEBOOK

To Find A Group

To find a mutual aid self-help group for your concern, you may want to begin by reviewing the section on **Self-Help Clearinghouses** to see if there is a clearinghouse which serves your community. Self-help clearinghouses can provide you with information on existing local self-help groups, especially on many of those local "one-of-a-kind" groups that are not affiliated with any of the national self-help organizations listed in this directory.

Next, check the **table of contents** in the front of the book, and the **key word index** section at the end of the book to find page references for a specific self-help group issue. The index will refer you to pages in the directory where any groups related to that listing will be found.

In the self-help group listing section, please note the various types of entries included. Most of the entries are for **national self-help organizations**. In italics, we have noted the area served (national or international), the number of affiliated groups, and the year founded. You can then use the information in the group listing to contact these national groups to determine if they have any local meetings or chapters in your area. Even if they have no group in your area, you may want to subscribe to their newsletter or participate in any other mutual support activities they offer (e.g. correspondence or phone network, conferences, etc.). In addition, they may be able to provide you with information on starting a group in your area.

We have also included **model** groups which have only one meeting or are limited to one geographic area. **We have included the model groups primarily to help those persons who may be interested in starting such a group in their local community,** so they do not have to "reinvent the wheel." We kindly request that you only contact model groups if you are interested in developing such a group in your community, since model groups often are very limited in their ability to respond to more general inquiries.

There are some issues for which we have been unable to identify any national or model self-help groups (e.g. rape). However, there are resources available to help those persons interested in developing support systems around such issues. Entries entitled **Resource** (organizations providing technical support and/or information & referrals), and **Guide** (manual or how-to material) offer assistance that may be of benefit to you.

To Form a Group

If you are indeed interested in starting a new group in your local area, we have included some suggestions in our "How-To Ideas for Developing Groups" section at the end of the book. In that same section we have included some separate guidelines for the professional who seeks to help start a self-help group, ideally serving as an "on tap, not on top" consultant to persons interested in developing a group. If you are interested in forming a group, check with the national and/or model groups listed herein, as well as with any local self-help clearinghouses, to learn more about how they might assist you in starting the new group. In most cases, national groups can provide you with assistance and printed guidelines for starting a local affiliated group or chapter.

In Contacting any Group

When writing to a group, always include a **self-addressed stamped envelope** to make it easier for them to respond. Many of the national group headquarters actually operate out of "kitchen table offices" and most run on "shoestring budgets." When phoning a group, keep in mind that many of these phone contacts are home numbers so please be considerate of the hour at which you phone, and keep in mind the different time zones. Please understand that several tries may be necessary.

Other Sourcebook Sections

For persons interested in finding or forming a self-help group for a relatively rare disorder or genetic illness, we have additional sections on Resources for Rare Disorders and Genetic Illnesses. In addition, we have noted resources for the Homeless, and for Housing. There is also a brief review of the use of Home Computers for networking and on-line conference meetings - a medium that is only in its infancy but has potential for expanding to meet the needs of persons who cannot attend a local face-to-face group meeting.

Just as self-help groups provide free information on resources and ways that help people deal with a wide variety of human problems, there are an increasing number of national toll-free helplines that help reduce the frustration in finding such information. Although these are not run by self-help groups, we continue to include a full section on National Toll-Free Helplines since they can be helpful, cost-free sources of information for individuals and groups alike.

If you would like to read more about self-help groups, there are a number of references in the Bibliography section.

To Better Understand the Term "Self-Help Groups"

Have you ever noticed when you have a problem, how it helps to talk with someone who has had a similar problem? Simply finding others who have "been there" and then realizing that "you are not alone" can be very comforting and helpful. The Sourcebook has been compiled to help you more easily find and form a self-help group--one that can provide such needed support, as well as practical information, education and sometimes needed advocacy.

The self-help groups listed on the following pages can better be described as Mutual Aid Self-Help groups because they derive their energy from members helping one another, without forms or fees. In examining the hundreds of national organizations, societies and foundations that exist for different illnesses, addictions, parenting and other stressful life situations and transitions, we have sought to identify those organizations that provide these mutual help opportunities. In addition to "mutual support," three other key characteristics of self-help groups that constitute our general criteria are: that the group be composed of "peers," people who share a common experience or situation; that the group or network be primarily run by and for its members, who therefore have a sense of "ownership" for the group or network; and that the group be voluntary, non-profit, i.e., they can "pass the hat," charge dues, or fundraise, but there are no fees for services.

Dr. Silverman, in her introduction to self-help groups on page 18, describes some of the characteristics and dynamics of self-help groups, and how these differ from professionally-run groups and services. Self-help groups can provide benefits that professional services cannot. But self-help groups are not meant to replace needed professional services, although they supplement, support and sometimes even develop them, as well as often prevent the very need for them.

We should point out that there are other types of community organizations that are sometimes described as self-help, including civic, housing, fraternal, business, ethnic and political groups. However, these groups, by their very numbers and broader focus, would warrant or already have separate directories of their own.

Also, please understand that the quality of individual self-help groups will differ, sometimes even among those with the same name. Contact and visit the group to see if it is for you. While initial research reflects the value of self-help groups, the ultimate evaluation and very survival of any self-help group is determined by those who attend it and decide to stay and contribute to it.

Please Note

The Clearinghouse has made every effort to include as many different self-help groups as possible. However, the Clearinghouse reserves the right to include or exclude any names, groups or telephone contacts at its absolute discretion. Omission of an organization does not signify disapproval. Inclusion of an organization does not signify approval. The use of any of the materials herein is entirely the responsibility of the reader. The Clearinghouse further disclaims any and all liability for any use or non-use of the materials herein. There are no warranties implied or expressed in any of the data provided herein. The information provided herein is based upon data supplied by the groups themselves. The Clearinghouse is not responsible for printing, insertion or deletion errors.

Know of a National or Model Group that Should be Included In the Next Edition of the Sourcebook?

We would be most grateful if you would let us know about any new or existing groups that you suggest be included in the next edition of the Sourcebook. We also would appreciate your comments and suggestions as to how the Sourcebook may be improved. Simply advise us by writing to us at: The American Self-Help Clearinghouse, Attn: Sourcebook Suggestion, St. Clares-Riverside Medical Center, 25 Pocono Rd., Denville, N.J. 07834.

"Today, the benefits of mutual aid are experienced by millions of people who turn to others with a similar problem to attempt to deal with their isolation, powerlessness, alienation, and the awful feeling that nobody understands...The future of health care in these troubled times requires cooperation between organized medicine and self-help groups to achieve the best care for the lowest cost."

- Former Surgeon General C. Everett Koop, for the Forward of the book, Self-Help: Concepts and Applications, Charles Press, 1992, p. xviii.

ABOUT THE CLEARINGHOUSE

The Sourcebook is the result of two self-help clearinghouse programs. Work in supporting self-help group efforts first began in 1978, when here at St. Clares-Riverside Medical Center we started to pull together a listing of "hard to find" self-help groups for a wide variety of stressful life problems. Most hospital and mental health center staff knew of only a few groups. When we advised them of others, they reported back how grateful their patients were to find out that they were not alone and that there was such a support group available. In 1979, we compiled the first directory of self-help groups in New Jersey. Unlike other directories, we added national and model groups that didn't exist in New Jersey, in order to show people what new self-help groups they could develop if they were willing to join with others. At the same time, we had seen how easy it was for us to link interested people together resulting in the development of many new groups.

In 1980, we submitted a proposal to the New Jersey State Division of Mental Health and Hospitals to establish the first statewide self-help clearinghouse in order to increase the awareness, utilization, and development of self-help groups. Subsequently, in January of 1981, the New Jersey Self-Help Clearinghouse was started. With additional new state directory editions, our listings of national and model groups grew - as did the number of people who were able to start new groups throughout the state with assistance from a national or model group listed in the directory. Since its start, the New Jersey Self-Help Clearinghouse has assisted in the development of over 580 new groups in the state. A wide variety of consultation, training, information and referral services are available to those persons in New Jersey who simply dial us at 800-FOR-M.A.S.H. (Mutual Aid Self-Help).

In 1982, we began to share our national listings with other self-help clearinghouses through our MASHnet computer program and database which has been used by 18 other self-help clearinghouses in the U.S. and Canada. Our M.A.S.H. Networking Project service was then started in 1984 to help individuals outside New Jersey start new networks that didn't previously exist anywhere in the country. Names of persons interested in starting new types of groups were listed on that same database alongside existing groups. In that way, interested callers could be referred to join those starting groups. Over a dozen new "first-of-their-kind" self-help groups or networks were started as a result.

The Clearinghouse listing of national and model groups had proved so helpful to others outside New Jersey, that with funding from Hoffmann La Roche, Inc., the first edition of The Self-Help

Sourcebook, was published in 1986 to make that information on those groups more widely available and known.

One way that we have sought to help more people learn about self-help groups is through our outreach efforts to the media. Prior mailings of the Sourcebook, with cover letters suggesting coverage of self-help groups, resulted in significant articles in Psychology Today, USA Today, American Health, FIRST for Women, Parade, New Age, New Physician, Better Homes & Gardens, and many other national magazines and professional newsletters.

In 1990, with funding from the St. Clares-Riverside Medical Center and the St. Clares-Riverside Foundation, and with the help of additional volunteers, the American Self-Help Clearinghouse program was added. In addition to the Sourcebook, it provides the following services:

Information and Referral For information on a group, phone 201/625-7101, or via TDD 201/625-9053, between 9am and 5pm Eastern time. Staff and volunteers can provide callers with information and contacts on any national self-help groups that deal with their particular concern. If no appropriate national group exists and the caller is interested in the possibility of joining with others to start a local group, we can often provide information on model groups operating in other parts of the country, or individuals who are starting networks and seeking others to help develop them. We also provide callers with information on any local self-help clearinghouse that may exist to serve them in their area.

Consultation - If there is no group or support network that exists anywhere in the country for your problem and you are interested in starting a mutual help group or network, contact the Clearinghouse for help with suggestions, materials, and networking.

We firmly believe **the most powerful potential of self-help is in the ability of people who are in need to come together and start needed new groups and networks.** Through the work of both self-help clearinghouses, we strive to help more people tap that potential for the benefit of themselves and for so many others.

AN INTRODUCTION TO SELF-HELP GROUPS

- Phyllis Silverman, Ph.D.

Let me begin by describing my own personal experience in a mutual help group. The first group that I became formally involved in was the La Leche League. It was of interest to me because at that time I was having difficulty in nursing my first child. She was nursing frequently and for excessively long periods of time, she slept very little and fussed when left alone in the crib. A mother of ten said to me: Get an infant seat for the table so she can watch the family and lie down in bed with her when you nurse. With those two statements she changed my entire relationship with my newborn and made the first year of her life a very wonderful and exciting period. That experience introduced me to the value of a "mutual help" group and the knowledge it can provide and helped join my personal and professional interests. (It was at this time that I discovered in my work that another widow was the most appropriate helper for newly widowed.)

A mutual help exchange occurs when people, who share a problem or predicament, come together to help one another. This occurs, for example, when parents form a baby-sitting cooperative. In the broadest sense, such exchanges of resources and care are the basis of society, and no social life is possible without mutual aid. Usually this aid is casual and informal, but natural helping networks sometimes develop into voluntary organizations, intentional communities in which members control the resources and make policy decisions. The help they offer is usually based on the experiences of veteran members. Although such groups are called self-help groups, the term "mutual help" is more appropriate.

As you will see in glancing over the pages of this directory, in our heterogeneous, mobile society of the late 20th century, the number and variety of mutual help groups has been increasing. This is partly a reaction to the expansion of professionalism and the accompanying depersonalization of consumers. There are others who believe that the mutual help movement can democratize and "humanize" the human service system by involving consumers more in their own care. But the development of these organizations is mainly due to people's need to find others like themselves who have experienced a similar problem. Mutual help groups are especially attractive to persons undergoing a transition that requires a shift in social roles -- whether they are recovering alcoholics, former mental patients or new parents.

Mutual help groups are more fluid than bureaucracies or professional organizations, but over time they tend to formalize their policies and practices. Some groups, such as Gray Panthers and the Mental Patient Liberation Movement, are governed wholly by consensus. "Liberation" groups usually avoid hierarchical organization, sacrificing efficiency for maximum participation. Other groups, such as Parents Without Partners, follow parliamentary procedures in establishing committees and electing officers. The La Leche League and others are organized as service delivery systems with authority vested in a national office and leadership recruited through an elaborate ascending hierarchy, always from people who have been helped by the group. But when a hierarchy exists, leaders have no way to enforce their authority, and members leave when the group stops meeting their needs. In many groups an informal consensus determines policy and rules are invented as required.

Actually, most local groups are small (10-20 people) and constantly struggling to survive. The simplest type of national organization is a loose network of autonomous groups. The most common is an association supported by dues from affiliated local branches or chapters that are authorized to use its name. Many of these national associations have paid staff who develop program materials for the local groups and provide consultants from regional offices. Examples are: Alcoholics Anonymous, Parents Without Partners, La Leche League and Compassionate Friends (for parents who have lost a child).

The support provided by mutual help organizations has a special meaning. The helper and the beneficiary are peers and everyone in the group can be both. Not being bound to the role of either helper or recipient may in itself have therapeutic value. Discovering that others have the same problem, members of mutual help groups no longer feel alone. Their feelings and experiences are legitimized, and they are provided with a framework for coping: "The most important thing for me was finding someone like me. When I walked into the room and found 50 other widows, I can't explain the good feeling it gave me."

Each organization develops a body of relevant information and strategies: "When I get nervous now I follow the guidelines I learned at the meeting; it really works." The best known of these is the "Twelve Steps" of Alcoholics Anonymous, which have been adapted to the needs of many other anonymous groups that you will find in the directory dealing with problems such as gambling, overeating and drug abuse.

Groups concerned with disabilities or with such universal problems as bereavement use a more flexible approach. The wisdom of experience amassed in these organizations provides a unique contribution distinct from the professional knowledge learned in schools. One member of such a group commented "When she said she understood, I knew she meant it. I needed to hear how she managed before anything else." Another person said, "I needed to have a name for what was bothering me. I could figure out what to do when someone explained what I needed, given my situation."

Methods of Helping The assistance provided by mutual help groups may include educational seminars, one-to-one exchanges and social gatherings, in addition to the basic sharing of personal experiences and small informal meetings. "When I got up at a meeting to talk and everyone listened, I can't tell you how much confidence it gave me," says a member of a Laryngectomy Club."

Some organizations have hotlines for immediate aid to persons in need. Many have outreach programs in which members make unsolicited offers of help; for example, members of Mended Hearts visit patients in the hospital before and after coronary surgery, and programs for widows and widowers often send a note to the bereaved shortly after the funeral. One widow said "I would never have gotten out, but when she called and said she was a widow I asked her to come right over. I didn't think I would be able to get up in the morning. She told me everyone feels that way; she did too. If she has energy to help me now, I realized I would be all right. She said it takes time. I needed to know that too."

Many organizations have formal orientation or training programs for outreach volunteers, facilitators in small group discussions, and for officers and leaders of other programs. Observing the usefulness of mutual help groups, professional agencies have begun to sponsor groups of their own, choosing the participants and convening the meetings themselves. Since members do not control resources and direct policy, these are technically not mutual help groups and do not accomplish the same ends. The context in which help is offered may critically change its nature and effects. The more professionals are involved, the more likely it is to resemble group therapy or another professional service under a different name. This can be unintentionally deceptive.

Professional human service agencies and mutual help groups sometimes have a tense and competitive relationship. Group members sometimes believe themselves to have been ill-served by professional helping systems, and members may be encouraged to only consult one another. Historically, professionals have sometimes tried to co-opt mutual help organizations, and they are often regarded as intruders. When groups turn to agencies for assistance, a struggle for control may result.

But most mutual help organizations are not anti-professional and collaboration is possible if there is a mutual respect and understanding. For example, La Leche League, the Ostomy society (for people who have undergone ileostomy and related surgery), and Recovery, Inc. (serving former mental patients) have professional advisory committees that provide medical information enabling members to become competent consumers of the services they need. Parents Anonymous (for child abusers) has also brought professionals into its programs.

Self-help clearinghouses, which are also listed in this directory, have been instrumental in promoting the increased identification, awareness and utilization of groups through their information, referral and consultation services. Some, like the NJ Self-Help Clearinghouse, have focused their primary efforts on the development of needed new mutual help groups.

In summary, mutual help groups are a powerful and constructive means for people to help themselves and each other. The basic dignity of each human being is expressed in his or her capacity to be involved in a reciprocal helping exchange. Out of this compassion comes cooperation. From this cooperation comes community. With the increased awareness and understanding of these national groups and models, as this resource directory seeks to promote, the number of mutual help communities will continue to grow -- and continue to provide their members with the direction, values and hope they need. In a sense, they speak for all of us since even those of us who study these groups as professionals are consumers. ♦

Dr. Silverman is a Professor on the faculty of the Institute of Health Professions of Massachusetts General Hospital and is the Co-Director of the Child Bereavement Study Project there. She also holds an appointment in the Dept. of Psychiatry at Harvard Medical School. She has served as consultant to several task forces on bereavement, mutual help and prevention and has worked in community agencies both as a case worker and as a researcher. Within the Lab of Community Psychiatry at Harvard Medical School, she developed the concept of the widow-to-widow program and directed the research that demonstrated its effect. In addition to her social work degree from Smith College of Social Work, she holds an MS in hygiene from Harvard School of Public Health and a Ph.D. from the Florence Heller School for Advanced Studies in Social Welfare at Brandeis University. Her works include Helping Each Other in Widowhood, If You Will Lift It I Will Lift It Too, Mutual Help Groups: A Guide for Mental Health Professionals, Mutual Help Groups: Organization and Development, Helping Women Cope with Grief and Widow to Widow.

THE SERENITY PRAYER

God grant me

the Serenity to accept the things I cannot change.

the courage to change the things I can,

and the wisdom to know the difference.

- Reinhold Niebuhr

The Serenity Prayer has been used by a wide variety of self-help groups for many years. In its simplicity, it has provided insight, support and courage to countless numbers of persons struggling with different addictions, disabilities, bereavement, illnesses and other stressful life problems.

ADDICTIONS

ADDICTION (GENERAL)
(also see also specific addiction)

Anesthetists in Recovery *National. Founded 1984.* Network of recovering anesthetists & their families. Referrals to groups. Information on treatment. Write: 2205 22nd Ave. South, Minneapolis, MN 55404. Call 612/724-8238.

Chemically Dependent Anonymous *Nat'l. 85 affiliated groups. Founded 1980.* Purpose is to carry the message of recovery to the chemically dependent person. For those with a desire to abstain from drugs/alcohol. Information & referrals, phone support, conferences. Group development guidelines. Write: P.O. Box 423, Severna Park, MD 21146. Call 301/647-7060.

I.C.A.P. (Intercongregational Alcoholism Program) *Int'l. Founded 1979.* Network of recovering alcoholic women in religious orders. Roman Catholic women who are (or have been) members of religious orders who are in need of help due to alcoholism or chemical dependencies. Information & referrals, assistance in meeting other members, phone support, conferences, newsletters. Write: 1515 N. Harlem Ave., #311, Oak Park, IL 60302. Call 708/445-1400; 445-1418 (FAX).

Int'l Doctors in A.A. *Int'l. Founded 1949.* Support network for doctors in the healing arts who suffer with alcoholism or chemical dependency in themselves or their families. Write: P.O. Box 199, Augusta, MO 63332. Call 314/781-1317.

Int'l Nurses Anonymous *Int'l* Fellowship of RNs, LPNs, & nursing students who are in recovery from chemical dependency, co-dependency, or involved in any 12 Step program. Quarterly newsletter. Write: c/o Pat G., 1020 Sunset Dr., Lawrence, KS 66044. Call 913/842-3893 or 913/749-2626 (day).

Int'l Pharmacists Anonymous *National. Founded 1987.* Fellowship of pharmacists & pharmacy students recovering from addiction to alcohol, drugs or gambling. Members must belong to a 12-step group. Newsletter, conferences, meetings, networking. Write: Nan, 32 Cedar Grove Rd., Annandale, NJ 08801. Call 908/735-2789 or 908/730-9072.

J.A.C.S. (Jewish Alcoholics, Chemically Dependent Persons & Significant Others) *National. Founded 1980.* For alcoholic & chemically dependent Jews, their families, & their communities. Networking, 12-step work, retreats, newsletter, literature. Help in starting local chapters. Speakers bureau. Write: 426 W. 58th St., New York, NY 10019. Call 212/397-4197.

"Just Say No" Int'l *Int'l. 13,000 clubs. Founded 1985.* Helps communities form "Just Say No Clubs" - groups of children (ages 7-14) who are committed to not using drugs, tobacco or alcohol. Offers educational, social, community service, & outreach activities. Newsletter, group development guidelines. Provides materials, technical assistance & training. Write: 2101 Webster St. #1300, Oakland, CA 94612. Call 800-258-2766.

Overcomers Outreach, Inc. *Int'l. 943 affiliated groups. Founded 1985.* Christian ministry of self-help groups for persons who could benefit from a secular 12-step group in the Christian community. Includes alcoholics, drug addicts, compulsive overeaters, gamblers, sexual addicts, co-dependents, etc. Newsletter, group development guidelines, conferences. Write: 2290 W. Whittier Blvd., Suite A/D, LaHabra, CA 90631. Call 213/697-3994.

Overcomers, Victory Through Christ *Int'l. 120 affiliated groups. Founded 1987.* A recovery program dealing with every aspect of addiction & dysfunction (spiritual, physical, mental, emotional, & social). Uses the Overcomers Steps which are Christ-centered. Newsletter, information & referrals, groups meetings. Assistance in starting groups. Literature. Write: 4905 N. 96th St., Omaha, NE 68134. Call 402-397-3317 (day).

Psychologists Helping Psychologists *National network. Founded 1980.* For doctoral level psychologists, including students, who had a personal experience with alcohol or drugs. Primary purpose to support each other in our recovery and to help others to recover. Tries to educate psychology community. Regional/national get-togethers, newsletter. Write: Jane Skorina, Ph.D., 17023 Cambridge St., Allen Park, MI 48101-3112. Call 313/278-1314; or Martha Dugan, Ph.D., 240 Waverly Pl., #54, NY, NY 10018. Call Martha 212/989-7628.

Rational Recovery Systems *Int'l. 350 groups. Founded 1986.* Helps persons achieve recovery from substance abuse & addictive behavior through self-reliance & self-help groups. Non-religious; based on rational-emotive therapy. Newsletter, group development guidelines; Member-run groups with professional advisors. Write: P.O. Box 800, Lotus, CA 95651. Call 916/621-4374.

RCA (Recovering Couples Anonymous) *National. 50 groups. Founded 1988.* 12-step group that helps couples restore intimacy, communication, trust & learn healthier tools for maintaining these elements. For couples involved in a committed relationship. Provides information & referrals, support group meetings. Group development guidelines. ($25). Write: P.O. Box 27617, Golden Valley, MN 55422. Call Deb M. 612/473-3752.

Secular Organizations for Sobriety (Save Ourselves) *Int'l. 1000 groups. Founded 1986.* Mutual help for alcoholics & addicts who want to acknowledge their disease & maintain sobriety as a separate issue from religion or spirituality. Newsletter. Guidelines & assistance available for starting groups. Write: P.O. Box 5, Buffalo, NY 14215. Call 716-834-2922.

Social Workers Helping Social Workers *National. 3 groups. Founded 1980.* To promote recovery from chemical dependency among social workers or matriculating students. Newsletter, annual retreat, group development guidelines. Write: 25 South St., Goshen, CT 06756. Call 203/489-3808 (answering service).

(Model) **Adoptive & Foster Parents of FAS & Drug-Affected Children** A support network for adoptive & foster parents of children affected by fetal alcohol syndrome or pre-natal drug use. Open to those who suspect their adopted/foster child may be affected as well. Support group meetings, literature. Write: BCCA & DA, P.O. Box 626, Paramus, NJ 07653. Call Ronnie Jacobs 201/261-1450.

(Model) **Chapter Nine Group of Hollywood** *Founded 1989.* 12-Step program of recovering couples (addictions/substance abuse) in which partners work together. Group name comes from Chapter Nine of the A.A. Big Book "The Family Afterward," based on the belief that members of the family or couple should meet upon the common ground of tolerance, understanding & love. Write: Don Justice, 1168 White Sands Dr., Lusby, MD 20657. Call 301/586-1425.

(Model) **Chemically Dependent Anonymous** *90 affiliated groups. Founded 1980.* Purpose is to carry the message of recovery to the chemically dependent person. For those with a desire to abstain from drugs/alcohol. Information & referrals, phone support, conferences. Group development guidelines. Write: P.O. Box 423, Severna Park, MD 21146. Call 301/647-7060.

Please remember: Model groups should be used primarily by those interested in starting similar groups in their area.

(Model) **Clergy Serving Clergy** *Founded 1987.* Volunteer group of recovering clergy giving help & support to one another. Assists in the identification, early intervention, proper treatment & productive recovery from the abuse of alcohol or other chemicals by clergy & family members. Quarterly newsletter. Write: 3509 Dana Dr., Burnsville, MN 55337. Call 612/894-4582.

(Model) **Dentists Concerned for Dentists** *Founded 1978.* Assists dentists with recovery from alcoholism or chemical dependency, or other human problems (family/marital, mental health, financial, etc). Group development guidelines. Write: 450 N. Syndicate #117, St. Paul, MN 55104. Call 612/641-0730.

(Model) **Dual Disorders Anonymous** *23 groups in Illinois. Founded 1982.* Fellowship of men & women who come together to help those members who still suffer from both mental disorder & alcoholism and/or drug addiction. Uses the 12-step program of A.A. Group development guidelines. Write: P.O. Box 4045, Des Plaines, IL 60016. Call 708-462-3380.

(Model) **Recovering Counselors Network** *Founded 1988.* Support for recovering counselors who are working in the field of chemical dependency. Group development guidelines. Write: 425 S. Lexington Parkway, St. Paul, MN 55105. Call 612/690-0306.

ALCOHOLISM
(also see Addictions - General)

A.A. (Alcoholics Anonymous) World Services, Inc. *Int'l. 94,000 groups. Founded 1935.* Fellowship sharing experience, strength & hope with each other so they may solve their common problem & help others achieve sobriety. A.A.'s sole purpose is to help the sick alcoholic recover through the 12 Steps of A.A. A.A. literature is interpretive of the A.A. program, not the general subject of alcoholism. Write: General Service Office, A.A. World Services, Inc., 475 Riverside Dr., 11th Fl., New York, NY 10115. Call 212-870-3400. For local meeting info look up A.A. in your local phone book or newspaper.

Adult Children of Alcoholics World Service Organization *Int'l. 1800+ meetings. Founded 1976.* A 12-step program of discovery and recovery for adults who realize that the characteristics which allowed them to survive as children in an alcoholic dysfunctional home now prevent them from fully experiencing life. Group development guidelines. Newsletter. Write: ACA, P.O. Box 3216, Torrance, CA 90510. Call 310/534-1815.

Al-Anon Family Groups *Int'l. 32000+ groups. Founded 1951.* Fellowship of men, women, children & adult children whose lives have been affected by the compulsive drinking of a family member or friend. Follows the 12-steps adopted from A.A. Guidelines for starting groups. Literature available in 29 languages. Write: P.O. Box 862, Midtown Station, New York, NY 10018-6106. Call 212/ 302-7240 or 800-344-2666 (meetings) or 800-356-9996 (general).

Alateen/Ala-preteen/Alatot *Int'l. 4100+ chapters. Founded 1957.* Fellowship of young Al-Anon members, usually teenagers, whose lives have been affected by someone else's drinking. Adult member of Al-Anon serves as a sponsor for each group. Based on the 12-steps. Group development guidelines. Literature available in 29 languages. Call 212/302-7240 or 800-344-2666. Write: P.O. Box 862 Midtown Station, New York, NY 10018-0862

Calix Society *National. 44 chapters. Founded 1947.* Helps Catholic alcoholics maintain their sobriety through Alcoholics Anonymous. Concerned w/total abstinence, spiritual development & sanctification of the whole personality of each member. Bi-monthly newsletter. Assistance in chapter development. Write: c/o Rolf Olson, 7601 Wayzata Blvd., Minneapolis, MN 55426. Call 612/546-0544 (mornings only).

I.L.A.A. (Int'l Lawyers in Alcoholics Anonymous) *Int'l. 40+ affiliated groups. Founded 1975.* Serves as a clearinghouse of support groups for lawyers who are recovering alcoholics. Newsletters, annual conventions. Group development guidelines. Write: 14643 Sylvan St., Van Nuys, CA 91411.

Nat'l Assn. for Native American Children of Alcoholics *National. 13 independent regional groups. Founded 1988.* Support network for Native American children of alcoholics. Provides education & training, newsletter, & conferences. Training manual ($20). Write: P.O. Box 18736, Seattle, WA 98118. Call 206/322-5601.

Women For Sobriety *Int'l. 350 groups. Founded 1976.* Program designed specifically to help the woman alcoholic achieve sobriety. Addresses need to overcome depression & guilt. Monthly newsletter, information & referrals, phone support, group meetings, pen pals, conferences, & group development guidelines. Write: P.O. Box 618, Quakertown, PA 18951-0618. Call 215/536-8026 or 800-333-1606.

CO-DEPENDENCY
(also see Addictions - General)

Co-Dependents Anonymous *Int'l. 3500+ groups worldwide. Founded 1986.* Fellowship of men, women & teens whose common problem is an inability to maintain functional relationships. Members desire healthy, fulfilling relationships with others & themselves. Follows the 12-step program adapted from A.A. Newsletter, literature, audio tapes. Write: P.O. Box 33577, Phoenix, AZ 85067-3577. Call 602/277-7991; 602/274-6111 (FAX).

Codependents Anonymous for Helping Professionals (CODAHP) *Int'l. 20+ affiliated groups. Founded 1985.* 12-Step group for professionals working in human services who are in recovery from codependency. Quarterly newsletter, group development guidelines ($5). Write: P.O. Box 42253, Mesa, AZ 85212. Call 602/468-1149.

(Model) **Nat'l Assn. of Adult Children of Dysfunctional Families** *Regional. Founded 1990.* Aims to raise awareness regarding the adult child of dysfunctional family syndrome. Facilitates networking of survivors & professionals alike, to assist Adult Children to move from victims to advocates through recovery. Newsletter, workshops, booklets, conferences; 12-step Starter Packets ($5). Write: Amy D., P.O. Box 463, Fond du Lac, WI 54936-0463. Call 414/921-6991.

DEBT / OVERSPENDING
(also see Addictions - General)

Debtors Anonymous General Service Board *National. 400+ groups. Founded 1976.* Fellowship that follows the 12-step program for mutual help in recovering from compulsive indebtedness. Primary purpose of members is to stay solvent & help other compulsive debtors achieve solvency. Newsletter, phone support network. Write: P.O. Box 400 Grand Central Station, New York, NY 10163-0400. Call 212/642-8222 for recorded message or 212/642-8220 to leave message.

DRUG ABUSE
(also see Addictions - General)

Co-Anon Family Groups *Int'l. 42 groups. Founded 1985.* 12-step program for friends & family of people who have problems with cocaine or other drugs. Phone support, help in starting new groups. WEST: P.O. Box 64742-66, Los Angeles, CA 90064. Call 714/647-6698 or 818/377-4317 (CA). EAST: P.O. Box 1080 Cooper Station, NY, NY 10276-1080. Call 212/713-5133 or 203/647-3694.

Cocaine Anonymous *Int'l. 1500 chapters. Founded 1982.* Fellowship of men & women who share their experiences, strengths & hopes that they may solve their common problem & help others to recover from addiction. Quarterly newsletter. Group starter kit available. Write: 3740 Overland Ave., #H, Los Angeles, CA 90034. For meeting info. call 800-347-8998 (24 hr.) or 310/559-5833 (business office).

Drugs Anonymous (formerly Pills Anonymous) *National. 10 groups.* Self-help, self-supporting, anonymous 12-step program, based on A.A., for those who want to help themselves & others recover from chemical addiction. Call 212/874-0700.

Families Anonymous *National. 500 groups. Founded 1971.* Mutual support for relatives & friends concerned about the use of drugs or related behavioral problems. Based upon the 12-step program adopted from A.A. Bi-monthly newsletter. Write: P.O. Box 528, Van Nuys, CA 91408. Call 800-736-9805 or 818/989-7841.

Nar-Anon, Inc. *Int'l. Founded 1967.* World-wide organization offering self-help recovery to families & friends of addicts. A 12-step program structured like Al-Anon. Provides group packet for starting new groups. Write: P.O. Box 2562, Palos Verdes, CA 90274-0119. Call 310/547-5800.

Narcotics Anonymous *Int'l. 22,000 groups. Founded 1953.* Fellowship of men & women for whom drugs had become a major problem. Recovering addicts meet regularly to help each other stay clean. Monthly magazine. Pen pal program, group development guidelines. Literature in Braille, 7 languages, audiotapes. Write: P.O. Box 9999, Van Nuys, CA 91409. Call 818/780-3951.

National Federation of Parents for Drug-Free Youth *National. 84 chapters. Founded 1980.* Information, networking, newsletter, & guidelines for parents forming groups to address drug abuse problems among adolescents. Youth training program, telephone support network, Red Ribbon Campaign (3rd week Oct.). Write: NFP, 11159-B S Towne Sq., St. Louis, MO 63123 Call 314/968-1322.

Pill Addicts Anonymous *Int'l. 6 groups. Founded 1979.* Fellowship for all who seek freedom from addiction to prescribed & over-the-counter mood-changing pills & drugs. Sharing of experience, strength & hope to stay clean & help others achieve sobriety. Follows the 12-Steps of A.A. Group development guidelines ($10). Write: P.O. Box 278, Reading, PA 19603. Call 215/372-1128.

GAMBLING
(also see Addictions - General)

Gam-Anon Family Groups *Int'l. 380 groups. Founded 1960.* Provides help for family members & friends of compulsive gamblers by offering comfort, hope & friendship through shared experiences. Newsletter. Gam-a-teen groups for teens. Group development guidelines & literature available. Write: P.O. Box 157, Whitestone, NY 11357. Call 718/352-1671 (Tues. & Thurs. only btwn. 9am-noon).

Gamblers Anonymous *Int'l. 1200 chapters. Founded 1957.* Fellowship of men & women who share experiences, strength & hope with each other to recover from compulsive gambling, following a 12-step program. Chapter development kit. Monthly bulletin for members. Write: P.O. Box 17173, Los Angeles, CA 90017. Call 213/386-8789.

OVEREATING
(also see Addictions - General; Health - Overweight)

Food Addicts Anonymous *National. 37 affiliated groups. Founded 1987.* Fellowship of men & women who are willing to recover from the disease of food addiction. Primary purpose is to maintain abstinence from sugar, flour & wheat. Follows 12-step program. Provides info. & referral, pen pal, conferences. Assistance in starting groups. Write: P.O. Box 057394, W. Palm Beach, FL 33405-7394.

National Association to Advance Fat Acceptance (NAAFA) *National. 60 chapters. Founded 1969.* Assists members in developing self-esteem & self-confidence in themselves as they are. Public education regarding obesity. Provides a forum for peer support. Membership organization $35/year. Monthly newsletter, phone network, pen pals, & annual convention. Chapter development guidelines. Write: P.O. Box 188620, Sacramento, CA 95818. Call 916/443-0303.

Overeaters Anonymous *Int'l. 9,968 groups. Founded 1960.* A 12-step fellowship who meet to help one another understand & overcome compulsive eating disorders. Also groups & literature for young persons & teens. Monthly magazine, bi-monthly newsletter, group development guidelines. Write: P.O. Box 92870, Los Angeles, CA 90009. Call 310/618-8835 or look in white pages of phone book for local number.

O-Anon *Int'l. 50 Affiliated groups. Founded 1975.* Fellowship of friends & relatives of compulsive overeaters. Follows the 12-Step Program adapted from Alcoholics Anonymous. Newsletter. Group development guidelines. Write: P.O. Box 4305, San Pedro, CA 90731. Call 310/547-1430.

T.O.P.S. (Take Off Pounds Sensibly) *Int'l. 11,500 chapters. Founded 1948.* Helps overweight persons attain & maintain their goal weights. Promotes a sensible approach to weight control. Chapters meet weekly for discussion & programs to provide support & competition. Newsletter. Chapter development guidelines. Write: P.O. Box 07630, 4575 S. 5th St., Milwaukee, WI 53207. Call 800-932-8677.

SEX/LOVE ADDICTION
(also see Addictions - General; Misc. - Women)

Augustine Fellowship, Sex & Love Addicts Anonymous *Int'l. 1000 affiliated groups. Founded 1976.* 12-step fellowship based on A.A. for those who desire to stop living out a pattern of sex & love addiction, obsessive/compulsive sexual behavior or emotional attachment. Newsletter, journal, information & referrals, conferences, phone support. Group development guidelines ($5). Write: P.O. Box 119, New Town Branch, Boston, MA 02258. Call 617/332-1845.

Co-Sex and Love Addicts Anonymous *Int'l. 25 groups. Founded 1989.* Fellowship of relatives, friends & significant others who share their experience, strength & hope in order to find solutions to the problems in dealing with co-sex & love addiction. Newsletter, phone support, group development guidelines, conferences, pen pals. Write: P.O. Box 614, Brookline, MA 02146-9998.

COSA (Codependents of Sex Addicts) *National. 50+ affiliated groups.* A self-help program of recovery using the 12 steps adapted from A.A. & Al-Anon, for those involved in relationships with people who have compulsive sexual behavior. Assistance in starting new groups. Write: P.O. Box 14537, Minneapolis, MN 55414. Call 612/537-6904.

S-Anon *Int'l. 65 affiliated groups. Founded 1984.* 12-step group for persons who have a friend or family member with a problem of sexual addiction. Assistance available for starting groups. Conferences. Quarterly newsletter. Write: P.O. Box 5117, Sherman Oaks, CA 91413. Call 818/990-6910.

Sex Addicts Anonymous *National. 500 groups. Founded 1977.* Fellowship of men & women who share their experience, strength, & hope with one another that they may solve their common problem & gain freedom from compulsive sexual behavior. Guidelines for starting new groups. literature. Monthly newsletter. Write: P.O. Box 3038, Minneapolis, MN 55403. Call 612/339-0217.

Sexaholics Anonymous *Int'l. 700 chapters. Founded 1979.* Program of recovery for those who want to stop sexually self-destructive thinking & behavior. Mutual support to achieve & maintain sexual sobriety. Telephone network, qtrly newsletter, literature & books; chapter development guidelines $4. Write: P.O. Box 300, Simi Valley, CA 93062. Call 818/704-9854 or 805/581-3343.

Sexual Compulsives Anonymous *Int'l. 100+ groups. Founded 1982.* Fellowship of men & women who share their experience, strength & hope that they may solve their common problem & help others to recover from sexual compulsion. Newsletter, information & referrals, phone support, conferences. Materials on starting new groups ($5.50). Write: P.O. Box 1585, NY, NY 10113-0935. Call 212-439-1123 (NY); 312-589-5856 (CHICAGO); 213-859-5585 (WEST COAST).

(Model) **Adult Children of Sexual Dysfunction** *Regional. 6 groups. Founded 1988.* Support & education for adults with a desire to recover from the effects of growing up in a sexually dysfunctional family (i.e. compulsive sexual behavior, incest, sexual rigidity or other dysfunctions). Follows 12-step program. Phone support, pen pals. For help in starting new groups send Self-addressed stamped envelope w/$0.35 postage. Write: P.O. Box 8084, Lake St. Station, 110 E 31st, Minneapolis, MN 55408.

SMOKING

Nicotine Anonymous World Services *Int'l. 500+ groups. Founded 1985.* Self-help group using the 12-step program of recovery for people who want to help themselves & others recover from nicotine addiction & live free of nicotine in all forms. Newsletter. Assistance available for starting groups. Write: 2118 Greenwich St., San Francisco, CA 94123. Call 415/922-8575.

Please remember: When writing to a group for information, always enclose a self-addressed stamped envelope. Model groups are not national organizations, and should be contacted primarily by those interested in starting a local chapter.

BEREAVEMENT

BEREAVEMENT (GENERAL)
(see also AIDS)

Rainbows for All God's Children *Int'l. 4000 affiliated groups. Founded 1983.* Establishes peer support groups in churches, schools or social agencies for children & adults who are grieving a death, divorce or other painful transition in their family. Groups are led by trained adults. Newsletter, information & referrals. Write: 1111 Tower Rd., Schaumburg, IL 60173. Call 708/310-1880.

Survivors *National. Founded 1987.* Mutual help & 12-step program to recover from the lasting effects of grief resulting from the death of a loved one. Assistance/literature on starting groups. Write: Timothy Quinn, 993 "C" S. Fanta Fe Ave., Vista CA 92083.

Twinless Twin Support Group *Int'l network. Founded 1985.* Mutual support for twins who have lost their twin. Provides information & referrals, phone support, pen pals, conferences. Newsletter. Group development guidelines. Provides assistance in starting local groups. Annual meeting. Write: c/o Dr. Brandt, 11220 St. Joe Rd., Fort Wayne, IN 46835-9737. Call Dr. Raymond Brandt 219/627-5414.

Victims of Pan Am 103, "The Truth Must Be Known" *National.* Mutual support for families & friends who lost a loved one on Pan Am Flight 103. Political activities, grief counseling & peer-counseling. Meets various times. Write: 135 Algonquin Parkway, Whippany, NJ 07981.

DEATH OF A CHILD / FETAL LOSS
(see also Crime Victims, Suicide)

Alive Alone, Inc. *National network. Founded 1988.* Self-help network of parents who have lost an only child or all of their children. Provides education & publications to promote communication & healing, to assist in resolving grief, & to develop means to reinvest lives for a positive future. Write: c/o Kay Bevington, 11115 Dull Robinson Rd., Van Wert, OH 45891.

A.M.E.N.D. (Aiding Mothers & Fathers Experiencing Neo-natal Death) *National. Founded 1974.* Offers support & encouragement to parents having a normal grief reaction to the loss of their baby. One-to-one peer counseling with trained volunteers. Write: 4324 Berrywick Terrace, St. Louis, MO 63128. Call 314/487-7582.

CLIMB, Inc. (Center for Loss In Multiple Birth) *Int'l network. Founded 1987.* Support by & for parents who have experienced the death of one or more of their children during a multiple pregnancy, birth, in infancy, or childhood. Newsletter, group development guidelines, pen pals, phone support. Materials for twins clubs & helping professionals, loss support groups. Write: P.O. Box 1064, Palmer, AK 99646. Call 907/746-6123.

Compassionate Friends, The *National. 665 chapters. Founded 1969.* Offers support, friendship & understanding to parents & siblings bereaving the death of a child. Telephone support, information on the grieving process, monthly chapter meetings. National newsletter $10/year & Sibling newsletter $5/year. Chapter leaders manual. Resource library. Write: P.O. Box 3696, Oak Brook, IL 60522-3696. Call 708/990-0010.

National Council of Guilds for Infant Survival *National. 15 chapters. Founded 1962.* Support & education for parents who have lost a child to sudden infant death syndrome (SIDS) & for families using in-home monitors for high risk infants. Quarterly newsletter, group development guidelines, correspondence. Write: P.O. Box 3586, Davenport, IA 52808.

Open ARMS (Abortion Related Ministries) *National. 11 affiliated groups. Founded 1986.* Christian post-abortion support group open to anyone suffering from abortion's emotional aftermath. Provides newsletters, phone support, conferences, information & referrals. Group development guidelines $10. Write: Patti Goodoien, P.O. Box 1056, Columbia, MO 65205. Call 314/449-7672.

Parents of Murdered Children *National. 325 chapters & contact persons throughout US & Canada. Founded 1978.* Provides self-help groups to support persons who have experienced the violent death of someone close, as they seek to recover. Newsletter; court accompaniment also provided in many areas. Write: 100 E. 8th St., 8-41, Cincinnati, OH 45202. Call 513/721-5683 (office); 513/721-5685 (FAX).

SHARE: Pregnancy & Infant Loss Support, Inc. *National. 250 chapters. Founded 1977.* Mutual support for bereaved parents & families who have suffered a loss due to miscarriage, stillbirth or neonatal death. Provides newsletter, pen pals, information re: professionals, caregivers & pastoral care. Chapter development guidelines. Write: c/o St. Joseph's Health Ctr., 300 First Capital Dr., St. Charles, MO 63301. Call 314/947-5000.

SIDS Alliance (Sudden Infant Death Syndrome) *National. 82 chapters. Founded 1962.* Provides emotional support for families of SIDS victims through local chapters. Supports research, educates the public. Newsletter, telephone support network, chapter development guidelines. Write: 10500 Little Patuxent Parkway #420, Columbia, MD 21044-3505. Call 800-221-7437 or 410/964-8000 (within Maryland).

Tender Hearts (Sponsored by Triplet Connection) *Int'l. Founded 1983.* Network of parents who have lost one or more children in multiple births. Newsletter information & referrals, phone support & pen pals. Write: c/o Triplet Connection, P.O. Box 99571, Stockton, CA 95209. Call 209/474-0885.

Unite, Inc. *National. 10 groups. Founded 1975.* Support for parents grieving miscarriage, stillbirth & infant death. Support for parents through subsequent pregnancies. Group meetings, phone help, newsletter, annual conference. Group facilitator & grief counselor training programs. Professionals in advisory roles. Write: Janis Heil, Jeanes Hospital, 7600 Central Ave., Philadelphia, PA 19111. Call 215/728-3777 (tape) or 215/728-2082.

(Model) **Abortion Survivors Anonymous** *2 affiliated groups. Founded 1989.* A 12-Step program to facilitate recovery & support of those affected by an abortion loss & wish to recover from the impact of abortion in their lives & relationships. Group development manual ($10). Write: P.O. Box 1533, Alpine, CA 91903. Call Sarah 619/445-1247 or Tim 303/221-3703.

(Model) **In Loving Memory** *2 groups. Founded 1989.* Mutual support, friendship & understanding for parents who have lost their only, or all of their children. Phone help, newsletter, socials, group development guidelines. Write: Elizabeth Anderson, 15007 114th Ave. Ct. E., Puyallup, WA 98374-3459; call 206/840-2375 (day); or Linda Nielsen, 1416 Green Run Lane, Reston, VA 22090; call 703/435-0608.

SUICIDE

Ray of Hope, Inc. *National. 7 affiliated groups. Founded 1977.* Mutual support groups for after-suicide bereavement. Educational materials on suicide postvention. Includes book, "After Suicide: A Ray of Hope," Lynn Publications, 240 pgs. Consultation provided for starting survivor support groups. Write: P.O. Box 2323, Iowa City, IA 52244. Call 319/337-9890.

S.O.S. (Survivors of Suicide) *National. 350 independent groups. Founded 1980.* Helps families & friends of suicide victims cope with the sorrow. Referrals to other survivor groups. Manual & materials for starting groups ($7). Guest speakers available for increasing public awareness. Write: c/o Sharry Schaefer, 3251 N. 78th St., Milwaukee, WI 53222. Call 414/442-4638.

(Model) **Heartbeat** *13 groups. Founded 1981.* Group of mutual support for those who have lost a loved one through suicide. Information & referrals, phone support, chapter development guidelines $10. Write: 2015 Devon St., Colorado Springs, CO 80909. Call 719/596-2575.

WIDOWS / WIDOWERS
(see also Single Parenting; Bereavement General)

COPS (Concerns of Police Survivors, Inc.) *National. 13 chapters.* Peer support for spouses & families of law enforcement officers who died in the line of duty. Quarterly newsletter, group development guidelines, peer support, conferences. Write: c/o Suzie Sawyer, 9423A Marlboro Pike, Upper Marlboro, MD 20772. Call 301/599-0445.

National Association of Military Widows *National. Founded 1976.* To provide assistance to all military widows through changes in legislation & making referrals. Newsletter. Dues $10/year. Members in all 50 states & the District of Columbia. Write: 4023 25th Rd., N. Arlington, VA 22207. Call Jean Arthurs 703/527-4565.

Society of Military Widows *National. 29 chapters. Founded 1968.* Support & assistance for widows/widowers of members of all U.S. uniformed services. Help in coping with adjustment to life on their own. Promotes public awareness. Newsletter. Dues $12. Chapter development guidelines. Write: 5535 Hempstead Way, Springfield, VA 22151. Call 703/750-1342.

THEOS (They Help Each Other Spiritually) *Int'l. 100+ chapters. Founded 1962.* Assists widowed persons of all ages & their families to rebuild their lives through mutual self-help. Network of local groups. Quarterly newsletter, chapter development guidelines ($5). Write: 717 Liberty Ave., 1301 Clark Bldg., Pittsburgh, PA 15222-3510. Call 412/471-7779.

Please remember to include a self-addressed stamped envelope when writing to a group for information.

T.L.A. (To Live Again) *National. 28 chapters. Founded 1974.* Mutual help organization covering the greater Delaware Valley, for widowed women & men supporting one another through the grief cycle. Monthly meetings, social programs, chapter development assistance, Reach-Out program, conferences, newsletter. Write: P.O. Box 415, Springfield, PA 19064. Call 215/353-7740.

Widowed Persons Service *National. 232 groups. Founded 1973.* A program run in cooperation with A.A.R.P. & local community groups, providing one-to-one peer support for widows & widowers. Provides manuals on starting support groups, quarterly newsletter, referral services & public education. Write: 601 E Street, NW, Washington, DC 20049. Call 202/434-2260.

PET BEREAVEMENT

(Resource) **Pet Loss.** For those who are having difficulty coping with the death of a pet, there are some pet bereavement support groups around the country. The Delta Society, P.O. Box 1080, Renton, WA 98057-1080 maintains a national listing of pet loss resource persons, a few of whom have support groups. For a local referral, send a self-addressed stamped envelope to or call 206/226-7357 (weekdays).

"Who then can so softly bind up the wound of another as he who has felt the same wound himself."

- Thomas Jefferson

TOGETHER WE'LL WALK THE STEPPING STONES

Come, take my hand, the road is long.
We must travel by stepping stones.
No, you're not alone, I'll go with you.
I know the road well, I've been there.
Don't fear the darkness, I'll be there with you.
We must take one step at a time.
But remember we may have to stop awhile.
It is a long way to the other side
And there may be obstacles.

We have many stones to cross, some are bigger than others,
Shocks, denial and anger to start.
Then comes guilt, despair and loneliness.
It's a hard road to travel, but it must be done.
It's the only way to reach the other side.

Come, slip your hand in mine.
What? Oh, yes, it's strong, I've held so many hands like yours.
Yes, mine was one time small and weak like yours.
Once, you see, I had to take someone's hand in order to take the
first step.
Oops! You've stumbled; go ahead and cry.
Don't be ashamed; I understand.
Let's wait here awhile and get your breath.
When you're stronger we'll go on, one step at a time.
There's no need to hurry.
Say, it's nice to hear you laugh. Yes, I agree,
The memories you shared are good.
Look, we're halfway there now; I can see the other side.
It looks so warm and sunny.
Oh, have you noticed, we're nearing the last stone and you're
standing alone?
We've reached the other side.

But wait, look back, someone is standing there.
They are alone and want to cross the stepping stones.
I'd better go, they need my help.
What? Are you sure?
Why, yes, go ahead, I'll wait, you know the way, you've been there.
Yes, I agreed, it's your turn, my friend --
To help someone else cross the stepping stones.

- by Barb Williams, The Compassionate Friends, Ft. Wayne, IN.
Reprinted with permission from <u>We Need Not Walk Alone</u>, pub. by
Compassionate Friends, PO Box 3696, Oak Brook, IL 60522.

DISABILITIES

AMPUTATION / LIMB DEFICIENCY
(seel also: Physical Disability)

AFTER *National. 5 affiliated groups. Founded 1979.* Created to meet the special needs of persons with amputations or limb deficiency (0 to 25). Groups for families & young adults. Hospital & home visits, monthly support groups, telephone support, info. & referral, newsletter, resource lending library, special events. Write: 8408 W. McNab Rd., Tamarac, FL 33321. Call 305/721-1140.

American Amputee Foundation, Inc. *National. 18 chapters. Founded 1975.* Information, referrals & peer support for amputees. Hospital visitation & counseling. Magazine, group development guidelines, conferences. Financial assistance program. Write: P.O. Box 250218, Little Rock, AR 72225-0218. Call 501/666-2523.

National Amputation Foundation, Inc. *National. 20 affiliated chapters. Founded 1919.* Mutual support for amputees of all ages. "Amp to Amp" program links individuals with others with similar amputations. Membership dues $15. Newsletter, library of information, advocacy, vocational guidance, information & referrals. Write: 12-45 150th St., Whitestone, NY 11357. Call 718/767-0596.

(Model) **A.I.M. (Amputees In Motion)** *Founded 1973.* Mutual support for amputees & their families. Discussions, help with rehabilitation, outreach to new amputees in hospitals, matching peers with similar circumstances. Social & sports activities, speakers program, assistance in starting new groups, newsletter. Write: P.O. Box 2703, Escondido, CA 92033. Call 619/454-9300.

(Model) **Families & Amputees In Motion** *Founded 1981.* Information, resources & peer support to amputees & their families. Instrumental in developing a nationwide coalition of amputee groups. Assistance in starting groups. Quarterly newsletter. Write: 10046 S. Western Ave. #201, Chicago, IL 60643. Hotline 708/524-0600.

(Model) **In Step** *Founded 1982.* Support for persons with congenital or acquired loss of limb. Peer support, informational & social meetings. Training program for caretakers of amputees. Monthly newsletter, telephone support network. Dues $15/year. Write: c/o Englewood Hospital, 375 Engle St., Englewood, NJ 07631. Call 201/886-0228.

(Model) **LEAPS Across the Heartland (Lower Extremity Amputees Providing Support)** *Midwest Regional.* (Affiliated with American Amputee Foundation) Peer support & understanding to individuals who have undergone or are about to undergo amputation surgery. Newsletter, monthly meetings, help in starting groups, visitation program. Write: P.O. Box 15961, Lenexa, KS 66215. Call 816/361-3206.

(Model) **Mutual Amputee Aid Foundation** *Founded 1973.* Peer support & understanding to help persons who have undergone, or who are about to undergo, amputation surgery. Visitation service by volunteer amputees who meet with patients & families. Info. & referrals, newsletter, assistance in starting groups. Write: P.O. Box 1200, Lomita, CA 90717. Call 818/509-3400.

(Model) **P.A.C.T. (Parents of Amputee Children Together)** *Founded 1975.* Support for families of children with congenital or traumatic amputees. Links parents, serves as forum to share concerns & information. Newsletter, bibliography. Write: c/o Kessler Rehab. Institute, Pleasant Valley Way, W. Orange, NJ 07052. Call Felice Celikyol or Sue Souza 201/731-3600 Ext 291 or 800-648-0296.

AUTISM

ANI (Autism Network International) *Int'l. Founded 1992.* Organization run by & for autistic people. Provides peer support & tips for coping & problem-solving. Information & referrals. Developing computer network, Big Pals network matching autistic adults & children for one-on-one computer correspondence. Advocacy, public education. Newsletter ($15). Write: P.O. Box 1545, Lawrence, KS 66044.

Autism Society of America *National. 185 chapters. Founded 1965.* Parents, professionals & citizens working together via education, advocacy & research for children & adults with autism. Quarterly newsletter, mail order bookstore, annual conference. Write: 8601 Georgia Ave., #503, Silver Spring, MD 20910. Call 301/565-0433 or 301/565-0834 (FAX).

*Please remember: Model groups are **not** national organizations. They should be contacted primarily by persons interested in starting such a group in their local community. Also, always include a self-addressed stamped envelope when requesting information from a group.*

BLIND / VISUALLY IMPAIRED

American Council of The Blind *National. 64 affiliates. Founded 1961.* Aims to improve the well-being of all blind & visually impaired people & their families through education, support, & advocacy. National conference, support groups, information & referrals, phone support, pen pals. Newsletter. Chapter development guidelines. Write: 1155 15th St. NW, #720, Washington, DC 20005. Call 800-424-8666 or 202/467-5081.

Association for Macular Diseases, Inc. *National. 12 local chapters. Founded 1978.* Support for persons suffering from macular diseases & their families. Distributes information on vision aids & research. Provides an eye bank devoted solely to macular disease research. Quarterly newsletter, phone network, group development guidelines. Write: 210 E. 64th St., New York, NY 10021. Call 212/605-3719.

Blinded Veterans Association *National. 38 groups. Founded 1945.* Information, support & outreach to blinded veterans. Help in finding jobs, information on benefits & rehabilitation programs. Bi-monthly newsletter. Chapter development guidelines. Regional meetings. Write: 477 H St., NW, Washington, DC 20001. Call 202/371-8880 or 800-669-7079.

Council of Citizens with Low Vision International *Int'l. State, regional & local chapters. Founded 1978.* Enables low vision people to make full use of vision through use of aids, technology & services. Education & advocacy. Newsletter, information & referrals, group development guidelines, scholarships, conferences. Speakers bureau. Dues $10. Write: Patricia Price, 5707 Brockton Dr. #302, Indianapolis, IN 46220-5481. Call 317/254-1185 or 800-733-2258 (in Indiana only).

Council of Families with Visual Impairments *National network. Founded 1979.* Support for sighted parents with blind children, blind parents with sighted or blind children, & other interested persons. Education, information & referrals. Newsletter, conferences, pen pals, support groups, advocacy, phone support. Help in starting groups. Dues $5. Write: c/o Nola Webb, 14400 Cedar Rd., University Heights, OH 44121. Call 216/381-1822.

National Assn. For Parents of The Visually Impaired, Inc. *Nat'l. 16 groups. Founded 1980.* Outreach & support for parents of visually impaired children. Assists in the formation of local parent support groups. Increases public awareness. Quarterly newsletter. Dues $20/family. Write: 2180 Linway Dr., Beloit, WI 53511. Call 608/362-4945 or 800-562-6265.

National Association for Visually Handicapped *National. 7 affiliated groups. Founded 1954.* Support for partially-seeing persons. Groups have professional advisors & provide mutual support, social contacts & education. Newsletter; phone support; information & referrals; literature on starting new groups. Write: c/o J. Eckstein, 22 W. 21st St., New York, NY 10010. Call 212/ 889-3141.

National Federation of the Blind *Nat'l. 51 affiliates. Founded 1940.* Serves as both an advocacy & a public information vehicle. Contacts newly blind persons to help with adjustment. Provides info. on services & applicable laws. Student scholarships. Assists blind persons who are victims of discrimination. Literature, monthly meetings & magazine. Write: 1800 Johnson St., Baltimore, MD 21230. Call 410/659-9314 (general info.); 800-638-7518 (service for blind seeking employment).

Parents of Blind Children (Nat'l Federation of the Blind) *National.* Support for parents of blind children. Serves as both an advocacy & public information vehicle. Provides information & services on services available. Offers positive philosophy & insights into blindness & practical guidance in raising a blind child. Newsletter, parent seminars, free information packet, conventions. Write: 1800 Johnson St., Baltimore, MD 21230. Call Carol Castellano 201/377-0976 (NJ).

R.P. Foundation Fighting Blindness *National. 50 affiliated groups.* Supports research into causes, prevention & treatment of Retinitis Pigmentosa & allied retinal degeneration. Information & referral, conferences. Retina Donor Program. Confidential registry. Newsletter. Write: 1401 Mt. Royal Ave., 4th Fl, Baltimore, MD 21217-4245. Call 800-683-5555 or 410/225-9400; 225-9409 (TDD); or 410/225-3936 (FAX).

Usher's Syndrome Self-Help Network *National network. Founded 1983.* A listing of individuals with Usher's or their families who are available to share their experiences with others. Write: c/o R.P. Fdn. Fighting Blindness, Usher's Syndrome Self-Help Network, 1401 Mt. Royal Ave., 4th Fl, Baltimore, MD 21217. Call 800-683-5555 or 410/225-9400; TDD 410/225-9409.

Vision Foundation, Inc. *National. 20 groups. Founded 1970.* Information & support network for persons coping with sight loss. Sponsors support groups for elders & "mixed" ages. Outreach services, career mentor program, phone support, large print literature & cassettes, pen pals, newsletter. Write: 818 Mt. Auburn St., Watertown, MA 02172. Call 617/926-4232, or 800-852-3029 (in MA only).

(Model) **Eye Openers** *NJ Statewide. Founded 1985.* Mutual support for individuals of all ages with any type of eye conditions, & their families. Education, advocacy, & social activities. Guidelines & literature available. Write: c/o NJ Self-Help Clearinghouse, St. Clares-Riverside Medical Center, 25 Pocono Rd., Denville, NJ 07834. Call 201-625-9565.

(Model) **Sight-Loss Support Group of Central Penna, Inc.** *Founded 1982.* Mutual help for people of all ages with varying degrees of sight loss. Information & referral, self-help group meetings, buddy phone exchanges, computer & reader/scanner training, monthly newsletter, art-through-touch program, speakers panel. Dues $5. Group development guidelines. Write: 111 Sowers St., #310, State College, PA 16801. Call 814/238-0132.

(Model) **Vision Northwest** *35 groups. Founded 1984.* The mission of Vision Northwest is to reach out with compassion, encouragement & understanding to those coping with vision loss, their families & friends to help them to become more independent by providing a network of support groups & information & referral services. Quarterly newsletter. Write: 4370 NE Halsey, Portland, OR 97213. Call 503/284-7560 or 800-448-2232.

BURN SURVIVORS

Burns United Support Group *National. 2 affiliated groups. Founded 1986.* For those who have survived being burned, no matter how major or minor the burn. Also for the family & friends. Outreach visitation, newsletter, pen pals, phone support, assistance in starting groups. Write: Donna Schneck-Smorol, 441 Colonial Court, Grosse Pointe Farms, MI 48236. Call 313/881-5577.

National Burn Victim Foundation *Int'l. Founded 1974.* Advocates for burn victims. Provides educational programs & seminars, mental health services to burn victims & their families in post-hospital period. Assists in formation of groups to achieve full recovery through mutual support & visitation. Write: 32 Scotland Rd., Orange, NJ 07050-1418. Call 201/676-7700.

Phoenix Society for Burn Survivors, Inc., The *Int'l. 260 chapters. Founded 1977.* Recovered burn victims work with severely burned people & their families during & after hospitalization. Pen pal network, chapter starter kit, quarterly newsletter, phone network, national & int'l conferences, books, & audio-visual materials. Write: 11 Rust Hill Rd., Levittown, PA 19056. Call 800-888-2876 or 215/946-2876.

CEREBRAL PALSY
(also see Parents of Disabled)

United Cerebral Palsy Associations, Inc. *National. 180 affiliates. Founded 1949.* Supports local affiliates that sponsor programs for families with developmentally disabled children. Local programs include support groups for parents & young adults with C.P. Qtrly magazine, newsletter, research reports. Write: 7 Penn Plaza, #804, New York, NY 10001. Call 800-872-1827 or 212/268-6655.

DEAF / HEARING IMPAIRED / TINNITUS

American Society for Deaf Children *National. 120 affiliates. Founded 1967.* Information & support for parents & families with children who are deaf or hard of hearing. Quarterly newsletter, telephone support network. Group development guidelines. Write: 814 Thayer Ave., Silver Spring, MD 20910. Call 800-942-ASDC (voice & TDD).

American Tinnitus Association *National. 106 groups. Founded 1971.* Educational information for patients & professionals. Provides network of services through clinics & self-help groups. Supports research. Quarterly newsletter. Group development guidelines. Write: P.O. Box 5, Portland, OR 97207. Call 503/248-9985.

Cochlear Implant Club International *Int'l. Founded 1985.* Support through fellowship for implant recipients & their families. Pre- and post-op counseling, information on new technology. $15 dues/year. Speakers bureau. Quarterly newsletter. Chapter development guidelines. Write: P.O. Box 464, Buffalo, NY 14223-0464. Call 716/838-4662 (voice & TDD).

Meniere's Network *National. 35 groups. Founded 1987.* Education for persons with Meniere's disease about the condition, treatment alternatives & coping strategies. Education for the public & professionals. Quarterly newsletter. Group development guidelines, phone buddies, pen pals. Dues $25/yr. Write: 2000 Church St., Box 111, Nashville, TN 37236. Call 800-545-4327.

National Association of The Deaf *Nat'l. 50 chapters. Founded 1880.* Oldest & largest consumer organization of people with disabilities in the U.S. with more than 22,000 members. Serves as an advocate for the more than 22 million deaf & hard of hearing people in America. Info & referral, newsletter, magazine, Jr. NAD, Youth Leadership camp. Write: 814 Thayer St., Silver Spring, MD 20910-4500. Call 301/587-1789 (TTY); 301/587-1788 (Voice).

National Fraternal Society of The Deaf *National. 85 divisions. Founded 1901.* Self-help organization for deaf & hearing impaired persons, their families & concerned professionals that provide low-cost life insurance, scholarships for students, info. & referrals. Fellowship & advocacy. Bi-monthly newsletter. Membership dues vary. Write: 1300 W. Northwest Hwy., Mt. Prospect, IL 60056. Call 800-676-NFSD (voice or TDD) or 708/392-9282.

Parents Section, A.G. Bell Assn. for the Deaf *Int'l. 20 affiliated groups. Founded 1958.* Enables parents of hearing impaired children to speak with unified strength on issues which concern them. Serves as clearinghouse to exchange ideas. Newsletter, phone support & conferences. Group development guidelines. Write: 3417 Volta Pl., NW, Washington, DC 20007. Call 202/337-5220.

S.H.H.H. (Self-Help for Hard of Hearing People, Inc.) *Int'l. 260+ chapters & groups. Founded 1979.* A volunteer, educational organization devoted to the welfare, interests & membership of hard of hearing people, their families & friends. Bi-monthly journal, local group & chapter referrals. Write: 7800 Wisconsin Ave., Bethesda, MD 20814. Call 301/657-2248 or 301/657-2249 (TDD).

Usher's Syndrome Self-Help Network *National network. Founded 1983.* A listing of individuals with Usher's or their families who are available to share their experiences with others. Write: c/o R.P. Fdn Fighting Blindness, Usher's Syndrome Self-Help Network, 1401 Mt. Royal Ave., 4th Fl, Baltimore, MD 21217. Call 800-683-5555. Within MD 410/225-9400; TDD 410/225-9409.

(Model) A.L.D.A. (Association of Late-Deafened Adults) *Regional. 20 affiliated groups. Founded 1987.* Serves the needs of people who become deaf during adulthood. Newsletter, social activities, information & referrals, assistance in starting groups. Write: c/o Bill Graham, 2445 W. Cuyler St., Chicago, IL 60618. Call 312/604-4192 (TDD); 312/604-4190 (voice) or 312/604-5209 (FAX).

HEAD INJURY / BRAIN TUMOR / COMA

Acoustic Neuroma Association *National. 34 chapters. Founded 1981.* Support & info. for patients who have experienced acoustic neuromas or other tumors affecting the cranial nerves. Provides public & professional education. Newsletter, annual national symposium, telephone network, chapter development guidelines. Write: P.O. Box 12402, Atlanta, GA 30355. Call 404/237-8023.

ABTA (American Brain Tumor Association) *National. Founded 1973.* To raise funds for research, promote local group development, & increase public awareness of prevalence of brain tumors. Provides support, info. & materials to patients & their families. Tri-annual newsletter. How-to materials available for starting groups. Write: 3725 N. Talman Ave., Chicago, IL 60618. Call 312/286-5571; or 800-886-2282 (patient services).

Brain Tumor Society, The *National network. Founded 1989.* Provides brain tumor patients & their loved ones with access to psychosocial support through groups & phone networks. Also provides educational material, fund-raising for research, conferences, information, newsletter. Attempts to raise public awareness. Write: 258 Harvard St., Suite 308, Brookline, MA 02146. Call Bonnie Feldman 617/243-4229.

Coma Recovery Association *National. 3 chapters. Founded 1980.* Support & advocacy for families of coma victims. Provides information & referrals, socialization programs for recovering coma victims & a transitional apartment program. Quarterly newsletter. Write: 377 Jerusalem Ave., Hempstead, NY 11550. Call 516/486-2847.

National Head Injury Foundation *Nat'l. 400 chapters. Founded 1980.* To improve the quality of life of individuals who have sustained a head injury & their families, & to prevent head injuries. Provides mutual support, education, information, resources, advocacy, public awareness & prevention programs. Newsletter. Dues $35 (free for patients & families). Write: 1140 Connecticut Ave., NW #812, Washington, DC 20036. Call 800-444-NHIF or 202/296-6443.

Perspectives Network, The *Int'l Network. Founded 1990.* Emotional support & networking for survivors of brain injury, their families & professionals through coordination of non-location dependent peer support groups. Qtrly magazine, pen pals, phone support, information & referrals, exchange of information from professionals & survivors. Write: 9919 Orangevale Dr., Spring, TX 77379-5103. Call 713/251-8939 (day).

(Model) Illinois Pediatric Brain Injury Resource Center *Founded 1991.* Aims to improve the quality of life for brain injured children & their families. Offers support group, Great Expectations, for parents of brain injured children, birth to 18. Provides information & referrals, conferences, phone support, newsletter, resource library, education, assistance in starting groups. Write: IPBIRC, P.O. Box 681096, Schaumburg, IL 60168. Call 708/658-5067 (day).

LEARNING DISABILITIES /
ATTENTION DEFICIT DISORDER

AD-IN (Attention Deficit Information Network), Inc. *National. 40 chapters. Founded 1984.* Mutual support for parents of children with attention deficit disorder. Education, information & sharing of ideas for parents, educators & medical personnel. Group starter kit ($20). Write: P.O. Box 790, Plymouth, MA 02362-0013. Call 508/747-5180.

ADDA (Attention Deficit Disorder Association) *National.* Coalition of support groups for parents of, or adults with, attention deficit disorder. Responds to needs of existing groups & underserved individuals. Provides newsletter, info. & referrals, assistance in starting groups, adult pen pal program, advocacy & speakers bureau. Write: 19262 Jamboree Blvd., Irvine, CA 92715, Call Linda Phillips 800-487-2282 for support services.

C.H.A.D.D. (Children with Attention Deficit Disorder) *Int'l. 300+ affiliated groups. Founded 1987.* Support for parents with children with A.D.D. Provides information for parents, teachers & professionals. Newsletter. Guidelines & assistance on starting self-help groups. Dues $30/year. Write: 1859 N. Pine Island Rd., #185, Plantation, FL 33322. Call 305/587-3700.

Feingold Associations of the U.S. *National. 12 chapters. Founded 1976.* Help for families of children with learning or behavior problems. Supports members in implementing the Feingold program. Generates public awareness re: food & synthetic additives. Newsletter. Telephone support network. Write: Box 6550, Alexandria, VA 22306. Call 703/768-3287.

Learning Disabilities Association of America *National. 500 chapters. Founded 1963.* Organization formed by concerned parents, devoted to defining & finding solutions for the broad spectrum of learning problems. Information & referrals, advocacy. Bi-monthly newsletter. Chapter development guidelines. Write: Jean Peterson, L.D.A. of America, 4156 Library Rd., Pittsburgh, PA 15234. Call 412/341-1515.

National Network of L.D. Adults *National. 38 affiliated groups. Founded 1980.* Consumer-directed self-advocacy organization for adults with learning disabilities to improve their image, develop communication skills, encourage formation of support groups. Quarterly newsletter. Chapter development guidelines. Write: P.O. Box 32611, Phoenix, AZ 85064-2611. Call 602/941-5112.

MENTAL RETARDATION / DOWN SYNDROME
(also see Health: under specific disorder)

ARC, The *National. 1200 chapters. Founded 1950.* Provides support for people with mental retardation & their families. Advocacy groups & direct services. Bi-monthly newsletter. Chapter development guidelines. Write: 500 E. Border St. #300, Arlington, TX 76010-7444. Call 817/261-6003.

National Down Syndrome Congress *National. 500 parent group networks. Founded 1974.* Support, information & advocacy for families affected by Down Syndrome. Promotes research & public awareness. Serves as clearinghouse & network for parent groups. Newsletter, annual convention, phone support, chapter development guidelines. Write: 1800 Dempster St., Park Ridge, IL 60068-1146. Call 800-232-NDSC; or 708/823-7550 (day).

People First Int'l *National. 33 groups. Founded 1977.* Self-help advocacy organization created by & for people with developmental disabilities. Provides help in starting new chapters. Quarterly newsletter. Write: P.O. Box 12642, Salem, OR 97309 or 932 6th St., Clarkston, WA 99403-2079. Call 503/362-0336.

Sibling Information Network *National network. Founded 1981.* Clearinghouse of information related to siblings & families of individuals with developmental disabilities. Quarterly newsletter, pen pal program. Information, referral, guidelines & resources on sibling support groups. Write: 991 Main St., E. Hartford, CT 06108. Call 203/282-7050.

(Model) **Speaking for Ourselves** *6 groups. Founded 1982.* Self-help advocacy group for people with developmental disabilities. Monthly chapter meetings. Members help each other resolve problems, gain self-confidence, learn leadership skills. Chapter development guidelines. Newsletter. Write: 1 Plymouth Meeting, #530, Plymouth Meeting, PA 19462. Call 215/825-4592.

PARENTS OF DISABLED / ILL
(also see Health: under specific disorder)

Association of Birth Defect Children *National network.* Information & support for families of children with birth defects believed to be caused by the mother's exposure to drugs, radiation, chemicals, pesticides or other environmental agents. Quarterly newsletter. Parent-to-parent networking. National birth defect registry. Write: 5400 Diplomatic Circle, #270, Orlando, FL 32810. Call 407/629-1466.

MUMS (Mothers United for Mutual Support) *National. 17 affiliated groups. Founded 1979.* Mutual support & networking for families dealing with children with any disorder, delay or disability. Provides newsletter, information & referrals, phone support. Assistance in starting groups for rare disorders. Write: 150 Custer Crt., Green Bay, WI 54301. Call 414-336-5333 (7am-3pm CST).

SKIP Nat'l (Sick Kids Need Involved People) *National. 22 affiliated groups. Founded 1983.* Purpose is to assist families to procure services necessary for their child with complex health care needs to return and/or stay at home. Information & referrals, phone support. Write: 990 Second Ave., New York, NY 10022. Call 212/421-9160.

(Model) **Association of Hispanic Handicapped of New Jersey.** Support for Hispanic parents of handicapped children & adult Hispanic disabled persons. Information & referrals, advocacy, recreation, training, employment respite care. Assistance in starting groups. Dues $25/year. Write: 16 Jackson St., Paterson, NJ 07510. Call Ligia Freire 201/279-0212 (day).

(Model) **Children in Hospitals** *Founded 1972.* Education & support for parents in coping with the hospitalization of a child or parent. Works to promote hospital policies that recognize the needs of all family members. Quarterly newsletter. Consumer directory of all Mass. hospitals. Phone support. Write: c/o Barbara Popper, 31 Wilshire Park, Needham, MA 02192. Call 617/482-2915.

(Model) **Parents Helping Parents** *2 groups. Founded 1976.* Education & support for families of disabled children. Parent/family rap groups, program of activities & support for siblings. Annual symposium, task forces. Peer counseling training, outreach visitation. Newsletter. Group development guidelines. Resource center for families with special needs children. Write: 535 Race St. #140, San Jose, CA 95126. Call 408/288-5010.

(Model) **Pilot Parents Program** *Founded 1971.* Emotional support, factual information, & updated community resources for parents of newly diagnosed handicapped children. Newsletter. Assistance in starting a support program. How-to material available $10.50. Write: 3610 Dodge St., Omaha, NE 68131. Call 402/346-5220.

*Please note: Model groups are **not** national organizations and should be contacted primarily by those persons interested in starting a similar group in their area.*

(Model) **Washington PAVE** *Statewide. Founded 1979.* Parent directed organization to increase independence, empowerment & opportunities for special needs children & their families through training, info., referrals & support. Provides newsletter, phone support, conferences, assistance in starting new chapters. Write: Elma Rounds, Washington PAVE, 6316 S. 12th, Tacoma, WA 98465. Call 206/565-2266 or 800-5-PARENT (WA only).

PHYSICALLY DISABLED (GENERAL)

American Society of Handicapped Physicians *National. Founded 1981.* Support & advocacy for handicapped people who have chosen a career in medicine or health. Promotes unity, continuing education & increased employment opportunities. Encourages & enables networking; phone support system. Qtrly. newsletter. Write: c/o Will Lambert, 105 Morris Dr., Bastrop, LA 71220. Call 318/281-4436.

C.U.S.A. (Catholics United for Spiritual Action) *National. 120 correspondence groups. Founded 1947.* A Catholic group correspondence organization for the handicapped & chronically ill. Open to persons of all faiths. Emphasis on spiritual values & mutual support. Through group letters members find close relationships, understanding & courage. Dues $10/yr. (can be waived). Write: 176 W. 8th St., Bayonne, NJ 07002. Call 201/437-0412 (day).

Disabled Artists' Network *National network. Founded 1985.* Mutual support & exchanging of information for professional artists with physical or emotional disabilities. Provides information & referrals, pen pal program & reports to active members only. Send self-addressed stamped envelope to: P.O. Box 20781, New York, NY 10025.

Disabled Journalists of America *National network. Founded 1988.* To unite disabled journalists in newspaper, broadcasting, public relations & advertising. Aims to share employment information. Write: David Shapiro, 484 Hammond Dr., Griffin, GA 30223. Call 404/228-6491.

Hear Our Voices *Int'l network. Founded 1991.* Support, advocacy & empowerment for alternative & augmentative communication users & persons with severe speech impairments. Provides phone support, information & referrals, newsletter. Write: 105 West Pine St., Wooster, OH 44691. Call 216/262-4681.

National Council on Independent Living *National. 90 centers. Founded 1982.* Advocacy to strengthen independent living centers through technical assistance & other membership services. Newsletter, info. & referrals, conferences. Write: 2539 Telegraph Ave., Berkeley, CA 94704. Call 510/849-1243.

National Shut-In Society *National. 5 branches. Representatives in 27 states. Founded 1877.* Offers a network for communication & encouragement among people who are chronically disabled & housebound. Members correspond through letters & tapes. Quarterly publication. Dues $5/year. Write: P.O. Box 986 Village Station, New York, NY 10014-0986. Call Patricia M. Erikson 212/222-7699.

National Spinal Cord Injury Association *National. 60 chapters & support groups. Founded 1948.* Information & referrals on many topics to persons with spinal cord injuries, their families & professionals. Group development guidelines, quarterly newsletter, support groups, peer counseling. Write: 600 W. Cummings Park, #2000, Woburn, MA 01801. Call 617/935-2722 or 800-962-9629.

Siblings for Significant Change *National. 2 chapters. Founded 1981.* For siblings of handicapped persons. Trains siblings to be advocates for themselves & their families. Networking for support & socializing. Quarterly meetings. Newsletter, phone network, chapter development guidelines. Write: 105 East 22nd St., New York, NY 10010. Call 212/420-0776.

Spinal Cord Society *Int'l. 175 chapters.* Organization of the spinal-injured, families & friends, dedicated scientists & physicians. Ultimate goal is to find a cure through improved treatment & research, promotes public awareness & community outreach. Monthly newsletter. Write: c/o Charles Carson, Wendell Rd., Fergus Falls, MN 56537. Call 218/739-5252.

(Model) **Coalition for Disabled Musicians, Inc.** *Founded 1986.* Introduces disabled musicians to each other who have an understanding of disability related problems. Assistance, education & workshops for disabled children & adults, whether beginners, amateurs or professional musicians. Newsletter, group development guidelines. Specializes in adaptive equipment & techniques. Write: P.O. Box 1002M, Bay Shore, NY 11706. Call 516/586-0366.

Remember to include a self-addressed stamped envelope when requesting information or literature from a group.

(Model) **D.A.W.N. (Dis-Abled Women's Network)** *Regional. 10+ chapters. Founded 1985.* Feminist organization controlled by & comprised of women with disabilities. Support & advocacy to assist women with disabilities to become self-determined. Bridge between the disabled consumer movement & the women's movement. Write: Maria Barile, 7785 Louis Hebert, Montreal, Canada 82E 2Y1; phone 514/725-4123 or Pat Israel, 4 Warner Ave., Toronto, Ontario, Canada M4A 1Z3, 406/288-8147.

(Model) **DisAbilities Anonymous** *Founded 1988.* 12-Step program aimed to help members live with more serenity, dignity & comfort with whatever disability, chronic illness, or dysfunction they may have. Provides assistance in starting new chapters. Literature. Call Rich 212/228-2313 or Dianne W. 212/989-3416.

POWERFUL MEDICINE

Research continues to show how friends or social support can play a significant role in maintaining good health. One study examined 1,368 heart patients over time. The Duke University study found that those persons who lacked a spouse or confidant were three times as likely to die within 5 years of diagnosis than those who were married or had a close friend. The New York Times of Feb. 5, 1992 notes that the researchers concludes...

"A support group may be as effective as costly medical treatment. Simply put, having someone to talk to is very powerful medicine."

HEALTH

ACIDEMIA, ORGANIC

Organic Acidemia Association, Inc. *Int'l. Founded 1982.* Support, information & networking for families affected by organic acidemia & related ureacycle disorders. Membership dues $18. Pen pal program, telephone network. Write: 522 Lander St., Reno, NV 89509. Call 702/322-5542.

ADRENAL / ADDISON'S DISEASE

National Adrenal Diseases Foundation *National. 6 groups. Founded 1984.* Dedicated to serving the needs of those with adrenal diseases (such as Addison's) & their families, especially through education, support groups where possible & buddy arrangements. Research is a planned goal. Newsletter, group development guidelines. Write: 505 Northern Blvd., Great Neck, NY 11021. Call 516/487-4992.

AICARDI SYNDROME

Aicardi Syndrome Newsletter, Inc. *Int'l. Founded 1983.* Support for families who have affected daughters. Information & referrals, resources, research projects. Phone support network, research group, newsletters. Dues $15/year. Write: c/o Denise Raynor, 5115 Troy Urbana Rd., Casstown, OH 45312. Call 513/339-6033.

A.I.D.S

AFTER AIDS Bereavement Support Group *National. Founded 1989.* Provides a safe place of comfort, hope & strength to anyone who has lost a loved one to AIDS. Offers phone support, get togethers between meetings. Assistance in starting new groups. Newsletter being developed. Write: P.O. Box 10488, Rochester, NY 14610.

Family Centered HIV Project *National network. Founded 1989.* Network of families caring for children with HIV/AIDS. Provides educational materials, advocacy skills, & mutual support. Three meetings per year. Open to biological, foster or adoptive parents. Newsletter, information & referrals, phone support, conferences, assistance in starting groups. Write: c/o ACCH, 7910 Woodmont Ave. #300, Bethesda, MD 20814. Call 301/654-6549 (day).

Gay Men's Health Crisis *Regional. Founded 1981.* Support & information for people affected by AIDS. Support groups for PWA's, PWARC's, care partners, & parents. Provides financial help, phone counseling, outreach, educational materials & legal assistance. Bimonthly newsletter. Write: 129 West 20th St., New York, NY 10011. Call 212/807-6655.

HIVIES *Int'l. Founded 1987.* A 12-step self-help group for those who are HIV+. Mutual support in learning to live with HIV. Group manual available for $15 ($20 for international mailing). Write: c/o Dan, 610 Greenwood, Glenview, IL 60025. Call 708/724-3832.

National Association of People With A.I.D.S. *National. 102 affiliated groups. Founded 1986.* Network of persons with AIDS. Information-sharing, collective voice for health, social & political concerns. Phone mail & electronics network, speakers bureau. Monthly newsletter $55 annual subscription. Write: 1413 K St., NW, #10, Washington, DC 20005-3405. Call 202/898-0414 (day).

(Model) **BEBASHI (Blacks Educating Blacks About Sexual Health Issues)** *Founded 1985.* Information & education among the African American & Latino communities about sexual health issues, especially AIDS. Peer-counseling, guest speakers, workshops, phone help. Write: 1528 Walnut St., #200, Philadelphia, PA 19102. Call 215/546-4140.

(Model) **Body Positive of New York** *Founded 1987.* Education & support for people affected by HIV. Information & referrals, public forums, social activities. National magazine. Three-week course on living with HIV. Write: Frank Carbone, 2095 Broadway, #306, New York, NY 10023. Call 212/721-1618.

(Model) **We the People Living with AIDS/HIV of the Delaware Valley** *10 affiliated groups. Founded 1987.* To help HIV+ people become aware of & make use of services provided. To encourage self-empowerment through support from other HIV+ people. Newsletter, group development assistance. Write: David Fair, 425 S. Broad St., Philadelphia, PA 19147. Call 215/545-6868.

ALBINISM

NOAH (Nat'l Organization for Albinism & Hypopigmentation) *National. 17 chapters. Founded 1982.* Support & information for individuals, families & professionals about albinism & other forms of hypopigmentation. Encourages research. Newsletter, chapter development guidelines, national conference. Dues $10/ind; 15/family. Write: 1500 Locust St., #1816, Philadelphia, PA 19102-4316. Call 215/545-2322 or 800-473-2310.

ALOPECIA AREATA

A.A.R.F. - H.A.I.R. *National network. Founded 1983.* Information, & support for people with alopecia areata hair loss. Education for patients & professionals. Promotes research. Local support meetings & members internationally. Periodical notices. Write: P.O. Box 1875, Thousand Oaks, CA 91358. Call 805/494-4903.

National Alopecia Areata Foundation *National. 43 chapters. Founded 1981.* Support network for people with alopecia areata, totalis, & universalis. Provides education, fundraising for research, support groups. Newsletter, support group guidelines. Write: P.O. Box 150760, San Rafael, CA 94915-0760. Call 415/456-4644.

A.L.S.

A.L.S. Association *National. 150+ chapters & support groups. Founded 1972.* Dedicated to finding the cause, prevention & cure of amyotrophic lateral sclerosis, & to enhance quality of life for ALS patients & their families. Quarterly newspaper, chapter development guidelines. Write: 21021 Ventura Blvd., #321, Woodland Hills, CA 91364. Call 818/340-7500 or 800-782-4747.

ALZHEIMER'S DISEASE
(See also MISC - Caregivers)

Alzheimer's Disease & Related Disorders Assoc., Inc. *National. 215 chapters, 1,600 support groups. Founded 1980.* Information & assistance for caregivers of Alzheimer's patients. Quarterly newsletter, literature, chapter development kit. Write: ADRDA, 919 N. Michigan Ave., #1000, Chicago, IL 60611-1676. Call 800-272-3900 or 312/335-8700; TDD 312/335-8882.

ANEMIA

Aplastic Anemia Foundation of America *National. 12 chapters. Founded 1983.* Provides public information & awareness, increased funds for research, counseling & support for patients & families. Quarterly newsletter, chapter development guidelines, support systems through local chapters. Write: P.O. Box 22689, Baltimore, MD 21203. Call 301/955-2803 or 800-747-2820.

Cooley's Anemia Foundation *National. 15 chapters. Founded 1957.* Education & networking for families affected by Cooley's anemia. Fund-raising, newsletter, annual seminars, research grants, young adult group, patient services, chapter development guidelines. Write: 105 E. 22nd St., #911, New York, NY 10010. Call 800-221-3571; 212/598-0911 or 800-522-7222 (in NY).

Fanconi's Anemia Support Group *Int'l. Founded 1985.* Provides support & exchange of information re: medical advances. Fundraising for research. Newsletter, phone support, Semi-annual newsletter, phone support, pen pals & networking. Write: 66 Club Rd., #390, Eugene, OR 97401. Call 503/687-4658.

National Assn. for Sickle Cell Disease, Inc. *National. 74 chapters. Founded 1971.* Education for the public & professionals about sickle cell disease. Support & information for persons affected by the disease. Support research. Quarterly newsletter, chapter development guidelines, phone network, films. Write: 3345 Wilshire Blvd., #1106, Los Angeles, CA 90010-1880. Call 213/736-5455 or 800-421-8453.

ANKYLOSING SPONDYLITIS

Ankylosing Spondylitis Association *Int'l. 29 affiliated groups. Founded 1983.* Support & education for patients, their families & friends, & health professionals concerned with A.S. Links members geographically for local support & programs. Publications, videotapes, newsletter & pharmacy service. Write: 511 N. LaCienega Blvd., #216, Los Angeles, CA 90048. Call 800-777-8189 or 301/652-0609 (in California).

APNEA, SLEEP

AWAKE Network *Int'l. 95 affiliated groups. Founded 1988.* Provides sleep disordered breathing patients & their families with education, support & social interaction. Groups are coordinated by professionals & persons familiar with sleep apnea. Assistance & guidelines for starting groups ($7.50). Newsletter. Write: P.O. Box 534, Bethel Park, PA 15102. Call 412/831-1024.

ARACHNOIDITIS

Arachnoiditis Information & Support Network *National network. Founded 1990.* Information & mutual support for persons suffering from arachnoiditis. Quarterly newsletter ($15). Write: P.O. Box 1166, Ballwin, MO 63022. Call Cheryl Ahearn 314/394-5741

ARNOLD-CHIARI MALFORMATION

Arnold-Chiari Family Network *Int'l network. Founded 1985.* Informal network of families affected by symptomatic Arnold-Chiari Malformation. Also network for adults. Provides referrals, phone support, newsletter, & networking of families. Write: c/o Maureen & Kevin Walsh, 67 Spring St., Weymouth, MA 02188. Call 617/337-2368.

ARTERIO VENOUS MALFORMATION

AVM Support Group, The *Int'l. 8 groups. Founded 1983.* Networking for persons who are being, or who have been treated for cerebral AVM by surgery, radiation or embolization. Meetings, phone support, pen pals, info. & referrals. Audio tapes of regional/national meetings ($15-$20). Newsletter. Dues: $50. Write: 107 Bella Vista Way, San Francisco, CA 94127. Call 415/334-8012.

ARTHRITIS

Arthritis Foundation *National. 70 chapters. Founded 1948.* Education, support & activities for people with arthritis & their families & friends. Self-help instruction programs. Bimonthly magazine. Groups for children & parents. National conferences. Write: P.O. Box 19000, Atlanta, GA 30326. Call 800-283-7800.

(Model) **R.A.S.H. (Rheumatoid Arthritis Self-Helpers)** *Founded 1983.* Offers moral support, friendship & information for people who have rheumatoid arthritis. Promotes research & rehabilitation by the self-help approach. Quarterly meetings & newsletters. Call 502/581-1945. Write: 1172 E. Broadway, Louisville, KY 40204

(Model) **Young Et Heart** *22 affiliated groups. Founded 1984.* Education & support for young adults with arthritis & other related diseases, their families & friends. Newsletter, group development package & assistance, Write: Amye Leong, MBA, 11 Coral Tree Lane, Rolling Hills Estates, CA 90274-4800. Call: 310/544-3346 or FAX 310/377-2266.

ARTHROGRYPOSIS

Avenues: A National Support Group for Arthrogryposis *National network. Founded 1980.* Connects families affected by Arthrogryposis with each other for mutual support & sharing of information. Educates medical & social service professionals. Semi-annual newsletter $7.50/year. Write: P.O. Box 5192, Sonora, CA 95370. Call 209/928-3688.

ATAXIA

National Ataxia Foundation *National. 25 groups. Founded 1957.* Assists families with ataxia. Education for patients & professionals, encourages prevention through genetic counseling, promotes research. Newsletter, info. & referral, assistance in starting support groups. Write: Donna Gruetzmacher, 15500 Wayzata Blvd., Wayzata, MN 55391. Call 612/473-7666 or 612/473-9289 (FAX).

BATTEN'S DISEASE

Battens Disease Support & Research Association *Int'l. 2 affiliated groups. Founded 1987.* Emotional support for persons with Battens Disease. Information & referrals, support group meetings, phone support, conferences, newsletter. Assistance provided for starting new groups. Write: 2600 Parsons Ave., Columbus, OH 43207. Call 800-448-4570.

BECKWITH-WIEDEMANN

Beckwith-Wiedemann Support Network *National network. Founded 1989.* Support & information for parents of children with Beckwith-Wiedemann Syndrome & interested medical professionals. Newsletter, parent directory, information & referrals, phone support. Aims to increase public awareness & encourages research. Write: c/o Susan Fettes, Pres., 3206 Braeburn Circle, Ann Arbor, MI 48108. Call 313/973-0263.

BENIGN ESSENTIAL BLEPHAROSPASM

Benign Essential Blepharospasm Research Fdn., Inc. *National. 165 groups. Founded 1981.* Organization of support groups nationwide. Education & research. Networks people with similar symptoms. Doctor referrals, bimonthly newsletter. Local group development guidelines. Voluntary contributions. Write: B.E.B. Fdn., P.O. Box 12468, Beaumont, TX 77726-2468. Call 409/832-0788 or Mrs. Mattie-Lou Koster, Pres. 409/832-0788.

BONE MARROW TRANSPLANT

Bone Marrow Transplant Family Support Group *National. Founded 1988.* Support network of patients who have undergone bone marrow transplants, as well as those who have assisted someone through the transplant. Information, referrals, phone support, home visits when possible, pen pals. Write: Sandra Connel, P.O. Box 845, Avon, CT 06001. Call 203/646-2836.

BREAST IMPLANTS
(also see Cancer)

AS-IS (American Silicone Implant Survivors, Inc.) *National. Founded 1991.* Education & support for women who have had problems with breast implants. Sharing of experiences & solutions for everyday problems that arise from silicone-related issues. Provides newsletter, info. & referrals, phone support, seminars, meetings. Assistance in starting local groups. Write: 1288 Cork Elm Dr., Kirkwood, MO 63122. Call 314/821-0115.

B.I.I.F. (Breast Implant Information Foundation) *Int'l. 40 affiliated groups. Founded 1989.* Mutual support for women who have had silicone implants. Meetings include guest speakers on current implant topics, info. on dangers of implants & latest findings regarding treatment of silicone disease. Newsletter, phone support, conferences, info. & referrals. Assistance in starting local groups. Write: 25301 Barents St., Laguna Hills, CA 92653. Call 714/830-2433.

Command Trust Network (Breast Implant Info. Network) *National. 40 groups. Founded 1988.* Provides education & support for women who have had problems with breast implant surgery, & for women considering breast implants. Informal networking. Newsletter ($15/yr). Information & referral. For information send $1 in self-addressed stamped envelope to: P.O. Box 17082, Covington, KY 41017. Call 606/331-0055.

CANCER
(also see DES, Int. Mult. Polyposis, Laryngectomee)

Candlelighters Childhood Cancer Foundation *Int'l. 400 groups. Founded 1970.* Support for parents of children & adolescents with cancer. Links parents, families & groups to share feelings, exchange info., identify patient & family needs. Long-term survivors network. Newsletter, Youth newsletter. Educational materials. Network for off-treatment survivors. Write: 1312 18th St., NW, 2nd Fl., Washington, DC 20036-1808. Call 800-366-2223 or 202/659-5136.

Leukemia Family Support Group Program *National. 35 affiliated professionally-maintained groups. Founded 1984.* Mutual support for people with leukemia & its related diseases (Hodgkin's disease, lymphoma, multiple myeloma), their families & friends. Meetings held once or twice monthly. Write: 733 Third Ave., New York, NY 10017. Call Dana Naughton 212/573-8484 or 800-284-4271.

National Coalition for Cancer Survivorship *National. 400 member organizations. Founded 1986.* Clearinghouse for information, publications, & programs working on issues of survivorship. Advocacy for the interests of cancer survivors. Assistance in starting cancer support & networking systems. Newsletter. Conferences. Write: 1010 Wayne Ave., Silver Spring, MD 20910. Call 301/585-2616.

PAACT (Patient Advocates for Advanced Cancer Treatment) *Int'l. 84 affiliated groups. Founded 1984.* Provides support & advocacy for prostate cancer patients, their families & general public at risk. Information relative to the advancements in the treatment of prostate cancer. Information, referrals, phone help, conferences, newsletters. Group development guidelines. $50 contribution. Write: P.O. Box 141695, Grand Rapids, MI 49514-1695. Call 616/453-1477.

Reach to Recovery Discussion Groups Local outgrowth of Reach to Recovery Program which in most areas is a one-to-one visitation program for women with breast cancer, but in some areas is a support group. Contact your local or state chapter of American Cancer Society to determine availability of such groups.

Retinoblastoma Support Group *Int'l network. Founded 1988.* Aims to reach out with encouragement & knowledge to families afflicted by this childhood cancer. Undertakes projects that promote early detection to prevent blindness & save lives. Newsletter, phone support, pen pal program, conferences, assistance in starting new groups, social activities. Write: Russ & Susan Laventure, 603 Fourth Range Rd., Pembroke, NH 03275. Call 603/224-4085.

Us Too *Int'l. 64 affiliated groups. Founded 1990.* Mutual support, information & education for prostate cancer patients, their families & friends. Provides newsletter, information & referrals, phone support, assistance in starting new groups. Write: P.O. Box 7173, Oakbrook Terrace, Il 60181 or 300 W. Pratt St. #401, Baltimore, MD 21201. Call 800-82-US-TOO.

Y-ME Nat'l Org. for Breast Cancer Info. & Support *National. 12 affiliated groups. Founded 1978.* Information & peer support for breast cancer patients & their families during all stages of the disease. Hotline, newsletter, group development guidelines, conferences. Write: 18220 Harwood Ave., Homewood, IL 80430. Call 800-221-2141 (day) or 708/799-8228 (24 hours).

(Model) AABCA (African American Breast Cancer Alliance) *Founded 1990.* Support & advocacy for Black women with breast cancer, & their families. Provides information & referrals, education, & a forum for women to discuss issues & concerns. Open to anyone interested in supporting & working with this grass-roots organization. Write: AABCA, P.O. Box 8981, Minneapolis, MN 55408. Call 612/644-1224 or 612/644-7119.

(Model) Bay Area Multiple Myeloma Support Group *Founded 1990.* Sharing of information & support for persons with multiple myeloma. Exchange of current treatment & techniques. Phone support, information & referrals, hospital visits, health advocates, assistance in starting local groups. Write: c/o Evelyn Hall, 252 Wayne Ave., Apt. F, Oakland, CA 94606. Call 510/763-6911.

(Model) **Cancer Support Network** *Regional. 9 affiliated groups. Founded 1988.* Support network for cancer survivors, their families & friends through peer support & health care professionals in a variety of activities. Groups for men also. Newsletter, information & referrals, phone support. Write: c/o Barbara Seltman, 5850 Ellsworth Ave., #303, Pittsburgh, PA 15232. Call 412/361-8600.

(Model) **SHARE: Self-Help for Women with Breast Cancer** *Founded 1966. (Bi-lingual)* Support for women faced with the emotional, social & non-medical problems of breast or ovarian cancer. Groups for family & significant others. Groups led by trained leaders who have had cancer. Educational programs, newsletter, walkathon, phone support, education programs. Write: 19 W. 44th St. #415, NY, NY 10036-5902. Call 212-382-2111 (24 hr.) or 212/719-0364 (office).

(Model) **SPOHNC (Support for People with Oral & Head & Neck Cancer)** *Founded 1991.* Patient-directed self-help program offering encouragement, support, acceptance & self-expression for persons with oral & head & neck cancer. Offers small group meetings, phone support, educational programs, one-on-one support, & information & referrals. Assistance in starting groups. Write: 20 Valley Ave., Locust Valley, NY 11560. Call 516/671-7637.

CARPAL TUNNEL SYNDROME

American Carpal Tunnel Syndrome Association *Int'l. Founded 1990.* To support, educate, & protect persons with CTS & related repetitive motion injuries. Aims to prevent CTS for persons at risk. Newsletter, information. Write: P.O. Box 6730, Saginaw, MI 48608.

CELIAC SPRUE

American Celiac Society/Dietary Support Coalition *National. 20 chapters. Founded 1976.* Mutual support & information for celiac-sprue patients, families & health care professionals. Buddy system, visitation, phone help, participation in educational efforts. Newsletter. Write: c/o Annette Bentley, 58 Mustano Ct., W. Orange, NJ 07052. Call 201/325-8837.

Celiac Sprue Association/United States of America, Inc. *National. 51 chapters. Founded 1979.* Provides educational materials on celiac sprue & dermatitis herpetiformis to patients, parents of children, & professionals. Provides opportunities for support groups & networking with patients & professionals. Newsletter, conference. Group development guidelines. Write: P.O. Box 31700, Omaha, NE 68131-0700. Call 402/558-0600.

Gluten Intolerance Group of North America *National. 14 groups. Founded 1974.* Provides information & support to persons with celiac sprue or dermatitis herpetiformis, their families & health care professionals. Newsletter, information & referral, conferences, group development guidelines, cookbooks. Write: P.O. Box 23053, Seattle, WA 98102-0353. Call 206/325-6980.

CFC SYNDROME

CFC Support Network *Int'l network. Founded 1991.* Mutual support for parents of children with CFC Syndrome. Strives to find & disseminate information on this disorder. Offers newsletter, information & referrals, phone support, pen pal program. Write: c/o Nancy Carlson, 157 Alder Ave., Mckee City, NJ 08232. Call 609-646-5606.

CHARCOT-MARIE-TOOTH

Charcot Marie Tooth Association *Nat'l. 31 affiliated groups. Founded 1983.* Information & support for patients & families affected by Charcot-Marie-Tooth disorders (also known as peroneal muscular atrophy or hereditary motor sensory neuropathy). Referrals, newsletter, phone help, VCR tapes, support groups, conferences. Write: c/o Crozer Mills Enterprise Ctr., 600 Upland Ave., Upland, PA 19015. Call 215/499-7486.

C.M.T. International *Int'l. 10 groups. 2000+ members in 16 countries. Founded 1984.* Sharing & caring for those with C.M.T., or peroneal muscular atrophy. Information to patients & professionals. CMT/PMA registry to encourage research. Pen pals, bimonthly newsletter, bi-annual convention. Write: One Springbank Dr. 91/06, St. Catharines, Ontario, Canada L2S 2K1. Call 416/687-3630 (Mon. through Thurs. only btwn. 9-4:40).

CHARGE SYNDROME

CHARGE Syndrome *Nat'l network. Founded 1991.* Networking of families affected by CHARGE Syndrome (Coloboma of the eye; Heart Defect; Atresia of the nasal passages; Retardation of growth and/or development; Genital hypoplasia; Ear malformations). Offers booklets, newsletter, information & referrals. Dues $12/yr. Write: Marion A. Norbury, 2004 Parkade, Columbia, MO 65202. Call 314/442-7604.

Remember to send a self-addressed stamped envelope when writing to a group for information.

CHEMICAL HYPERSENSITIVITY /
ENVIRONMENTAL ILLNESS
(also see Chronic Fatigue Syndrome)

H.E.A.L. (Human Ecology Action League, Inc.) *National. 100+ chapters. Founded 1976.* Support, information for persons affected by multiple chemical sensitivities. Education to increase awareness of toxic substances. Resource list. Helps local chapters to achieve mutual objectives. Newsletter. Chapter development guidelines. Write: P.O. Box 49126, Atlanta, GA 30359-1128. Call 404/248-1898.

National Center for Environmental Health Strategies *Nat'l network. Founded 1986.* Support, networking, education, research & advocacy for chemically, environmentally or occupationally caused illnesses & anyone interested in indoor pollution & chemical sensitivity. Phone help, referrals, publications, newsletter. Dues: $10-15/individuals; $20/professionals. Call Mary Lamielle 609/429-5358 or write: 1100 Rural Ave., Voorhees, NJ 08043.

National Foundation for the Chemically Hypersensitive *National. 40 chapters. Founded 1986.* Information & networking for people who have a chemically induced immune system disorder. Devoted to research, education, & development of local chapters. Information & referrals, pen pals, conferences. Write: P.O. Box 222, Ophelia, VA 22530-0222. Call 517/697-3989.

CHROMOSOME DISORDERS
(See also specific disorder & Parenting: of Disabled)

Chromosome Deletion Outreach *National network. Founded 1992.* Support for families having a child diagnosed with any type of chromosome deletion. Provides phone support, newsletter. Dues $5/year. Write: P.O. Box 164, Holtsville, NY 11742. Call Christine Barr 516/736-6754.

Chromosome 18 Registry & Research Society *Int'l network. Founded 1990.* Education for families, physicians & the public about the disorders of chromosome 18. Encourages & conducts research into areas that impact families. Links affected families & their physicians to the research community. Newsletter, phone support, info. & referrals, pen pals. Dues $20-25. Write: Jannine Cody, 6302 Fox Head, San Antonio, TX 78247. Call 512/657-4968.

Please remember to enclose a self-addressed stamped envelope when requesting information from a group.

CHRONIC FATIGUE/EPSTEIN BARR SYNDROME
(also see Environmental Illness)

CFIDS Association, Inc. *National.* For people affected by chronic fatigue & immune dysfunction syndrome. Education, advocacy, funding of research. CFIDS Chronicle newsletter ($25 US; $35 Canada; $45 Overseas/Airmail). Write: P.O. Box 220398, Charlotte, NC 28222-0398. Call 800-442-3437.

National Chronic Fatigue Syndrome Association, Inc. *National. 600 affiliated groups worldwide. Founded 1985.* To educate patients, the public & medical profession about chronic fatigue syndrome. Support groups, quarterly newsletter, funds research, conducts seminars. Literature available for patients & physicians. Guidelines & assistance available for starting support groups. Write: 3521 Broadway #222, Kansas City, MO 64111. Call 816/931-4777 (24 hotline).

CLEFT PALATE

National Cleft Palate Association *Nat'l. 50 groups. Founded 1984.* Support & assistance for families of children with cleft palate or cleft lip & other cranio-facial anomalies. Hopes to build a coalition of parent support groups. Promotes public awareness & encourages research. Provides annual conferences, newsletter. Dues voluntary. Group development guidelines. Write: 1218 Grandview Ave., Pittsburgh, PA 15211. Call 800-242-5338 or 412/481-1376.

(Model) **Prescription Parents, Inc.** *Founded 1973.* Support group for families of children with cleft lip & palate. Education for parents of newborns, presentations by professionals. Family social events, newsletter, phone support network, group development guidelines. Write: P.O. Box 161, W. Roxbury, MA 02132. Call Laura Cohen 617/527-0878.

COFFIN-LOWRY SYNDROME

Coffin-Lowry Syndrome Foundation, The *Int'l network. Founded 1991.* Provides support through a database of real-life experiences & information on achievements that can be accomplished through love & early intervention for affected families. Newsletter, pen pal program, phone support, information & referrals. Write: Mary Illa, 6790 N.E. Day Rd. West, Bainbridge Island, WA 98110. Call 206/842-1523.

Please note: Model groups should be contacted primarily by those persons interested in starting a similar group in their area.

CONGENITAL CENTRAL HYPOVENTILATION SYNDROME

CCHS Family Support Network *Int'l network. Founded 1990.* Mutual support to help parents cope with having a child with Congenital Central Hypoventilation Syndrome (aka Ondine's Curse). Family newsletter, physician directory, phone support, information & referrals. Aids in research. Write: c/o Mary Vanderlaan, 71 Maple St., Oneonta, NY 13820. Call 607/432-8872.

CORNELIA DE LANGE

Cornelia de Lange Syndrome Foundation, Inc. *Int'l. 800+ member families. Founded 1981.* Provides parent & family support & education to support research & create public awareness. Newsletter. Family album for networking & mutual support. Annual convention. Write: Julie Mairano, 60 Dyer Ave., Collinsville, CT 06022. Call 800-223-8355. In Connecticut 800-753-2357 or 203/693-0159.

CRI DU CHAT (5P) SYNDROME
(See also Chromosome Disorders)

5P- Society *National.* Support organization for families having a child with 5P- Syndrome, genetic disorder characterized by a high-pitched cry. Dedicated to facilitating flow of info. among affected families & interested medical professionals. Listing of families in U.S & Canada. Newsletter. Annual meeting. Write: 11609 Oakmont, Overland Park, KS 66210. Call 913/469-8900.

CROHNS / COLITIS

Crohn's & Colitis Foundation of America (CCFA) *National. 90 chapters. Founded 1967.* Gives patients & their families an opportunity to share their feelings & reduce the isolation of living with these diseases. Funds for research, newsletter, educational seminars, films, videotapes, chapter development guidelines. Dues $25/year. Write: 444 Park Ave. South, 11th Fl., New York, NY 10016. Call 800/932-2423 or 212/685-3440.

CUSHING'S DISEASE
(also see Pituitary Disorders)

National Cushing's Association *National network. Founded 1988.* Education & support for persons with Cushing's disease. Physician referral, medical information, phone support, pen pal program, Dues $25/year. Write: 4645 Van Duys Blvd., Sherman Oaks, CA 91403. Call 818-788-9239 (day).

DALKON SHIELD

Dalkon Shield Information Network *National.* Support & information for women who are Dalkon Shield survivors. Referrals to allied organizations. Conferences. Write: P.O. Box 53, Bethlehem, PA 18016. Call 812/333-4507.

DES

DES-Action U.S.A. *National. 45 groups. Founded 1978.* For women who took DES during pregnancy & their children. Support groups, physician referrals, education for the public & health workers. Quarterly newsletter. Group development guidelines. East coast write: Long Island Jewish Medical Center, New Hyde Park, NY 11040. Call 516/775-3450. West coast write: 1615 Broadway #510, Oakland, CA 94612. Call 510/465-4011.

DES Cancer Network *National. Founded 1983.* For women who have had DES-related clear cell cancer. Peer support, information on medical & legal resources, research advocacy. Newsletter. Regional meetings. Write: P.O. Box 10185, Rochester, NY 14610. Call 716/473-6119.

DIABETES

American Diabetes Association *National. 54 affiliates. Founded 1941.* Seeks to improve the well-being of people with diabetes & their families. Fund raising for research. Affiliates & chapters provide many support services. Free newsletter. $24 dues includes magazine. Write: 1660 Duke St., Alexandria, VA 22314. Call 800-232-3472 (day).

JDF International, The Diabetes Research Foundation *Int'l. 130+ chapters in No. America; 140+ worldwide. Founded 1970.* Fund raising for research to find the cause, cure, treatment & prevention of diabetes & its complications. Peer support groups through local chapters. Quarterly magazine. Chapter development guidelines. Write: 432 Park Ave. South, New York, NY 10016. Call 212/889-7575 or 800-223-1138.

(Model) **Diabetes Anonymous** *Founded 1990.* Fellowship of men & women who share their experience, strength, hope & recovery with each other. Primary purpose is the management of diabetes. Phone support, assistance in starting new groups. Write: P.O. Box 60905, Sunnyvale, CA 94088-0905. Call James 408/746-2022.

DPT VACCINE INJURY

Nat'l Vaccine Info. Ctr. (Dissatisfied Parents Together) *Nat'l. Reps in all states. Founded 1982.* NVIC/DPT is a support, information & advocacy group for parents whose children were adversely affected by vaccines. Advocates for safety reforms in the mass vaccination system & safer vaccines. Promotes education for parents & professionals. Various literature ($5-13); newsletter. Dues $20/yr. Write: NVIC, 204-F Mill St., NE #F, Vienna, VA 22180-4500. Call 703/938-DPT3.

DYSAUTONOMIA

Dysautonomia Foundation, Inc., The *Int'l. 16 chapters. Founded 1951.* Information, referrals & fundraising for research & clinic maintenance. Peer support for families affected by dysautonomia. Newsletter. Informal pen pal & phone support network. Dues $25/year. Write: 20 E. 46th St., #302, New York, NY 10017. Call 212/949-6644.

DYSMOTILITY, CHRONIC

Chronic Dysmotility Support Group *National network.* Telephone & mail network providing support & information for patients & families. Write: c/o Sandra Domask, 114 West 4th St., Palmyra, NJ 08065. Call 609/829-0377.

DYSTONIA

Dystonia Medical Research Foundation *National. 24 chapters. Founded 1976.* Education, support groups & fund-raising for research. Newsletter, information & referrals, conferences. In Canada, write: Lois Raphael, E.D., First City Bldg, #1800, 777 Hornby St., Vancouver, BC V6Z 2K3 Canada. Call 604/661-4886. In US write: Dana Klosner, Dystonia Med. Research Fdn., 8383 Wilshire Blvd., #800, Beverly Hills, CA 90210. Call 213/852-1630.

EAR ANOMALIES

Ear Anomalies Reconstructed: Atresia/Microtia Support Group *Int'l. 3 affiliated groups. Founded 1986.* Networking for families whose members have microtia, atresia, or craniofacial microsomia. Sharing of experiences & medical information. Phone support, visitation, conferences. Support group meets periodically in New York City. Write: c/o Betsy Old, 72 Durand Rd., Maplewood, NJ 07040. Call Betsy Old 201/761-5438 or Jack Gross 212/947-0770.

EATING DISORDERS (ANOREXIA/BULIMIA)
(see also Addictions: General)

American Anorexia/Bulimia Association, Inc. *National. 4 affiliated groups. Founded 1978.* Information & education for persons with eating disorders, their families & professionals. Referrals to support groups. Offers speakers bureau, newsletter, group development assistance, professional conferences, lecture series. Dues $50/yr. per family. Groups are member-run with professionals used as resource persons. Write: 418 E. 76th St., NY, NY 10021. Call 212/734-1114.

B.A.S.H. (Bulimia Anorexia Self-Help) *National network. Founded 1981.* Information & self-help groups for people with anorexia or bulimia & their families, as well with individuals struggling with mood disorders. Literature, meetings & discussion groups led by trained peer facilitators. Monthly magazine $25/yr. Annual conference each Spring. Group facilitator's manual. Write: P.O. Box 39903, St. Louis, MO 63138.

National Anorexic Aid Society, Inc. *National. Founded 1977.* Support & education for people suffering from anorexia, bulimia & related eating disorders, & their families & friends. Support groups, qtrly newsletter, information & referrals, audiotapes. Dues $20. Group development guidelines $5; info. packets $5. Write: 1925 E. Dublin Granville Rd., Columbus, OH 43229-3517. Call 614/436-1112.

Nat'l Assn. of Anorexia Nervosa & Associated Disorders, Inc. (ANAD) *Int'l. 300+ affiliated groups. Founded 1976.* Information on self-help groups, therapy, & referrals to professionals. Meetings led by members with professionals as sponsors. Newsletter. Group development guidelines. Write: P.O. Box 7, Highland Park, IL 60035. Call 708/831-3438.

ECTODERMAL DYSPLASIAS

National Foundation for Ectodermal Dysplasias *National network. Founded 1981.* Distributes information on symptoms & treatments; provides support programs for families; cooperates with research projects. Monthly newsletter. Annual family conference. Directory of members for informal contacts among families. Group development guidelines. Write: 219 E. Main St., Box 114, Mascoutah, IL 62258. Call 618/566-2020.

Remember to always include a self-addressed stamped envelope when requesting information or literature from a group.

EHLERS DANLOS SYNDROME

Ehlers-Danlos National Foundation *Nat'l. Founded 1985.* Emotional support & updated information to persons with Ehlers-Danlos Syndrome. Serves as a vital informational link to & from the medical community. Provides physician referral assistance, computerized database to link interested members to communicate w/each other, & conducts periodic learning conferences. Write: P.O. Box 1212, Southgate, MI 48195. Call 313/282-0180; 313/282-2793 (FAX).

ENDOMETRIOSIS

U.S. - Canadian Endometriosis Association *Int'l. 125 support groups & chapters. Founded 1980.* Information exchange, mutual support, educational materials & newsletter. Promotes research. Phone support network. Wide variety of literature available. Information & referrals. Dues $25/year. Chapter development guidelines. Write: 8585 N. 76th Pl., Milwaukee, WI 53223. Call 800-992-3636 or 414/355-2200.

EPILEPSY

Epilepsy Foundation of America *National. 85 affiliates. Founded 1967.* Information & support for people with epilepsy, their families & friends. Pharmaceutical program, newsletter for members. Affiliates' development kit. Referrals to local affiliates (many of which have employment related programs). Info. & referrals. Write: 4351 Garden City Dr., Landover, MD 70785. Call 301/459-3700. Prof. library; medical & psychosocial literature call 800-332-4050

(Model) **Epilepsy Society of Southern NY, Inc.** *Founded 1977.* Provides medical & neurological referrals, education, family support services, advocacy, crisis intervention, counseling, & medical & medicaid case management. Write: 4 Secor Rd., P.O. Box 371, Thiells, NY 10984. Call 914/942-0002.

EXSTROPHY OF BLADDER

National Support Group for Exstrophy of the Bladder *National. Founded 1979.* Networking for patients & their families. Seminars, educational meetings & social events. Newsletter, informal pen pal program & phone support network, information & referrals. Write: 5075 Medhurst, Solon, OH 44139. Call 216/248-6851 (eves).

EXTRACORPOREAL MEMBRANE OXYGENATION

ECMO Moms & Dads *Int'l network. 17 groups. Founded 1987.* Mutual support for parents who have agreed to extracorporeal membrane oxygenation procedure on their infant as a last resort to attempt to save the life. Phone support, newsletter, pen pal, conferences, info. & referrals, help in starting groups. Write: c/o Gail Willson, HCRI Box 255, Plainview, TX 79072. Call 806-889-3877.

FACIAL DISFIGUREMENT

AboutFace *Int'l. 38 chapters. Founded 1985.* Support & info. to those who have a facial disfigurement & their families. Networks families who have a similar concern. Programs of public education & awareness. Newsletter, info, & referrals, assistance in starting local groups. Write: 1002 Liberty Ln., Warrington, PA 18976. Call 800-AB5-FACE; or (Int'l) 99 Crowns Lane, 3rd Fl., Toronto, Canada M5R 3P4. Call 416/944-FACE.

Let's Face It *National.* Network for people with facial disfigurements & other facial disorders. (Does not include disfigurement caused by "botched" plastic surgery.) Phone help, pen pals, support groups meetings, hospital & home visitation. Networking support. Resource list. Write: 711, Concord, MA 01742. Call Betsy Wilson 508/371-3186.

Orofacial Outreach *Int'l network. Founded 1990.* Support, reassurance & education for families of children with Goldenhar Syndrome or Hemifacial Microsomia. Information & referrals, phone support, pen pals, & occasional trips. Write: 13962 Wake Ave., Irvine, CA 92718. Call Gretchen Garza 714/651-6151.

(Model) **Forward Face** *Founded 1978.* Mutual support & problem solving for people with craniofacial disfigurement & for their families. Liaison with medical personnel, community education. Newsletter. Videotapes. Dues $5. Phone support network. Write: c/o I.R.P.S., NYU Medical Ctr., 560 First Ave., NY, NY 10016. Call Patricia Chibbaro 800-422-3223 or 212/340-5205.

FAMILIAL ERYTHROPHAGOTIC LYMPHOHISTIOCYTOSIS

FEL Network *Int'l network. Founded 1990.* Network for parents of children with Familial Erythrophagotic Lymphohistiocytosis. Provides information, referral, networking, phone support & current resources. Write: c/o Kay Wojtek, 2519 W. Twohig, San Angelo, TX 76901. Call 915/949-4228.

FETAL ALCOHOL SYNDROME
(see also Parenting: Adoption; Parents of Disabled)

Fetal Alcohol Network *Int'l. Founded 1990.* Mutual support for parents of persons with fetal alcohol syndrome. Interested in advocacy, educational issues, behavioral problems & accessing community services. Newsletter, conferences, group development guidelines. Write: 158 Rosemont Ave., Coatesville, PA 19320. Call 215/384-1133.

(Model) **Adoptive & Foster Parents of FAS & Drug-Affected Children** *Founded 1991.* Support network for adoptive & foster parents of children affected by fetal alcohol syndrome or pre-natal drug use. Open to those who suspect their adopted/foster child may be affected, as well. Support group meetings, literature. Write: BCCA & DA, Attn: Ronnie Jacobs, P.O. Box 626, Paramus, NJ 07653. Call Ronnie Jacobs 201/261-1450.

FIBRODYSPLASIA OSSIFICANS PROGRESSIVA

Int'l Fibrodysplasia Ossificans Progressiva Association *National network. Founded 1988.* Information & support for people affected by F.O.P. Provides newsletter, pen pals, phone support, conferences, current research information, group development guidelines. Write: 1434 Howard St., Petoskey, MI 49770, phone 616/347-1833; or 910 N. Jerico, Casselberry, FL 32707, phone 407/365-4194.

FIBROMYALGIA

Fibromyalgia Assn. of Central Ohio *Regional. 85 groups. Founded 1987.* Education & support for persons with fibromyalgia. Distributes educational material to public & professionals. Information & referrals to support groups. Newsletter, phone support, conferences. Assistance in starting new groups. Write: 3545 Olentangy River Rd., #008, Columbus, OH 43214. Call 614/262-2000.

Fibromyalgia Network *National. Founded 1988.* Provides information on fibromyalgia, self-help groups/patients contacts & health care professionals, & other services to improve the quality of life for FMS patients. Offers newsletter, phone support, information & referrals, conferences. Write: 5700 Stockdale Hwy, #100, Bakersfield, CA 93309. Call 805/631-1950 (day).

FRAGILE X SYNDROME

Fragile X Association of America *National. Founded 1984.* Provides mutual support for parents & siblings of children with Fragile X Syndrome. Education for public & professionals. Pen pal program, telephone network. Write: Jackie Franklin, P.O. Box 39, Park Ridge, IL 60068. Call Dr. Kravis, Univ. of Chicago 312/702-6487 or Jackie Franklin 708/680-3317.

National Fragile X Foundation. The *Int'l. 46 groups. Founded 1984.* Provides information to promote education & research regarding Fragile X Syndrome, a genetic disorder, which is the leading cause of inherited mental retardation. Phone support, newsletter, information & referrals. Write: 1441 York St., #215, Denver, CO 80206. Call 800-688-8765 or 303/333-6155.

FREEMAN-SHELDON

Freeman-Sheldon Parent Support Group *Int'l network. Founded 1981.* Emotional support for parents of children with Freeman-Sheldon. Also for adults with this syndrome. Sharing of helpful medical literature library. Info. on growth & development of affected individuals. Members network by phone & mail Write: 509 E. Northmont Way, Salt Lake City, UT 84103. Call 801/364-7060.

GALACTOSEMIC CHILDREN

Parents of Galactosemic Children, Inc. *Int'l. 5 U.S./4 Int'l affiliated groups. Founded 1985.* Provides information & support for parents of galactosemic children. Newsletter, information & referrals, & phone support. Write: c/o Linda Manis, 20981 Solano Way, Boca Raton, FL 33433. Call 407/852-0266.

GAUCHER DISEASE

National Gaucher Foundation *Nat'l. 22 support groups. Founded 1984.* Information & assistance for those affected by Gaucher's Disease. Education & outreach to increase public awareness. Family support network, newsletter, telephone support, medical board. Write: 19241 Montgomery Village Ave. #E-21, Gaithersburg, MD 20879-2033. Call 301/990-3800.

GLYCOGEN STORAGE DISEASE

Association For Glycogen Storage Disease *U.S & Canadian network. Founded 1979.* Mutual support & information-sharing among parents of children with glycogen storage disease. Fosters communication between parents & professionals, creates public awareness, encourages research. Newsletter, phone support, conferences. Write: P.O. Box 896, Durant, IA 52747. Call 319/785-6038.

GRANULOMATOUS DISEASE, CHRONIC

Chronic Granulomatous Disease Assn. *Int'l network. Founded 1982.* Support & information for persons with CGD, their families & physicians. Networking of patients with similar CGD-related illnesses; support through correspondence & telephone. Newsletter publishes medical & research articles. National registry of patients. Write: 2616 Monterey Rd., San Marino, CA 91108. Call 818/441-4118 (9am-3pm, or anytime with special concerns).

GRAVES DISEASE

National Grave's Disease Foundation *Nat'l. 8 chapters. Founded 1990.* Aims to establish support groups, fund research, provide better treatment, & to increase public awareness. Newsletter, information & referrals, phone support, one-on-one programs, conferences. Group development guidelines $10. Write: c/o Dr. Nancy Patterson, 320 Arlington Rd., Jacksonville, FL 32211. Call 904/724-0770.

GUILLAIN-BARRE SYNDROME

Guillain-Barre Syndrome Foundation International *Int'l. 130 chapters. Founded 1983.* Emotional support, visitation, & education for people affected by Guillain-Barre Syndrome. Promotes research. Newsletter, pen pals, phone network, group development guidelines, international symposium. Write: P.O. Box 262, Wynnewood, PA 19096. Call 215/667-0131.

HEART DISEASE

Coronary Club, Inc. *National. 5 affiliated groups. Founded 1968.* Offers support to heart patients, & provides education on proper heart care & rehabilitation. Literature. Monthly bulletin "Heartline." $20/year. Networking & referrals. Group development guidelines. Write: 9500 Euclid Ave., Cleveland, OH 44106. Call 216/444-3690.

International Bundle Branch Block Association *Int'l. Founded 1979.* Support & information to help bundle branch block persons & families cope. Educates public. Sporadic newsletter. Pen pal program, informal phone support system. Guidelines & assistance for starting groups. Voluntary dues $10. Write: c/o R. K. Lewis, 6631 W. 83rd St., Los Angeles, CA 90045-2899. Call 310/670-9132.

Mended Hearts *National. 225 chapters. Founded 1951.* Self-help groups for persons who have heart disease, their families, friends, & interested persons. Newsletter. Chapter development kit. Write: 7320 Greenville Ave., Dallas, TX 75231. Call 214/706-1442.

United Patient's Assn. for Pulmonary Hypertension *National network. Founded 1990.* Support & information for patients with pulmonary hypertension (a cardio-vascular disease), their families & physicians. Encourages research, promotes awareness. Phone help, resource references, pen pals, help in starting groups. Newsletter ($10). Write: 116 Mattek Ave., Dekalb, IL 60115. Call Judy Simpson 815/758-4101 or Teresa Knazik 407/729-0256 (FL).

HEMIFACIAL MICROSOMIA

Hemifacial Microsomia/Goldenhar Syndrome Family Support Network *Int'l network. Founded 1988.* Mutual support & sharing of information re: treatment centers for parents of children with hemifacial microsomia or Goldenhar syndrome. Family & center resource list, medical library, newsletter, pen pals, phone help. Write: 6 Country Lane Way, Philadelphia, PA 19115. Call 215/677-4787.

HEMIFACIAL SPASM

Hemifacial Spasm Support Group *National network. Founded 1991.* Provides information & referrals regarding treatments & doctors for people suffering with hemifacial spasms. Phone support, pen pal program. Write: 9928 Clearfield Ave., Vienna, VA 22181. Call 703/242-2330.

HEMOCHROMATOSIS

Hemochromatosis Research Foundation, Inc. *National. 5 chapters. Founded 1982.* For hemochromatosis families & professionals. Promotes general awareness, encourages screenings to identify families; fundraising, videotapes, educational materials, genetic counseling, referrals, newsletter, conferences & periodic teleconferences. Send self-addressed stamped envelope to: P.O. Box 8569, Albany, NY 12208. Call 518/489-0972.

Iron Overload Diseases Assoc., Inc. *National. 6 groups. Founded 1981.* For hemochromatosis (excess iron) patients & their families. Encourages research & public awareness. Organizes self-help groups, acts as clearinghouse for patients & doctors. Bi-monthly newsletter "Ironic Blood." Membership dues $50/yr. Write: 433 Westwind Dr., N. Palm Beach, FL 33408. Call 407/840-8512, 407/840-8513 or 407/840-8514 (TDD).

HEMOPHILIA

National Hemophilia Foundation *National. 43 chapters. Founded 1948.* Service to persons with hemophilia & their families. Promotes research. Seeks to increase public awareness. Semi-annual newsletter, group development guidelines, annual meeting for patients & professionals. Dues vary. Write: c/o The Soho Bldg., 110 Green St. #303, New York, NY 10012. Call 800-42-HANDI or 212/219-8180.

National Hemophilia Fdn. Women's Outreach Network (WONN) *National. 48 groups. Founded 1990.* A peer-led hemophilia & HIV/AIDS support & education program designed to mobilize & empower any woman who has a relationship to someone with hemophilia, or who has a bleeding disorder herself. Newsletter, phone support, conferences, information & referrals, assistance in starting new groups. Write: 110 Green St., #303, New York, NY 10012. Call 212/219-8180.

HEREDITARY HEMORRHAGIC TELANGIECTASIA

HHT Foundation International, Inc *Int'l. Founded 1991.* Support for those interested in Hereditary Hemorrhagic Telangiectasia (aka Rendu-Osler-Weber Syndrome) by exchanging information & research. Aims to protect privacy. Newsletter, conferences, pen pals, scholarships, activities & brochures. Assistance in starting support groups. Dues $40/family. Write: 1159 Sudden Valley, Bellingham, WA 98226-4830. Call Sharon Victor 206/738-7605.

HERPES

Herpes Resource Center *National. 100 groups. Founded 1979.* Emotional support & medical info. for persons with herpes. Quarterly journal, telephone network, support group development guidelines. Dues $25/contribution. Also helps start HPV support groups. Free pamphlets. Write: P.O. Box 13827, Research Triangle Park, NC 27709. Call 919/361-8485 (office) or 919/361-8488 (hotline - 9am-7pm).

(Model) **Herpes Anonymous** *Founded 1984.* Educational & social support for persons with herpes & interested others. Dedicated to helping others overcome the social stigmas & embarrassing hardships brought on by this chronic disease. Dues $20/year. Newsletters, socials. Write: H.A., P.O. Box 278, Westbury, NY 11590. Call Lenny 516/334-5718.

HIRSCHSPRUNG'S DISEASE

American Hirschsprung's Disease Association, Inc. *Int'l. Founded 1984.* Information & support for parents of children with Hirschsprung's Disease. Videotaped educational meetings, parent-to-parent support, listing of patients & data, newsletter, conferences. Write: 22-1/2 Spruce St., Brattleboro, VT 05301. Call 802/257-0603.

HISTIOCYTOSIS-X

Histiocytosis Association of America *National network. Founded 1985.* Mutual support & information for parents & patients with this rare disorder. Parent-patient directory facilitates networking & communication. Encourages research. Bi-lingual literature & pamphlets. Newsletter. Write: 609 New York Rd., Glassboro, NJ 08028. Call 800-548-2758 (day) or Jeff & Sally Toughill 609/881-4911 (eve).

HUMAN PAPILLOMA VIRUS

HPV Support Program *National. Founded 1991.* Provides a safe, confidential environment in which to obtain information & share experiences with others with HPV. Information & referrals, help in starting groups. Write: c/o ASHA/HPV Prog. Coord., P.O. Box 13827, Research Triangle Park, NC 27709. Call 919/361-8400.

(Model) **Human Papilloma Virus Support Group** *Founded 1992.* Open to anyone who is, or has been, infected with the HPV virus, or those interested in gathering more information on this virus. Sponsored by American Social Health Assn. Write: Dick Conevoy, P.O. Box 9701, Washington DC 20016; call 202/244-7208 (eve).

HUNTINGTON'S DISEASE

Huntington's Disease Society of America *National. 32 chapters. Founded 1967.* Maintains chapters offering support groups for patients & families. Supports research. Educational materials. Newsletter. Chapter development guidelines. Write: 140 West 22nd St., 6th Fl., New York, NY 10011. Call 212/242-1968 or 800-345-4372.

HYDROCEPHALUS

HEALTHY (Hydrocephalics Encouraging Active Lives Through Helping Yourself) *Int'l. Founded 1986.* Communication among people with hydrocephalus & their families. Networking of adults with hydrocephalus. Provides phone support & pen pals.

Assistance in starting groups. Write: c/o Cheryl Wolkoff, 434 Cardinal Lane, Bedminster, NJ 07921. Call 908/781-2519.

Hydrocephalus Association *National network. Founded 1984.* Offers mutual support, education & advocacy for parents of children with hydrocephalus. Provides newsletter, phone support, conferences, information & referrals; assistance in starting new groups. Write: 2040 Polk St. #342, San Francisco, CA 94109. Call Emily Fudge 415/776-4713.

Hydrocephalus Parent Support Group *National. Founded 1982.* Support & education about various aspects of hydrocephalus & spina bifida. Family social events. Phone help, peer-counseling, visitation. National newsletter $10/year. Pen pals. Write: c/o Kathy McGowan, 6059 Rancho Mission Rd. #106, San Diego, CA 92108-2365. Call 619/282-1070.

National Hydrocephalus Foundation *National. 3 affiliated groups. Founded 1979.* Support & information for adults with hydrocephalus & for parents of children with hydrocephalus. Quarterly newsletter, reference library, VCR rentals of annual symposiums. Dues $10/yr. Write: 400 N. Michigan Ave., Suite 1102, Chicago, IL 60611-4102. Call 815/467-6548.

HYPOGLYCEMIA

Hypoglycemia Association, Inc. *Int'l network. Founded 1967.* Mutual support & education for persons with hypoglycemia & their families. Newsletter, information & referrals, meetings 5 times per year. Provides assistance in starting new groups. Write: Dorothy Schultz, Pres., 18008 New Hampshire Ave., Box 165, Ashton, MD 20861-0165. Call 202/544-4044 (recorded message).

HYSTERECTOMY

(Model) **HERS Foundation (Hysterectomy Educational Resources & Services)** *Founded 1982.* Provides information about alternatives to & consequences of hysterectomy. Helps network women together for support. Quarterly newsletter $20/year. Group development guidelines. Write: 422 Bryn Mawr Ave., Bala Cynwyd, PA 19004. Call 215/667-7757.

IMMUNE DEFICIENCY

Immune Deficiency Foundation *National. Chapters in 19 states. Founded 1980.* Provides support & education for families affected by primary immune deficiency diseases. Newsletter, handbook, videotape & educational materials for public & medical professionals. Scholarships & fellowship programs. Group development guidelines. Write: P.O. Box 586, Columbia, MD 21045. Call 410/461-3127.

IMPOTENCY

Impotents Anonymous & I-Anon *National. 100+ chapters. Founded 1983.* Information & support for impotent men & their partners. Uses an adaptation of the 12-Step program of AA. Quarterly newsletter. Physician reference list. Videotapes & audio cassettes. Chapter development guidelines. Send self-addressed stamped envelope. Write: P.O. Box 5299, Maryville, TN 37802-5299. Call 615/983-6064.

INCONTENTIA PIGMENTI

I P Support Network *National network. Founded 1991.* Mutual support & networking for families affected by Incontentia Pigmenti (Bloch-Siemens-Sulzberger Syndrome). Newsletter. Write: 34929 Elm, Wayne, MI 48184. Call 313/729-7912.

INCONTINENCE

Simon Foundation *National network. Founded 1983.* Support & advocacy for people suffering from incontinence. Quarterly newsletter, pen pal program, group development guidelines. Write: P.O. Box 815, Wilmette, IL 60091. Call 718/864-3913 or 800-23-SIMON.

INFERTILITY

Resolve *National. 52 chapters. Founded 1974.* Emotional support & medical referrals for infertile couples. Peer counseling, education for members & public. Quarterly newsletter, publications. Chapter development guidelines. Write: 1310 Broadway, Somerville, MA 02144-1731. Call 617/623-0744.

INTERSTITIAL CYSTITIS

Interstitial Cystitis Association *National. Coordinators in various states. 100 groups. Founded 1985.* Provides education, information & support groups for those with interstitial cystitis & their spouses & families. Quarterly newsletter. Write: P.O. Box 1553, Madison Square Station, New York, NY 10159. Call 212/979-6057.

Remember to always enclose a self-addresed stamped envelope when requesting information from a group.

INTESTINAL MULTIPLE POLYPOSIS

IMPACC (Intestinal Multiple Polyposis And Colorectal Cancer) *Nat'l network. Founded 1986.* Support network for patients & their families. Provides referrals to local registries. Quarterly newsletter. Phone support network; pen pal program. Information & referrals. Write: c/o Dolores Boone, 1008 Brinker Dr. #101, Hagerstown, MD 21740-7420. Call 301/791-7526; or Anne Krush, Johns Hopkins 410/955-3875; FAX: 410/955-0484.

INTRAVENTRICULAR HEMORRHAGE

I.V.H. Parents *National. Founded 1984.* Support & education for parents of children with I.V.H., & professionals. On-going research. Professional information exchange. Quarterly newsletter, pen pal program, telephone support, computer networking. Membership dues $15/yr. Write: P.O. Box 56-111, Miami, FL 33256-1111. Call 305/232-0381 or FAX 305/232-9890.

JOSEPH DISEASE

International Joseph Diseases Foundation, Inc. *Int'l network. 3 affiliated groups. Founded 1977.* Voluntary, non-profit organization of concerned persons including patients, their families & friends, & health care professionals. Provides information about the disease, supports & conducts research, helps patients find services. Newsletter, group development guidelines. Write: P.O. Box 2550, Livermore, CA 94551-2550.

JOUBERT SYNDROME

Joubert Syndrome Parents-In-Touch Network *Int'l network. Founded 1992.* Mutual support & sharing of knowledge for parents of children with Joubert Syndrome. Aims to educate physicians & support team. Provides information & referrals, phone support & pen pal program. Write: c/o Mary J. VanDamme, 12348 Summer Meadow Rd., Rock, MI 49880. Call 906/359-4707.

KIDNEY DISEASE / HEMODIALYSIS

American Association of Kidney Patients (AAKP) *National. 20 chapters. Founded 1969.* Provides information, education & mutual support for patients, their families & friends. Consumer advocacy. Educational materials, quarterly newspaper, bi-annual magazine, chapter development guidelines. Write: 111 S. Parker St., Tampa, FL 33606-2354. Call 800-749-2257 or 813/251-0725.

PKR Foundation (Polycystic Kidney Disease) *Int'l. 13 affiliated groups. Founded 1982.* Provides emotional support & education for persons with polycystic kidney disease & their families. Promotes public awareness. Holds medical seminars & fundraisers. Conferences, phone support, newsletter, assistance in starting new groups. Write: 922 Walnut, #411, Kansas City, MO 64106. Call 800-PKD-CURE (day).

(Model) **Positive Renal Outreach Program (PROP)** *Founded 1984.* Support for kidney disease patients, families & friends. Education for the public on living with kidney disease. Newsletter, info & referrals, phone support, assistance in starting groups. Write: P.O. Box 32, Maryknoll, NY 10545-0032. Call 914/739-6436.

KLINEFELTER SYNDROME

Klinefelter Syndrome & Associates *National network. Founded 1989.* Support & information for families of boys with Klinefelter syndrome. Newsletter. Write: P.O. Box 119, Roseville, CA 95661-0119. (Please include self-addressed stamped envelope).

KLIPPEL-TRENAUNAY

Klippel-Trenaunay Support Group *National network. Founded 1986.* Provides mutual support & sharing of experiences among families of children with K.T., & adults with K.T. Newsletter, phone support, meetings every two years. Write: 4610 Wooddale Ave., Minneapolis, MN 55424. Call 612/925-2596.

LACTIC ACIDOSIS

Lactic Acidosis Support Group *National network.* Mutual support for parents dealing with lactic acidosis. Information & referrals, phone support, pen pals, conferences. Write: Sandy Glaser, P.O. Box 480282, Denver, CO 80248-0282. Call 303/287-4953.

LANDAU-KLEFFNER SYNDROME

CANDLE (Childhood Aphasia Autism Neurological Disorders LKS & Epilepsy) *Int'l.* Network of parents & professionals interested in Landau-Kleffner Syndrome/Acquired Epileptic Aphasia. Provides information on options, treatments, identification. Newsletter, listening & sharing of experiences, letter exchanges, conferences, information & referrals. Write: c/o Jane Rudick, 4414 McCampbell Dr., Montgomery, AL 36106. Call 205/271-3947.

LARYNGECTOMY

Int'l Assoc. of Laryngectomees *Int'l. 302 chapters. Founded 1952.* Acts as a bridge starting before surgery through rehabilitation, & for practical & emotional support. Newsletter. Chapter development guidelines. Write: c/o Amer. Cancer Soc., 1599 Clifton Rd., NE, Atlanta, GA 30329. Call 404/320-3333.

LEAD POISONING

(Model) **Coalition Against Lead Poisoning** *Founded 1986.* Mutual support & assistance for parents whose children have lead paint poisoning. Advocacy to reduce lead poisoning through legislative changes. Meetings, info. & referrals, phone support. Write: 10 S. Wolfe St., Baltimore, MD 21231. Call 301/727-4226.

LEUKODYSTROPHY

United Leukodystrophy Foundation, Inc. *National network. Founded 1982.* Provides information & resources for patients & their families. Network among families. Promotes research, public & professional awareness. Quarterly newsletter. National & regional conferences. Dues $25-50. Write: 2304 Highland Dr., Sycamore, IL 60178. Call 815/895-3211 or 800-728-5483.

LIFE-THREATENING ILLNESS

Center for Attitudinal Healing, The *National. 70+ affiliates. Founded 1975.* Support programs for children, adolescents & adults facing their own, or a family member's, life-threatening illness. All services free of charge. Quarterly newsletter. Write: 19 Main St., Tiburon, CA 94920. Call 415/435-5022.

Make Today Count *National. 300 chapters. Founded 1974.* Mutual support & discussion for persons facing a life-threatening illness. For relatives & friends also. National bimonthly newsletter, information & referrals. Chapter development guidelines. Write: P.O. Box 6063, Kansas City, KS 66106. Call 913/362-2866.

LISSENCEPHALY

Lissencephaly Network, Inc., The *National network. Founded 1991.* Support for families affected by lissencephaly (smooth brain surface) to help deal with the retardation & other health problems. Educates professionals. Phone support, pen pals, newsletter, info. & referrals. Equipment program, genetic counseling. Write: c/o Dianna Fitzgerald, 7121 Baer Rd., Fort Wayne, IN 46809. Call 219/747-1075.

LIVER DISEASE

American Liver Foundation *National. 28 chapters. Founded 1976.* Fights all liver diseases through research, education & patient self-help groups. Chapters organized & operated by lay volunteers. Newsletter, chapter development guidelines. Write: 1425 Pompton Ave., Cedar Grove, NJ 07009. Call 201/256-2550 or 800-223-0179.

LOWE'S SYNDROME

Lowe's Syndrome Association *Int'l. Founded 1983.* Fosters communication among families with Lowe's Syndrome. Provides medical/educational info. Supports research. Booklet available, newsletter 3X/year. Int'l conference. Dues $15 (can be waived). Write: 222 Lincoln St., W. Lafayette, IN 47906. Call 317/743-3634.

LUPUS

American Lupus Society *National. 25 chapters. Founded 1974.* Monthly meetings & rap groups for lupus patients & families. Stimulates public awareness, raises funds for lupus research. Free literature. Quarterly newsletter. Some chapters have phone networking. Dues $12/year. Write: 3914 Del Amo Blvd., Suite 922, Torrance, CA 90503. Call 310/542-8891 or 800-331-1802.

Lupus Foundation of America, Inc., The *National. 104 chapters. Founded 1977.* Information & materials about lupus, services to people with lupus & their families. Education & research programs. Newsletter & membership through local chapters. Write: 4 Research Pl., #180, Rockville, MD 20850-3226. Call 800-558-0121 or 301-670-9292.

LYME DISEASE

(Resource) **Lyme Borreliosis Fdn., Inc.** *Founded 1988.* Had previously referred to self-help groups. Currently provides information, packets on Lyme disease & doctor referrals. Write: P.O. Box 462, Tolland, CT 06084. Call 203/871-2900.

LYMPHEDEMA

National Lymphedema Network Inc. *National. 48 affiliated chapters. Founded 1988.* Support groups & information re: primary & secondary lymphedema. Newsletter, phone hotline, pen pal program, conferences, referrals to treatment centers, assistance in starting new groups. Dues $25/yr. Write: 2211 Post St., #404, San Francisco, CA 94115. Call 800-541-3259.

MALIGNANT HYPERTHERMIA

Malignant Hyperthermia Assn. of the U.S. (M.H.A.U.S.) *Nat'l network. Founded 1981.* Education & support for M.H. susceptible families. Information for health care professionals. Conducts limited research. Newsletters, annual conference. Write: P.O. Box 191, Westport, CT 06881-0191. Call 203/655-3007.

MAPLE SYRUP URINE DISEASE
(also see Neurometabolic Disorders)

Maple Syrup Urine Disease Family Support Group *National network. Founded 1981.* Opportunity for support & personal contact for those with MSUD & their families. Information on MSUD distribution. Strengthens the liaison between families & professionals. Encourages research & newborn screening. Three newsletters, $10/yr. Write: c/o Bonnie Lou Koons, 8017 Jonestown Rd., Harrisburg, PA 17112. Call 717/652-1386.

MARFAN SYNDROME

National Marfan Foundation *National. 25 chapters & support groups. Founded 1981.* Provides information to patients, families & physicians. Provides a means for patients & relatives to share experiences & support one another. Supports & fosters research. Conference, newsletter, publications. Chapter development guidelines. Write: 382 Main St., Port Washington, NY 11050. Call 800-862-7326.

MENKE'S DISEASE

Corporation for Menke's Disease *National. Founded 1984.* Parent & professional network that seeks to provide support & referrals. National seminar. Networks physicians. Parent newsletter, sibling pen pal program, telephone support network. Write: 5720 Buckfield Ct., Fort Wayne, IN 46804. Call 219/436-0137.

MENOPAUSE

(Model) **Women - Midlife & Menopause (WMM)** *Founded 1989.* Mutual support & sharing of experiences for women going through midlife changes & menopause. Discussion of solutions. Offers feedback, warmth, understanding mutual respect & humor. Provides information & referrals, phone support, meetings. Help in starting local groups. Group materials packet $5. Write: Clara Wood Anthony, 7337 Morrison Dr., Greenbelt, MD 20770.

METABOLIC DISORDERS

Research Trust for Metabolic Diseases in Children *Int'l network. Founded 1981.* Networks parents of children with any type of metabolic disorder for mutual support. Encourages research into the cures & pre-natal diagnosis of such disorders. Provides grants for treatment & cure. Info. & referral to support groups, newsletter, phone support, pen pals. Write: c/o Golden Gates Lodge, Weston Rd., Crewe, Cheshire CW1 1XN, England. Call 0270-250221 (day).

(Model) **Purine 24** *Founded 1986.* Mutual support for patients with purine metabolic disorders & their families. Fundraising for research. Phone support, newsletter, information & referrals. Assistance in starting new support groups. Write: c/o Tahma Metz, 5424 Beech Ave., Bethesda, MD 20814. Call 301/530-0354.

MILLER'S SYNDROME

Foundation for Nager & Miller Syndromes *Int'l. Founded 1989.* Networking for families that are affected by Nager or Miller Syndromes, or any cranio-facial disfigurement, limb anomalies or any rare condition. Provides referrals, library of information, phone support, newsletter, brochures. For Miller: contact Margaret Ieronimo, 333 Country Ln, Glenview, IL 60025; 708-729-0701; For Nager: contact Pam LeBaron, 721 S. Carlisle, South Bend, IN 46619; 219-289-5611.

MONOSOMY 9P
(also see Chromosome Deletions)

Support Group for Monosomy 9P *Int'l network. Founded 1983.* Provides information, parent-to-parent networking & technical support to parents of children with 9P-. Facilitates research to further understand monosomy 9P. Information, referrals, phone support. Write: c/o Jonathan Storr, 43304 Kipton Nickel Plate Rd., LeGrange, OH 44050. Call 216/775-4255.

MUCOPOLYSACHARIDOSES

National MPS Society *National. 9 regional contacts. Founded 1974.* For families with MPS & related disorders. Support groups, public education, fund-raising for research, parent referral service for networking. Quarterly newsletter. Telephone support network. Write: 17 Kraemer St., Hicksville, NY 11801. Call 516/931-6338.

MULTIPLE SCLEROSIS

Multiple Sclerosis Association of America *National. 4 affiliated groups. Founded 1970.* Self-help organization where many staff & board members have M.S. Offers support group meetings, newsletter, information & referrals, phone support, conferences, pen pals, & experienced, knowledgeable counseling. Help in starting local groups. Write: 601-05 White Horse Pike, Oaklyn, NJ 08107. Call 800-833-4MSA.

National Multiple Sclerosis Society *National. 1400 groups. Founded 1946.* Funds research in multiple sclerosis, provides information & referrals, support groups for patients & families, Professional education. Newsletter. Write: 733 Third Ave., New York, NY 11791. Call 800-624-8236 (general information package) or 800-227-3166 (M-Th, 11am-5pm) for other information.

(Model) **Multiple Sclerosis Service Organization, Inc.** *6 chapters. Founded 1949.* Dedicated to helping people with M.S. & their families. Chapters provide peer support, exercise programs, counseling, referrals & social activities. Bi-monthly newsletter $5. Conferences, workshops, drop-in center. Write: 146 Park Ave., Randolph, NJ 07869. Call 201/927-0204.

MUSCULAR DYSTROPHY

S.M.D.I. Int'l (Soc. for Muscular Dystrophy Information) *Int'l network. Founded 1983.* Purpose is to share & encourage the exchange of non-technical, neuromuscular disorder & disability related information. Directory of worldwide resources, referrals to support groups, qtrly. networking newsletter, pen pals, publication exchange. Dues $25-30. Write: P.O. Box 479, Bridgewater, NS Canada B4V 2X6. Call 902/682-3086.

MYALGIC ENCEPHALOMYELITIS

Myalgic Encephalomyelitis Association *Int'l. 480 groups. Founded 1976.* Mutual support for people who suffer from myalgic encephalomyelitis. Information to medical professionals, care agencies & general public. Fund-raising for research. Quarterly newsletter, pen pals, information & referrals, conferences, assistance in starting groups. Write: c/o Stanhope House, High St., Stanford-le-Hope, Essex SS17 OHA, United Kingdom. Call 0-375-642466.

Please remember. Model groups are not national organizations. They should be contacted primarily by persons interested in starting similar groups.

MYASTHENIA GRAVIS

Myasthenia Gravis Foundation *National. 53 chapters. Founded 1952.* Promotes research & education into myasthenia gravis, a chronic neuromuscular disease. Provides supportive services for patients & families. Information & referral. Newsletter, support groups, annual & scientific meetings, patient registry. Write: 53 W. Jackson Blvd., #660, Chicago, IL 60604. Call 312/427-6252 or 800-541-5454.

MYELOPROLIFERATIVE DISEASE

MPD Research Center, Inc. *Int'l. Umbrella organization. Founded 1989.* Support network enabling patients to share with each other their experiences & problems unique to Myeloproliferative Disease. Publishes information, sponsors educational programs, maintains database of physicians, & supports research. Newsletter, information & referrals, phone support, conferences. Write: 2220 Tiemann Ave., Baychester, NY 10469. Call 212-231-0270 or 800-HELP-MPD.

NAGER SYNDROME

Foundation for Nager & Miller Syndromes *Int'l. Founded 1989.* Networking for families that are affected by Nager or Miller Syndromes, or any cranio-facial disfigurement, limb anomalies or any rare condition. Provides referrals, library of information, phone support, newsletter, brochures. For Miller: contact Margaret Ieronimo, 333 Country Ln., Glenview, IL 60025; 708-729-0701; For Nager: contact Pam LeBaron, 721 S. Carlisle, South Bend, IN 46619; 219-289-5611.

NARCOLEPSY

American Narcolepsy Association *National. 40 support groups. Founded 1977.* Education, networking, & referrals for persons with narcolepsy. Quarterly newsletter. Write: P.O. Box 26230, San Francisco, CA 94126-6230. Call 415/788-4793 or 800-222-6085.

Narcolepsy Network *National. 30+ affiliated groups. Founded 1986.* Support & education for persons with narcolepsy & other sleep disorders, their families & interested others. Helps with coping skills, family & community problems. Provides advocacy & education, supports research. Newsletter, conferences, phone support & group development guidelines. Write: P.O. Box 1365, FDR Sta., NY, NY 10150. East Coast call: 914/834-2855; West Coast call: 415/591-7884.

NEUROFIBROMATOSIS

National Neurofibromatosis Fdn., Inc. *National. 26 chapters. Founded 1978.* For patients with neurofibromatosis & their families. Promotes & supports research on the causes & cure of NF. Provides information, assistance & education. Dues $25/individual; $35/family. Quarterly newsletter. Professional grants awarded for research. Write: 141 5th Ave., #7-S, New York, NY 10010. Call 800-323-7938.

NEURO-METABOLIC DISORDER

Association for Neuro-Metabolic Disorders *National. Founded 1981.* Education & support for families of children with neuro-metabolic disorders, such as PKU, MSUD & others. Parent support between families. Promotes research. Newsletter 3X/yr. Dues $5/yr. Telephone network, correspondence. Write: c/o Mrs. Cheryl Volk, 5223 Brookfield Lane, Sylvania, OH 43560-1809. Call 419/885-1497.

NEVUS, CONGENITAL

Nevus Network *National network. Founded 1990.* To provide a network of support & information for people with large congenital nevi. Write: c/o B.J. Bett, 1400 S. Joyce St., #C1201, Arlington, VA 22202. Call 703/920-2349 or 405/377-3403.

NIEMANN PICK TYPE C

Niemann Pick Type C Foundation, Inc., The *National network. Founded 1991.* Provides support to families affected by NPC, a severe neurological condition, to educate the public on this rare disorder, & to encourage research. Provides phone support, newsletter. Dues $20/family or $250/business. Write 1990 Je-To Lake E. Dr., Danville, IN 46122. Call 317/745-2738.

NOONAN SYNDROME

Noonan Syndrome Society *Int'l network. Founded 1989.* Support & information to help parents & professionals understand Noonan Syndrome. Aids in research. Newsletter, information & referral, phone support, parent contact program & conferences. Write: 1278 Pine Ave., San Jose, CA 95125. Call 408/723-5188.

OSTEOGENESIS IMPERFECTA

Osteogenesis Imperfecta Foundation *National. 4 chapters. Founded 1970.* Support for families dealing with O.I. Provides public education. Supports research. Provides literature. Quarterly newsletter. Telephone support network. Group development guidelines. Write: 5005 W. Laurel St. #210, Tampa, FL 33607-3836. Call 813/282-1161.

OSTEOPOROSIS

National Osteoporosis Foundation *Nat'l. Founded 1984.* Public & professional education. Direct support for biomedical research into causes, prevention & treatment of osteoporosis. Advocates for increased federal research. Newsletter, information & referrals, conferences. Support group development guidelines. Write: 2100 M Street, NW, #602, Washington, DC 20037. Call 202/223-2226.

OSTOMY

United Ostomy Association *National. 60 chapters. Founded 1962.* Dedicated to helping every person with an ostomy & related surgeries return to normal living. Provides education, support to local chapters, & national identity. Monthly newsletter, chapter development help, visitation program, magazine. Write: 36 Executive Park #120, Irvine, CA 92714-6744. Call 800-826-0826 or 714/660-8624.

(Model) **Pediatric Support Group for Ostomy & Colon Disease** *Founded 1988.* Information & support for families & others involved in the care of children with ostomies & colon disorders. Bi-monthly meetings for entire family which include professional speakers, education, social events & support. Newsletter, phone support, info. & referrals. Write: 11385 Cedarbrook Rd., Roscoe, IL 61073. Call 815/623-8034.

OVERWEIGHT
(see also Addictions: Overeating)

National Association to Advance Fat Acceptance (NAAFA) *National. 60 chapters. Founded 1969.* Assists members in developing self-esteem & self-confidence in themselves as they are. Public education regarding obesity. Provides a forum for peer support. Membership organization $35/year. Monthly newsletter, phone network, pen pals, & annual convention. Chapter development guidelines. Write: P.O. Box 188620, Sacramento, CA 95818. Call 916/443-0303.

T.O.P.S. (Take Off Pounds Sensibly) *Int'l. 11,500 chapters. Founded 1948.* Helps overweight persons attain & maintain their goal weights. Promotes a sensible approach to weight control. Chapters meet weekly for discussion & programs to provide support & competition. Newsletter. Chapter development guidelines. Write: P.O. Box 07630, 4575 S. 5th St., Milwaukee, WI 53207. Call 800-932-8677.

(Model) **Gastroplasty Support Group** *Founded 1985.* Group of volunteer patients & professionals who educate & provide support for persons contemplating, or who have had silicone gastric banding. Deals with problems associated with weight loss. Monthly update letter, phone network. videotapes. Write: 657 Irvington Ave., Newark, NJ 07106. Call Joan Scala 201/399-6031 or Dr. Lubomyr Kuzmak 201/374-1717 (Mon/Thurs/Fri).

OXALOSIS & HYPEROXALURIA

Oxalosis & Hyperoxaluria Foundation *National network. Founded 1989.* Support & current information for patients & families. Educates the public, supports research. Newsletter, information & referrals, phone support, pen pals, conferences. Write: P.O. Box 1632, Kent, WA 98035. Call 206/631-0386 (collect calls accepted from patients & families).

PAIN, CHRONIC

American Chronic Pain Association, Inc. *National. 575 chapters. Founded 1980.* Help for people suffering from chronic pain. Support, understanding & sharing skills to maintain wellness. Workbook for self-help recovery. Quarterly newsletter. Group development guidelines. Phone network. Outreach program to clinics. Write: P.O. Box 850, Rocklin, CA 95677. Call 916/632-0922.

National Chronic Pain Outreach Assoc., Inc. *National network. Founded 1980.* Clearinghouse for information about chronic pain & pain management. Aims at increasing public awareness & decreasing the stigma of chronic pain. Provides kit to develop local support groups, professional education, quarterly magazine & other materials. Write: 7979 Old Georgetown Rd. #100, Bethesda, MD 20814. Call 301/652-4948 or FAX 301/907-0745.

PALLISTER-KILLIAN

Pallister-Killian Family Support Group *Int'l network. Founded 1991.* Mutual support & education for families with children or adults with Pallister-Killian Syndrome. Provides information & referrals, newsletter, phone support, & siblings pen pal program. Write: 4255 5th S.W., Naples, FL 33999. Call 813/455-0400.

PARKINSON'S DISEASE

American Parkinson Disease Association, Inc. *National. 82 chapters. Founded 1961.* Network of 400 support groups for patients & families. Promotes research. Chapter development guidelines. Quarterly newsletter, information & referral centers nationwide. Write: 60 Bay St. #401, Staten Island, NY 10301. Call 718/981-8001 or 800-223-2732.

Parkinson's Disease Foundation, Inc. *Int'l. Founded 1957.* Aims to provide Parkinson patients a better quality of life through funding of research, in the hopes of finding the cause &, ultimately, the cure. Referrals to support groups, newsletter, information & phone support. Assistance in developing new groups. Write: c/o William Black Medical Research Bldg., 650 W. 168th St., New York, NY 10032. Call 212/923-4700 or 800-457-6676 (day).

Parkinson's Educational Program *National. 400+ groups. Founded 1981.* Information & support for Parkinson's families. Education for medical professionals. Free literature, referrals to groups & physicians, regional conferences, monthly newsletter $15. Group development guidelines. Write: M. Baughman, 3900 Birch St., #105, Newport Beach, CA 92660. Call 800-344-7872.

Parkinson's Support Groups of America *National. 150 groups. Founded 1980.* Educates patients & families on necessity for full participation in normal life. Encourages formation of support groups. Supports research & exchange of information. Annual convention. Speakers bureau. Newsletter, chapter development guidelines. Write: c/o Ida Raitano, 11376 Cherry Hill Rd., #204, Beltsville, MD 20705. Call 301/937-1545.

PEDIATRIC PSEUDO-OBSTRUCTION

North American Pediatric Pseudo-Obstruction Society, Inc. (NAPPS) *Int'l network. Founded 1988.* Education & support for families of children who have been diagnosed with this or other gastrointestinal motility disorder. Quarterly newsletter, pen pals, phone support, medical symposia & fundraising events to facilitate medical research. Write: NAPPS, P.O. Box 772, Medford, MA 02155. Call 617/395-4255.

PELVIC INFLAMMATORY DISEASE

(Model) Canadian P.I.D. (Pelvic Inflammatory Disease) Society *Founded 1986.* Info. & referrals, counseling & resources for women with pelvic inflammatory disease, professionals & general public. Provides public education, coordination & distribution of info.

including booklets, brochures & videos. Telephone support network, research. Write; P.O. Box 33804, Station D, Vancouver, B.C., Canada V6J 4L6. Call 604/684-5704 (Tue., 1-5pm PST).

PHENYLKETONURIA
(also see Neurometabolic Disorders)

Children's PKU Network *Int'l network. Founded 1991.* Provides support & services to families with the metabolic disease Phenylketonuria (PKU). Offers phone support, conferences, information & referrals to the public & professionals. Assistance in starting groups. Write: c/o Katie Andrews, 10525 Vista Sorrento Pky. #204, San Diego, CA 92121. Call 619/587-9421.

PITUITARY DISORDERS
(also see Disabilities: Head Injury)

Brain-Pituitary Foundation of America *Int'l network. Founded 1984.* Mutual support for patients & families affected by adult pituitary tumors (including acromegaly, Cushing's disease & prolactinomas). Exchange of information, referrals, phone support, counseling, patient profiles. Write: 281 E. Moody Ave., Fresno, CA 93720-1524. Call 209/434-0610.

Diabetes Insipidus & Related Disorders Network *National network. Founded 1990.* Offers mutual support for persons with pituitary and/or hypothalamus dysfunction & their families. Support is via newsletter & phone support. Write: c/o Beth Perry, Route 2 Box 198, Creston, IA 50801. Call 515/782-7838.

POLIO

International Polio Network *Int'l network. Founded 1958.* Information on late effects of polio for survivors & physicians. Int'l conferences, proceedings & tapes. Newsletter, annual directory. Guidelines & workshops for support groups. Membership $12. Handbook on late effects in several languages - $6.75. Write: 5100 Oakland Ave., #206, St. Louis, MO 63110. Call 314/534-0475.

POLYMYOSITIS/DERMATOMYOSITIS

National Support Group for Polymyositis/Dermatomyositis *National network. Founded 1989.* To provide emotional support, sharing of experiences, coping skills & hope for people with polymyositis or dermatomyositis, their families & friends. Offers newsletter, phone support, pen pals, medical advisory board, & member mailing list. Write: 1119 Spring Garden St., Bethlehem. PA 18017. Call 215/974-9832.

PORPHYRIA

American Porphyria Foundation *National. 40 groups. Founded 1982.* Supports research, provides education & information to the public, patients & physicians, networks porphyria patients & support groups. Quarterly newsletter, pen pal program, telephone network. Membership dues $20/yr. Write: P.O. Box 1075, Santa Rosa Beach, FL 32459. Call 904/654-4754.

PORT WINE STAIN BIRTH MARK

National Congenital Port Wine Stain Foundation *National. 12 groups. Founded 1984.* Disseminates information concerning the identification, treatment & prevention of congenital port wine stains. Establishes support groups for those afflicted & for parents. Fund-raising to support & establish research grants. Newsletter, brochures. Write: 125 East 63rd St., New York, NY 10021. Call 212/755-3820.

PRADER-WILLI SYNDROME

Prader-Willi Syndrome Association *National. 30 chapters. Founded 1975.* Support & education for parents of, & professionals in contact with children with Prader-Willi Syndrome. Bi-monthly newsletter. Membership dues $20. Pen pal network. Several publications. Chapter development kits available. Write: 6490 Excelsior Blvd., #E-102, St. Louis Park, MN 55426. Call 800-926-4797.

PROGRESSIVE SUPRANUCLEAR PALSY

Society for Progressive Supranuclear Palsy, Inc. *Int'l network. Founded 1990.* Provides advocacy for, & support of, patients with this disorder, their families & caregivers. Offers newsletter, information & referrals, phone support, conferences, pen pals, assistance in starting new groups. Dues $15/year. Write: 2904 Marnat Rd., Baltimore, MD 21209-2420. Call 410/484-8771 (day).

PROZAC

Prozac Survivors Support Group *National. 34 chapters. Founded 1990.* Mutual support & sharing of information for people who have been adversely affected by the antidepressant medication Prozac. Newsletter, group development guidelines. Write: c/o Bonnie Leitsch, 2212 Woodbourne Ave., Louisville, KY 40205. Call 502/459-2086.

PRUNE BELLY SYNDROME

Prune Belly Syndrome Network *National network. Founded 1984.* Mutual help for parents of children with Prune Belly Syndrome (also called Eagle Barrett). Sharing of information & experiences through phone contacts & pen pal program. Write: Barbara Hopkins, 1005 East Carver Rd., Tempe, AZ 85284. Call 602/838-9006 or 602/730-6364.

PSEUDOXANTHOMA ELASTICUM

Nat'l Assn. for Pseudoxanthoma Elasticum *National network. Founded 1988.* Support, education & advocacy for persons with PXE, & their families, professionals & interested others. Local self-help groups forming. Newsletter, information & referrals, phone support. Dues $20. Write: 82B Philip St., Albany, NY 12202. Call 518/426-0451.

RADIATION

(Model) **National Association of Radiation Survivors** *8 regional representatives. Founded 1982.* Public education on radiation health effects. Advocacy for health care & compensation for veterans & civilians exposed to radiation. Mutual support. Quarterly newsletter. Promotes research. Annual conference. Write: c/o Fred Allingham, P.O. Box 20749, Oakland, CA 94620. Call 510/655-4886 or 800-798-5102.

REFLEX SYMPATHETIC DYSTROPHY

Reflex Sympathetic Dystrophy Syndrome Association *National. 70 groups. Founded 1984.* Aims to meet the practical & emotional needs of R.S.D.S. patients & their families, while promoting research into the cause & cure, & educating the public & professionals. Quarterly newsletter. Group development guidelines. Write: 332 Haddon Ave., Westmont, NJ 08108. Call Audrey Thomas 215/955-5444 (day) or secretary 609/858-6553 (1pm-5pm).

RESPIRATORY DISEASE / EMPHYSEMA

Alpha 1 National Association *National. 8 affiliated groups. Founded 1988.* Emotional support & information for persons with Alpha 1 Antitrypsin & their families. Networking of members through newsletter. Sharing of current information on treatments & research. Pen pal program. Newsletter, group development Write: c/o Sandy Brandley, 1829 Portland, Minneapolis, MN 55404. Call 612/871-7332.

Asbestos Victims of America *National. 28 groups. Founded 1980.* Provides support groups, phone counseling, information, referral assistance for doctors & lawyers, links with hospices & other helping professionals. Info re: asbestos in the home, abatement, brochures, publications, newsletter. Speakers forum. Write: P.O. Box 559, Capitola, CA 95010. Call H. Maurer, Exec. Dir. 408/476-3646.

Asthma & Allergy Foundation of America *Int'l. 101 affiliated groups. Founded 1953.* Self-care, support & community education. National conferences for self-help group leaders. Newsletter, support groups, assistance in starting groups. How-to manual & tape. Some groups are professionally-maintained. Write: 1125 15th St. N.W., #502, Washington, DC 20005. Call 202/466-7643 (days).

Brown Lung Association *National. 12 chapters. Founded 1975.* Support, education & advocacy for cotton textile mill workers. Member of BLOC (Breath of Life Organizing Campaign). Monthly newsletter. Chapter development guidelines. Write: P.O. Box 7583, Greenville, SC 29610. Call 803/269-8048.

Emphysema Anonymous *National. Founded 1965.* Mutual assistance through education & encouragement for people with emphysema & other lung disorders, such as asthma. Bi-monthly newsletter "Batting the Breeze." Assistance available for starting groups. Provides referrals to groups & consumer information. Write: P.O. Box 3224, Seminole, FL 34642. Call 813/391-9977.

White Lung Association *National. 211 chapters. Founded 1979.* Educational support & advocacy for asbestos victims & their families. Public education on health hazards of asbestos. Education of workers on safe work practices. Chapter development guidelines. Quarterly newsletter. Films & videotapes available. Write: P.O. Box 1483, Baltimore, MD 21203. Call 410/243-5864.

RETT SYNDROME

Int'l Rett Syndrome Association (IRSA) *Int'l. Founded 1985.* For parents, interested professionals & others concerned with Rett syndrome. Information & referral, peer support among parents, & encourages research. Quarterly newsletter. Dues per year $30/int'l, $25/family, $20/single. Write: 8511 Rose Marie Dr., Fort Washington, MD 20744. Call 301/248-7031.

REYE'S SYNDROME

National Reye's Syndrome Foundation *National. Founded 1974.* 140 affiliates. Devoted to conquering Reye's Syndrome, primarily a children's disease affecting the liver & brain, but can affect all ages. Provides support, information & referrals. Encourages research. Local chapters usually formed by parents. $25 dues includes newsletter. Write: 426 N. Lewis St., Bryan, OH 43506. Call 800-233-7393. In Ohio call 800-231-7393.

RUBINSTEIN-TAYBI SYNDROME

Rubinstein-Taybi Parent Group *National network. Founded 1984.* Mutual support, information & sharing for parents of children with Rubinstein-Taybi Syndrome. Newsletter, phone support, parent contact list. Write: Garry & Lorrie Baxter, 414 E. Kansas, Smith Center, KS 66967. Call 913/282-6237.

RUSSELL-SILVER SYNDROME

Association for Children with Russell-Silver Syndrome, Inc. *Int'l network. Founded 1989.* Education & support to families of children with Russell-Silver Syndrome through periodic newsletters & parent-to-parent contact. Clearinghouse of information. Aims to increase public awareness & encourage research. Quarterly newsletter. Write: 22 Hoyt St., Madison, NJ 07940. Call 201/377-4531.

SARCOIDOSIS

National Sarcoidosis Resource Center *National network. Founded 1992.* Mutual support for Sarcoid patients & their families. Telephone support, networking, literature & education. Maintains national database, encourages research, provides support & physician referrals, resource guide. Dues $25/year. Write: P.O. Box 1593, Piscataway, NJ 08855-1593. Call 908/699-0733.

Sarcoidosis Foundation *National. 2 support groups. Founded 1982.* Support, information & referrals for families affected by Sarcoidosis. Increases public awareness. Telephone network & group development guidelines. Write: P.O. Box 22868, Newark, NJ 07101-2868. Call 900-988-0042 ext. 458. ($2/minute. All proceeds go to Foundation.) or 201/923-8818.

SCLERODERMA

Scleroderma Federation, Inc. *Int'l. 22 groups. Founded 1980.* Promotes the welfare of scleroderma patients & their families.

Provides education, support groups, phone help, referrals. Fund-raising for research. Newsletter & other educational materials. Group development guidelines. Write: 1182 Teaneck Rd., Teaneck, NJ 07666. Call 201/837-9826.

United Scleroderma Foundation *Int'l. 24 chapters. Founded 1975.* Educates the public, promotes medical research, helps patients make contacts. Brochures, handbook, Scleroderma Digest & newsletters. Chapter development guidelines. Write: P.O. Box 399, Watsonville, CA 95077-0399. Call 800-722-HOPE.

SCOLIOSIS

Scoliosis Association, Inc. *National. 52 affiliates. Founded 1976.* Information & support network. Organization of scoliosis patients & parents of children with scoliosis. Encourages school screening programs & establishes local patient & parent self-help groups. Supports research. Newsletter. Dues $12. Guidelines for starting chapters. Write: 2500 N. Military Trail #301, Boca Raton, FL 33431. Call 407/994-4435 or 800-800-0669.

SJOGREN'S SYNDROME

National Sjogren's Syndrome Association *Int'l. 13 chapters. Founded 1990.* Provides emotional support to patients & their families. Educational information to both patients & health professionals. Encourages research. Newsletter, support groups, information & referrals, phone support, conferences. Assistance in starting groups. Write: Barbara Henry, 3201 W. Evans Dr., Phoenix, AZ 85023. Call 602/993-7227 or 800-395-NSSA.

Sjogren's Syndrome Foundation Inc. *Int'l. 25 groups & contacts & overseas affiliates. Founded 1983.* Information & education for patients, families, health professionals & the public. Opportunities for patients to share ways of coping. Stimulates research for treatments & cures. Newsletter, chapter development guidelines, audio tapes, annual symposium, Sjogren's handbook. Write: 382 Main St., Port Washington, NY 11050. Call 516/767-2866.

SKIN DISEASE

DEBRA of America (Dystrophic Epidermolysis Bullosa Research Assn.) *National network. Founded 1980.* Support & information for families. Promotes research, provides education for professionals, pen pals, phone network, information & referrals, newsletter, regional conferences. Write: 141 Fifth Ave. #7-South, New York, NY 10010. Call 212/995-2220.

F.I.R.S.T. (Foundation for Ichthyosis & Related Skin Types) *National. 9 affiliated groups. Founded 1981.* Provides support & networking for people with ichthyosis. Provides public & professional education. Support group development guidelines. Supports research on treatment & cure. Newsletter, pen pals, annual conference. Dues $20. Write: P.O. Box 20921, Raleigh, NC 27619-0921. Call 919/782-5728.

National Vitiligo Foundation *National. 11 chapters. Founded 1985.* Mutual help & education for persons with vitiligo, a skin disorder affecting pigmentation. Fund-raising for research. Semi-annual newsletter. Telephone network. Write: P.O. Box 6337, Tyler, TX 75711. Call 903/534-2925.

National Psoriasis Foundation *National. Founded 1968.* Support & information for psoriasis patients. Education to increase public awareness of the disorder. Fund-raising for research. Bi-monthly newsletter. Pen pal program. Group development guidelines. Write: 6443 S.W. Beaverton Hwy., #210, Portland, OR 97221. Call 503/297-1545.

SOTOS SYNDROME

Sotos Syndrome Support Association *National network. Founded 1984.* To provide information & mutual support for families of children with Sotos syndrome. Newsletter, information & referrals, phone support, pen pals, annual conferences. Write: 4686 Vinton, Omaha, NE 68106. Call 402/556-2445.

SPASMODIC DYSPHONIA

Nat'l Spasmodic Dysphonia Association *National. 50+ affiliated groups. Founded 1990.* Promotes the care & welfare of those with spasmodic dysphonia & their families. Aims to increase public awareness & education. Encourage formation of local support groups. Quarterly newsletter. Write: P.O. Box 1574, Birmingham, MI 48009.

(Model) **Spasmodic Dysphonia Support Group of New York** *52 other S.D. groups. Founded 1987.* Provides members with the latest information regarding spasmodic dysphonia; emotional & practical support, workshops & discussions, encourages education for the public & physicians. Guest speakers, information & referrals, newsletter ($20/yr). Write: 156 5th Ave., #1033, New York, NY 10010-7002. Call 212/929-4099.

SPASMODIC TORTICOLLIS

National Spasmodic Torticollis Association *National. 27 chapters. Founded 1983.* Support group for S.T. victims & their families. Interest in research, public education & establishment of support groups throughout the U.S. Newsletter, pen pals, telephone network, chapter development guidelines. Write: P.O. Box 476, Elm Grove, WI 53122. Call 800-HURTFUL.

SPINA BIFIDA

Hydrocephalus Parent Support Group *National. Founded 1982.* Support & education about various aspects of hydrocephalus & spina bifida. Family social events. Phone help, peer-counseling, visitation. National newsletter $10/year. Pen pals. Write: c/o Kathy McGowan, 6059 Rancho Mission Rd. #106, San Diego, CA 92108-2365. Call Kathy McGowan at 619/583-4096.

Spina Bifida Association of America *National. 85 chapters. Founded 1972.* Encourages educational & vocational development of patients. Promotes public awareness, advocacy & research. Bi-monthly newsletter, chapter development guidelines, adoption referral program, film/videotapes. Write: 4590 MacArthur Blvd. NW, #250, Washington, DC 20007. Call 800-621-3141 or 202/944-3285.

SPINAL MUSCULAR ATROPHY

Families of S.M.A. (Spinal Muscular Atrophy) *Int'l. 3 chapters. Founded 1984.* Support & networking for families affected by spinal muscular atrophy including Werdnig-Hoffman, Oppenheim's & Kugelberg-Welander Disease & Aran-Duchenne Type. Provides educational resources, group development guidelines, newsletter, pen pals, phone support & videotapes. Write: P.O. Box 1465, Highland Park, IL 60035. Call 708/432-5551.

STREP, GROUP B

Group B Strep Association *Int'l network. Founded 1990.* Educates the public about Group B Streptococcal infections during pregnancy. Provides information & referrals, phone support, newsletter & assistance in developing state networks. Write: P.O. Box 16515, Chapel Hill, NC 27516. Call 919/932-5344.

STROKE

Courage Stroke Network *National. 808 groups. Founded 1979.* Promotes development of support groups. Provides leadership consultation. Information, referral & public education. "Stroke

Connection" newsletter. Annual seminar. Peer counselor training.
Group development guidelines ($12.95/members; $16.95/
non-members) + postage/handling). Write: c/o Courage Center,
3915 Golden Valley Rd., Golden Valley, MN 55422. Call
800-553-6321 or 612/520-0464.

National Stroke Association *National. 6 chapters. Founded 1984.*
Dedicated to reducing the incidence & severity of stroke through
prevention, medical treatment, rehabilitation, family support &
research. Research grants on prevention & treatment. Newsletter,
professional publications, information & referrals. Guidance for
starting stroke clubs & groups. Write: 300 E. Hampden Ave.,
#240, Englewood, CO 80110-2654. Call 303/762-9922 or 800-
STROKES.

Stroke Clubs *Int'l. Founded 1968.* Organization of persons who
have experienced strokes, their families & friends for the purpose
of mutual support, education, social & recreational activities.
Provides information & assistance to Stroke Clubs (which are
usually sponsored by local organizations). Newsletter, group
development guidelines. Write: 805 12th St., Galveston, TX 77550.
Call 409/762-1022.

STURGE-WEBER

Sturge-Weber Foundation, The *Int'l network. Founded 1987.*
Mutual support network for families affected by Sturge-Weber
Syndrome. Disseminates information, funds & facilitates research.
Quarterly newsletter, phone support, letter-writing among families.
Write: P.O. Box 460931, Aurora, CO 80046. Call 800-627-5482 or
303/360-7290.

SYRINGOMYELIA

American Syringomyelia Alliance Project *National network.
Founded 1988.* Support, networking, & information for people
affected by syringomyelia. Newsletter, phone support, pen pals,
conferences. Write: P.O. Box 1586, Longview, TX 75606-1586. Call
903/236-7079; 903/757-7456 (FAX).

TARDIVE DYSKINESIA/TARDIVE DYSTONIA

Tardive Dyskinesia/Tardive Dystonia National Association
National network. Founded 1988. Support for those suffering from
TD/TD & their families & friends. Provides advocacy, education &
promotes public awareness. Works in concert with professional &
lay communities. Helps with starting groups. Will help anyone
concerned about side effects of medication. Pen pals, seminars,

videos, cassettes & publications. Write: P.O. Box 45732, Seattle, WA 98145-0732. Call 206/522-3166.

Tardive Dyskinesia-Tardive Dystonia Nat'l Victims Assn. *Int'l. 12 groups. Founded 1991.* Networking of tardive dyskinesia-tardive dystonia victims to others in their area. Information & referrals, phone support, conferences, pen pal program, list of doctors. Write: 1011 Boren Ave. #131, Seattle, WA 98104. Call 206/725-9339.

TAY-SACHS DISEASE

Nat'l Tay-Sachs & Allied Diseases Association *National. 7 affiliated groups. Founded 1957.* Committed to the eradication of Tay-Sachs & allied diseases. Public & professional education, prevention, carrier screening, lab quality control, research, family services. Parent peer group program. Newsletter. Write: 2001 Beacon St., Brookline, MA 02146. Call 617/277-4463; 617/277-0134 (FAX).

THROMBOCYTOPENIA ABSENT RADIUS

T.A.R.S.A. (Thrombocytopenia Absent Radius Syndrome Assoc.) *Int'l network. Founded 1981.* Information, networking & support for families children with T.A.R. Syndrome (a shortening of the arms), & for affected adults. (Does not include ITP.) Annual newsletter, pen pal program, phone network. Write: 212 Sherwood Dr., RD1, Linwood, NJ 08221-9745. Call 609/927-0418.

TOURETTE SYNDROME

Tourette Syndrome Association *National. 48 chapters. Founded 1972.* Education for patients, professionals & public. Promotes research into the causes, treatments & cures. Provides services to families & professionals to enable patients to achieve optimum development. Chapter development guidelines, newsletter. Dues $35. Write: 42-40 Bell Blvd., Bayside, NY 11361-2861. Call 718/224-2999 or 800-237-0717.

TRACHEO ESOPHAGEAL FISTULA

Tracheo Esophageal Fistula Parent Network *National network. Founded 1985.* Emotional & practical help for parents of T.E.F. children. Telephone & correspondence networking between families. Bi-annual meetings to discuss mutual problems & provide encouragement. Write: Julia & George Knapp, 42 Saskatoon Dr., Etobicoke, Ontario, Canada M9P 2E9. Call 416/249-8710.

TRANSPLANT RECIPIENT (ORGAN)

Transplant Recipients International Organization (TRIO) *Int'l. 37 chapters. Founded 1983.* Peer support for transplant candidates, recipients & their families. Public education on organ donation. Association of member chapters. Monthly meetings. Annual international meeting, chapter development assistance. Newsletter. Write: TRIO, 244 N. Bellefield Ave., Pittsburgh, PA 15213. Call 412/687-2210; 412/687-7190 (FAX).

TREACHER COLLINS SYNDROME

Treacher Collins Foundation *National network. Founded 1988.* Support for families, individuals & professionals re: Treacher Collins Syndrome & related disorders. Provides networking, educational materials, newsletter, information & referrals, phone support, resource list, bibliography & central library. Write: P.O. Box 683, Norwich, VT 05055. Call 802/649-3020.

TRIGEMINAL NEURALGIA/TIC DOULOUREUX

Trigeminal Neuralgia Assn. (Tic Douloureux) *National. Founded 1991.* Provides information, mutual support & encouragement to patients & their families to reduce isolation of those affected. Aims to increase public/professional awareness, & promote research into cause & cure. Phone support, pen pal program. Local groups being formed in several states. Write: Claire Patterson, P.O. Box 785, Barnegat Light, NJ 08006. Call 609/361-1014.

TRISOMY
(see also specific disorder)

S.O.F.T. (Support Organization For Trisomy) *National. 62 chapters. Founded 1979.* Support & education for families of children with trisomy & related genetic disorders. Education & awareness for professionals. Quarterly newsletter. Pen pal program, phone network. Regional gatherings. Annual int'l conference, booklets. Write: c/o Barbara Van Herreweghe, 2982 S. Union St., Rochester, NY 14624. Call 716/594-4621.

TUBE-FEEDING

Oley Foundation, Inc. *National. Founded 1983.* Mutual support, education & advocacy for individuals on home parenteral or enteral nutrition. Maintains national registry (OASIS). Pen pals, bi-monthly newsletter free to patients, group development guidelines. Write: c/o Albany Medical Center, Room HUN-214, A-23, Albany, NY 12208. Call 518/445-5079 or 800-776-6539.

TUBEROUS SCLEROSIS

National Tuberous Sclerosis Association *National. 110 state reps. Founded 1975.* Encourages research, support & education among families of children with tuberous sclerosis. Newsletter, pen pal program, parent-to-parent program, support group meetings. Chapter development guidelines. Write: 8000 Corporate Dr., #120, Landover, MD 20785. Call 301/459-9888 or 800-225-NTSA.

TURNER'S SYNDROME

Turner's Syndrome Society *Int'l. 11 chapters in Canada. Founded 1981.* Support & education to Turner's Syndrome persons & families. Tapes, publications, referrals to groups in U.S. & Canada. Newsletter, pen pals, chapter development guidelines, annual conference. Write: Sandi Hofbauer, Exec. Dir., 7777 Keele St., Fl. 2, Concord, Ontario L4K 1Y7 Canada. Call 416/660-7766; 416/660-7450 (FAX).

Turner Syndrome Society of the U.S. *National. 20 chapters. Founded 1988.* Mutual support for women, girls, & their families affected by Turner's syndrome. Educates public. Newsletter, chapter development assistance, annual conference. Write: c/o Lynn Tesch, 768-214 Twelve Oaks, 15500 Wayzata, Wayzata, MN 55391. Call 612/475-9944, 612/475-9949 (FAX).

VENTILATOR-ASSISTED PERSONS

Care For Life, Inc. *National network. Founded 1980.* Creates awareness of issues facing ventilator-assisted persons & families. Educates & networks concerned families, professionals, individuals & organizations. Stimulates the development of treatment models. Write: 1018 W. Diversey Pkwy., Chicago, IL 60614. Call 708/831-3435 (Illinois Self-Help Ctr.), or 312/880-4630 (FAX).

International Ventilator Users Network *Int'l. Founded 1987.* Information sharing by ventilator users & health care professionals experienced in home mechanical ventilation. Biannual newsletter. Membership: users $8; health professionals $20. Handbook on ventilators & muscular dystrophy $6. Write: 5100 Oakland Ave., #206, St. Louis, MO 63110. Call 314/534-0475.

National Association for Ventilator Dependent Individuals *National. 2 affiliated groups. Founded 1990.* Support & education for ventilator-dependent individuals & their families. Info. & referrals, phone support, conferences. Group development guidelines. Groups professionally assisted. Write: P.O. Box 3666, Erie, PA 16508.

VESTIBULAR DISORDERS

Vestibular Disorders Association *National. 60 independent groups. Founded 1983.* Information, referrals & support for people affected by disorders caused by inner ear problems. Public education, group development assistance, quarterly newsletter, resource library, phone support, meetings. Write: P.O. Box 4467, Portland, OR 97208-4467. Call 503/229-7705; 503/229-8064 (FAX).

VON HIPPEL LINDAU

Von Hippel-Lindau Disease Syndrome Foundation, Inc. *Nat'l network. Founded 1992.* Information & support network for individuals affected by VHL. Provides fund-raising activities, assistance in starting support groups, advocacy, literature distribution, & phone support. Write: c/o Marirene Heisler, 1101 Carlow Dr., Toms River, NJ 08753. Call 908/244-7635.

WEGENERS GRANULOMATOSIS

Wegeners Foundation, Inc. *National network. Founded 1990.* Provides support & education for persons with Wegeners granulomatosis. Encourages research into the causes & treatment of this rare disabling disease. Provides information & referrals, phone support, newsletter. Write: Judith Williams, 9000 Rockville Pike Bldg. 31A B1W30, Bethesda, MD 20892. Call 301/496-8331.

WERDNIG HOFFMAN DISEASE
(also see Spinal Muscular Atrophy)

(Model) **Werdnig Hoffman Parents Group** Mutual support for parents of children with Werdnig Hoffman disease. Phone network, quarterly meetings, recreational activities, quarterly newsletter. Write: c/o M.D.A., 561 Pilgrim Dr. #C, Foster City, CA 94404. Call 415/570-6166.

WILLIAM'S SYNDROME

Williams Syndrome Association *National. 10 chapters. Founded 1983.* To encourage research related to Williams syndrome, find & support families with Williams syndrome, & share information among parents & professionals re: educational, medical & behavioral experiences. Newsletter. Write: Dana Vouga, P.O. Box 3297, Ballwin, MO 63022. Call 314/227-4411.

Remember to always include a self-addressed stamped envelope when writing to a group for information.

WILSON'S DISEASE

Wilson's Disease Association *National network. Founded 1979.* Provides information to the public & professionals about Wilson's disease. Provides mutual support & aid for those affected by the disease & their families. Promotes research into treatment & cure. Quarterly newsletter. Phone support network. Write: P.O. Box 75324, Washington, DC 20013. Call 703/636-3014 or 636-3003.

WOLF-HIRSCHHORN SYNDROME (4P-)
(also see Chromosome Deletion)

4P- (Wolf-Hirschhorn Syndrome) Parent Contact Group *National network. 1 group in England. Founded 1984.* Provides support & information to families of children with Wolf-Hirschhorn Syndrome. Offers phone support, biographies on other children with this syndrome. Newsletter. Write: 3200 Rivanna Ct., Woodbridge, VA 22192. Call 703-491-0309 (8am-9pm).

WOMEN'S HEALTH

National Black Women's Health Project/Self-Help Division *National. 130 groups. Founded 1981.* Committed to the empowerment of all women through wellness. Especially addresses health concerns of black women. Establishes black women's self-help groups. Quarterly newsletter, national conferences. Assistance in starting local groups. Dues vary. Send self-addressed stamped envelope ($2.90/postage): 1237 Ralph David Abernathy Blvd. SW, Atlanta, GA 30310-1731. Call 800-ASK-BWHP or 404/758-9590; 404/758-9661 (FAX).

(Model) **Por La Vida** *15 local groups. Founded 1988.* Bi-lingual program in which Hispanic women learn to lead groups of family & friends in discussions of nutrition, disease prevention, community living skills, family communication & other matters that affect their own & families' well-being. Educational materials. Assistance in starting new groups. Write: Joan Rupp, 6505 Alvarado Court, #101, San Diego, CA 92120. Call 619/594-2437.

Please note: Model groups are not national organizations and should be contacted primarily by persons wishing to start a similar group in their local area. Also, please enclose a self-addressed envelope when requesting information from any group. When calling a contact number, remember that many of them are home numbers so be considerate of the time you call. Keep in mind the different time zones.

MENTAL HEALTH

DEPRESSION / MANIC-DEPRESSION / POST-PARTUM DEPRESSION

Depressed Anonymous *Int'l. 8 affiliated groups. Founded 1985.* 12-step program to help depressed persons believe & hope they can feel better. Newsletter, phone support, info. & referrals, pen pals, workshops, conferences & seminars. Information packet ($5), group starter manual ($10.95). Newsletter. Write: 1013 Wagner Ave., Louisville, KY 40217. Call Hugh S. 502/969-3359.

Depression After Delivery *National. 85 chapters. Founded 1985.* Support & information for women who have suffered from post partum depression. Telephone support in most states, newsletter, group development guidelines, pen pals, conferences. Write: P.O. Box 1281, Morrisville, PA 19067. Call 215/295-3994 or 800-944-4773 (to leave name & address for info. to be sent).

Depressives Anonymous *National. Founded 1977.* Helps anxious & depressed persons change troublesome behavior patterns & attitudes about living. Professional involvement. Newsletter, chapter development guidelines. Write: 329 East 62nd St., New York, NY 10021. Call 212/689-2600 (answering service).

National Depressive & Manic-Depressive Association *National. 250 chapters. Founded 1986.* Mutual support & information for manic-depressives, depressives & their families. Public education on the biochemical nature of depressive illnesses. Annual conferences, chapter development guidelines. Newsletter. Write: NDMDA, 730 N. Franklin, #501, Chicago, IL 60610. Call 800-82-NDMDA or 312/642-0049.

NOSAD (Nat'l Organization for Seasonal Affective Disorder) *National. 4 groups. Founded 1988.* Provides information & education re: the causes, nature & treatment of Seasonal Affective Disorder. Encourages development of services to patients & families, research into causes & treatment. Newsletter. Write: P.O. Box 451, Vienna, VA 22180. Call 301/762-0768.

(Model) **Helping Hands** *Founded 1985.* A comfortable & homey atmosphere for people with manic-depression, schizophrenia or clinical depression who seek an environment that makes them more aware of themselves & eliminates a negative attitude. Group development guidelines. Write: c/o Rita Martone, 86 Poor St., Andover, MA 01810. Call 508/475-3388.

(Model) **MDSG-NY (Mood Disorders Support Group, Inc.)** *Founded 1981.* Support & education for people with manic-depression or depression & their families & friends. Guest lectures, newsletter, rap groups, assistance in starting groups. Write: P.O. Box 1747, Madison Square Station, New York, NY 10159. Call 212/533-MDSG.

FAMILIES OF MENTALLY ILL

Attachment Disorder Parents Network *National. 5 affiliated groups. Founded 1988.* To promote the understanding of attachment disorders. Information & support for parents dealing with children who have attachment disorders. Newsletter, phone support, information & referrals. Write: P.O. Box 18475, Boulder, CO 80308. Call 303/443-1446.

Federation of Families for Children's Mental Health *National. 10 affiliated groups. Founded 1989.* Parent-run organization focused on the needs of children & youth with emotional, behavioral or mental disorders & their families. Provides information & advocacy; newsletter, conferences. Write: c/o Marge Samels, 1021 Prince St., Alexandria, VA 22314-2971. Call 703/684-7710.

Forensic Committee of National Alliance for the Mentally Ill *National. Coordinators in 38 states. Founded 1984.* Support for families of mentally ill persons in prison or going through the criminal justice system. Advocacy for those in prison. Education for the criminal justice system. Quarterly newsletter. Write: c/o NAMI, 2101 Wilson Blvd., #302, Arlington, VA 22201. Call 703/524-7600.

Foundation for Elective Mutism *Nat'l. Founded 1992.* Mutual support for parents of children with elective mutism, a rare behavioral disorder in which children refuse to speak in social situations. Also open to adults who have, or outgrew, the disorder. Provides info. & referrals, phone support. Contact: Sue Leszcyk, P.O. Box 7845, Rego Park, NY 11374-9998, phone 718-997-0057; or Carolyn Miller, P.O.Box 13133, Sissonville, WV 25360.

Homeless and Missing Network *National. Local coordinators in most states. Founded 1986.* Support & advocacy for families with any mentally ill relative who is missing or homeless. Write: c/o NAMI, 2101 Wilson Blvd. #302, Arlington, VA 22201-3008. Call 703/524-7600.

Multiple Personality Dignity/LOOM (Loved Ones of Multiples) *Int'l. Founded 1989.* For persons with multiple personality or dissociative disorder. Also, Loved Ones of Multiples network. Pen/phone pals, newsletter, support groups. Non-religious 12-practices approach. Must obtain Guidebook ($15 sugg. donation) & sign confidentiality agreement before joining network. Due to curiosity seekers, only participants are given meeting info. Write: P.O. Box 4367, Boulder, CO 80306.

N.A.M.I. (National Alliance for the Mentally Ill) *National. 1000 affiliates. Founded 1979.* Network of self-help groups for relatives of the seriously mentally ill. Emotional & educational support. Bi-monthly newsletter, affiliate development guidelines. Write: 2101 Wilson Blvd., #302, Arlington, VA 22201-3008. Call 800/950-NAMI (group referrals), or 703/524-7600 (office).

Schizophrenia Society of Canada *National. 90 chapters. Founded 1979.* Information, support & advocacy for families & friends of persons with schizophrenia. Provides public awareness campaigns, advocacy & fund-raising. Newsletter, guidelines & assistance for starting self-help groups. Information & referrals, phone help, conferences, brochures, handbooks, videos. Dues $5. Write: 75 The Donway W. #814, Don Mills, Ontario Canada M3C 2E9. Call 416/445-8204.

Siblings & Adult Children's Network (SAC Network) *National. 100 affiliated groups. Founded 1982.* Support & information for siblings & children of persons with mental illness. Quarterly newsletter. How-to packet on starting a group ($10). Information & referrals. Conferences. Write: c/o NAMI, 2101 Wilson Blvd., #302, Arlington, VA 22201. Call 703/524-7600.

(Model) **DD-Anon** *Founded 1985.* Fellowship who share their experience, strength & hope with each other to maintain their own mental & physical health while remaining supportive of loved ones who are being treated for a dissociated disorder (usually Multiple Personality Disorder). Follows the 12-step program. Confidential. Write: P.O. Box 4078, Appleton, WI 54915.

(Model) **F.A.I.R. (Family And Individual Reliance)** *14 groups. Founded 1981.* Statewide mutual support groups for persons with present or past mental or emotional illness. Separate groups for family & friends of such persons. "How-To" manual $12. Facilitators training manual $5. Quarterly newsletter. Write: c/o Mary Dees, Mental Health Assn. in Texas, 8401 Shoal Creek Blvd., Austin, TX 78758. Call 512/454-3706.

(Model) **Parents Involved Network** *Regional. Founded 1984.* Self-help, advocacy, information & training resource for parents whose children & adolescents have serious emotional problems. Provides parents an opportunity to come together to share common concerns & experiences, exchange information & identify resources. Newsletter. Write: 311 S. Juniper St., Rm. 902, Philadelphia, PA 19107. Call 800-688-4226 or 215/735-2465.

(Model) **REACH ("Reassurance to Each")** *Statewide. Founded 1977.* Groups of families & friends of persons with a mental illness, for support & information. Groups are free, confidential & open to new participants at any time. Information & technical assistance available for starting new groups. WRITE: c/o Mental Health Assn. of MN, 328 E. Hennepin Ave., Minneapolis, MN 55414. Call 612/331-6840; or 800-862-1799 (in MN).

MENTAL HEALTH (GENERAL)

Children's & Youth Emotions Anonymous *National. 19 chapters. Founded 1971.* Program to help youth develop healthy emotions, attitudes, & habits, using the 12 step program. Youth groups led by adult members of E.A. Chapter development guidelines. Write: P.O. Box 4245, St. Paul, MN 55104. Call 612/647-9712.

Emotions Anonymous *National. 1200 chapters. Founded 1971.* Fellowship sharing experiences, hopes & strengths with each other, using the 12 step program, in order to gain better emotional health. Correspondence program for those who cannot attend meetings. Chapter development guidelines. Write: P.O. Box 4245, St. Paul, MN 55104. Call 612/647-9712.

Emotional Health Anonymous *National. 50 chapters. Founded 1970.* Fellowship of people who meet to share experiences, strengths & hopes with each other so they may solve common problems of mental health. Patterned after the 12 Step Program of Alcoholics Anonymous. Group development guidelines, newsletter. Write: P.O. Box 429, Glendale, CA 91202-0429. Call 818/240-3215.

International Association for Clear Thinking *Int'l. 100 chapters. Founded 1970.* For people interested in living their lives more effectively & satisfactorily. Uses principles of clear thinking & self-counseling. Newsletter; group handbook; chapter development kit; audio tapes, facilitator leadership training; self-help materials. Write: IACT, P.O. Box 1011, Appleton, WI 54912. Call 414/739-8311 or 800-236-8311 (in Wisconsin).

Isolators Anonymous *National. Founded 1988.* 12-step fellowship for people who feel uncomfortable connecting with other people. Aims to help members recognize & change the self-defeating behavior patterns that keep them feeling isolated. Write: 130 West 75th St., New York, NY 10023. Call 212/877-1808.

Neurotics Anonymous *Int'l. 158 U.S. groups. Founded 1964.* Fellowship of people banded together to solve their mental & emotional problems following the 12-steps. Sole purpose is to help mentally & emotionally disturbed persons recover from their illness & maintain their recovery. Info. & referrals, phone support, assistance for starting new groups, newsletter. Write: 11140 Bainbridge Dr., Little Rock, AR 72212. Call 501/221-2809.

Recoveries Anonymous *Int'l. 20 groups. Founded 1983.* A support group for those who know the 12-steps work & want to know how to use them. Fellowship focusing on the spiritual solutions contained in the 12-steps. Open to anyone, especially those who have yet to be successful in their search for recovery. Service package ($3); group starter kit ($25). Write: P.O. Box 1212, Hewitt Sq. Stn., E. Northport, NY 11731. Call 516/261-1212.

Recovery, Inc. *National. 850 chapters. Founded 1937.* A community mental health organization that offers a self-help method of will training; a system of techniques for controlling temperamental behavior & changing attitudes toward nervous symptoms & fears. Publication "Recovery Reporter" for members. Info. on starting groups. Leadership training. Write: 802 N. Dearborn St., Chicago, IL 60610. Call 312/337-5661; 312/337-5756 (FAX).

TARA (Total Aspects of Recovery Anonymous) *Int'l. 17 affiliated groups. Founded 1989.* 12-step recovery program to provide a loving & safe environment where members are free to address the entire spectrum of addictive & dysfunctional behaviors. Newsletter. Guidelines for developing groups. Write: 3799 Montclair, Cameron Park, CA 95682. Call 916/676-3366.

(Model) **California Consumers for Responsible Therapy** *Founded 1991.* Mutual help & information for people who have experienced a dual relationship (sexual or non-sexual) with a therapist, counselor, or minister. Local support groups for women. Information & referrals, assistance in starting new groups. Write: P.O. Box 2194, Garden Grove, CA 92642-2194. Call 714/870-8864.

Remember to always include a self-addressed stamped envelope when requesting information from a group.

(Model) **C.A.I.R. (Changing Attitudes in Recovery)** *20 groups in Calif. Founded 1990.* Self-help "family" sharing a common commitment to gain healthy esteem. Includes persons with relationship problems, addictions, mental illness, etc. Offers new techniques & tools that lead to better self-esteem. Assistance in starting new groups. Handbook ($9.95), audio tapes, leader's manual. Write: c/o Psych. Assoc. Press, 706 13th St., Modesto, CA 95354. Call 209/577-1667 (day).

(Model) **Mental Illness Anonymous** Fellowship of men & women with any type of mental illness, sharing their pain & hope with each other in order to attain recovery. Based on the 12-steps with a spiritual focus. Assistance in starting support groups. Write: Darrell F., c/o St. Mary's Episcopal Church, 1895 Laurel Ave., St. Paul, MN 55106. Call 612/646-6175.

(Model) **UNFAIR (United Network for Action Instead of Resentment)** *Founded 1990.* Support & assistance to help people learn how to stand up to unfair treatment by other individuals, employees, etc. Provides information & referrals, phone support & the creation of tool kits for handling problems. Assistance for starting groups. Write: 23 Currierville Rd., Newton, N.H. 03858. Call 603/382-7503.

MENTAL HEALTH CONSUMERS

Grow *Int'l. 100 groups in America. Founded in 1957.* 12-step mutual help program to provide know-how for avoiding & recovering from a breakdown. Caring & sharing community to attain emotional maturity & personal responsibility. Leadership training & consultation to develop new groups. Newsletter. Write: 225 Weymouth Rd., Box 212B, Vineland, NJ 08360. Call 609/794-1033 or 609/691-3663 (office).

National Association of Psychiatric Survivors *National network. Founded 1985.* Aids in the development of user-controlled alternatives to the mental health system, including self-help groups. Aims to improve quality of life for current & former mental patients. Group development guidelines. Newsletter. Write: P.O. Box 618, Sioux Falls, SD 57101. Call 605/334-4067.

National Mental Health Consumers' Association *National. 32 affiliated groups. Founded 1985.* Network of mental health consumers. Promotes local consumer controlled alternatives to improve the quality of life by addressing housing, employment & discrimination issues. Newsletter. Write: NMHCA, P.O. Box 1166, Madison, WI 53701.

Reclamation, Inc. *National. 3 affiliated groups. Members from 26 states. Founded 1974.* Alliance of former mental patients helping to eliminate stigma of mental illness. Helps patients with social, employment & housing problems. Newsletter. Staffed & funded by ex-patients. Write: HC4, Box 254, Blanco, TX 78606. Call 512/833-4946.

Schizophrenics Anonymous *National. Groups in 15 states. Founded 1985.* Organized & run by people with a schizophrenia-related disorder. Offers fellowship, support & information. Focuses on recovery using a 6-step program, along with medication & professional help. Weekly meetings, guest speakers, phone network, newsletter. Assistance in starting groups. Write: c/o Mental Health Assn., 15920 W. Twelve Mile, Southfield, MI 48076. Call Joanne 313/477-1983.

(Resource) **National Empowerment Center.** Technical assistance for psychiatric survivors & consumers who are, or want to be, involved in self-help. Provides referrals to support groups, lists of available newsletters, conferences. Write: 130 Parker St., Lawrence, MA 01843. Call 508/685-1518 or 800-POWER-2-U.

(Resource) **The National Mental Health Consumer Self-Help Clearinghouse.** Encourages the development of consumer self-help groups. Provides information, materials, help & referrals for a wide range of technical assistance issues from fund-raising to the development of consumer-run drop-in enters. Write: 311 S. Juniper St., #1000, Philadelphia, PA 19107. Call 215/735-6082 or 800-553-4539.

(Model) **FAIR (Family And Individual Reliance)** *14 groups. Founded 1981.* Statewide mutual support groups for persons with present or past mental or emotional illness. Separate groups for family & friends of such persons. "How-To" manual $12. Facilitators training manual $5. Quarterly newsletter. Write: c/o Mary Dees, Mental Health Assn. in Texas, 8401 Shoal Creek Blvd., Austin, TX 78758. Call 512/454-3706.

(Model) **Helping Hands** *Founded 1985.* For people with manic-depressive disorders, schizophrenia or clinical depression, Provides a comfortable & homey atmosphere for those who seek an environment that makes them more aware of themselves & eliminates a negative attitude. Group development guidelines. Write: c/o Rita Martone, 86 Poor St., Andover, MA 01810. Call 508/475-3388.

(Model) **On Our Own, Inc., of Baltimore** *4 chapters. Founded 1981.* Mutual support & advocacy for ex-mental patients. Promotes public education & awareness of conditions faced by ex-patients. Information & referral to community services. Drop-in center. Newsletter. Resource library. Group development guidelines. Write: 5422 Belair Rd., Baltimore, MD 21203. Call 800-553-9899.

(Model) **Well Mind Association of Greater Washington** *Founded 1967.* Provides education about mental illness as principally a metabolic disorder. Explores the connection between mental illness & environmental, biological & physiological factors. Provides newsletter, phone support, info. & referrals, monthly meetings, literature, books & tapes. Assistance in starting new groups. Write: 11141 Georgia Ave., #326, Wheaton, MD 20902. Call 301/949-8282.

OBSESSIVE-COMPULSIVE DISORDER

Obsessive-Compulsive Anonymous *National. 40 affiliated groups. Founded 1988.* 12-Step self-help group for people with obsessive-compulsive disorders. Assistance available for starting groups. Write: P.O. Box 215, New Hyde Park, NY 11040. Call 516/741-4901.

Obsessive-Compulsive Disorders Assn. of National Capital Area, Inc *National. 7 groups. Founded 1988.* Information, referrals & mutual support for persons with obsessive-compulsive disorder and/or trichotillomania, & their families. Newsletter, monthly teleconferences, telephone peer counseling, literature, advocacy, treatment referrals & prescription program. Assistance in starting groups. Write: P.O. Box 11837, Alexandria, VA 22311. Call 703/379-8510.

O.C. Foundation, Inc. *National. 2 chapters. Founded 1987.* Dedicated to early intervention in controlling & finding a cure for obsessive compulsive disorders & improving the welfare of people with O.C.D. & other related OCD spectrum disorders. Provides education, research, mutual support. Bi-monthly newsletter. Group development guidelines. Write: P.O. Box 9573, New Haven, CT 06535. Call 203/772-0565 (9-5).

(Model) **Council on Anxiety Disorders** *4 affiliated groups. Founded 1988.* Education, advocacy, & mutual support for people with anxiety disorders: general anxiety, panic disorders, phobias, obsessive-compulsive disorders, post-traumatic syndrome. Group development guidelines. Write: P.O. Box 17011, Winston-Salem, NC 27116. Call 919/722-7760.

PHOBIA / ANXIETY
(see also Mental Health General: Recovery)

A.I.M. (Agoraphobics In Motion) *National. 30 groups. Founded 1983.* Uses specific behavioral techniques to help people recover from agoraphobia, anxiety, & panic attacks. Relaxation techniques & small group discussions, field trips. Newsletter, pen pals. Group development guidelines - $27. Write: 1729 Crooks, Royal Oak, MI 48067-1306. Call 313/547-0400.

Anxiety Disorders Association of America *National network. Founded 1980.* Promotes welfare of people with phobias & related anxiety disorders. An organization for consumers, health care professionals & other concerned individuals. National Membership Directory; Self-Help Group Directory. ADAA Reporter & Network News newsletters. Write: 6000 Executive Blvd. #513, Rockville, MD 20852-3801. Call 301/231-9350 or 900-737-3400.

Fear of Success Anonymous *National. Founded 1989.* Gathering of men & women who are committed to obtaining & enjoying the benefits of success, as we individually define it, in all areas of our lives. Follows the 12-steps to overcome fears, avoid self-sabotaging behavior & take action. Group meetings, phone lists, workshops, assistance in starting groups. Write: 16161 Ventura Blvd. #727, Encino, CA 91436. Call 818/907-3953.

Phobics Anonymous *Int'l. 70+ affiliated groups. Founded 1985.* Fellowship for people with anxiety & panic disorders. Follows the 12-Step program of recovery. Group development manual & worksheets available. Send stamped self-addressed envelope to: P.O. Box 1180, Palm Springs, CA 92263. Call 619/322-COPE.

(Model) **ABIL, Inc.** *Statewide network. 18 groups. Founded 1986.* Mutual support, encouragement, hope, goal setting, & education for persons with agoraphobia, anxiety or panic-related disorders & their families & friends. Provides information & referrals, phone support, newsletter, assistance in starting new groups. Write: 1418 Lorraine Ave., Richmond, VA 23227. Call Shirley Green 804/266-9409.

(Model) **Council on Anxiety Disorders** *7 affiliated groups. Founded 1988.* Education, advocacy, & mutual support for people with anxiety disorders: general anxiety, panic disorders, phobias, obsessive-compulsive disorders, post-traumatic syndrome. Group development guidelines. Write: P.O. Box 17011, Winston-Salem, NC 27116. Call 919/722-7760.

GALLUP FINDING

In a magazine interview, national pollster George Gallup commented upon the despondency and apprehension that Americans feel in the face of the problems of the recession, poverty, crime, drugs, and education. When asked if all the trends were "doom and gloom," he answered: "Not at all...there is a widespread tendency among Americans to get together in small groups - support groups, self-help groups, groups of all kinds, really. According to our data, one American in three belongs to some kind of small support or self-help group. In our fragmented society, where loneliness and isolation are so prevalent, it is encouraging to see so many people reaching out to each other. It's a very hopeful sign for the future." (New Jersey Monthly, Jan., 1992, p. 32).

PARENTING / FAMILY

ADOPTION
(see also: Health - Infertility)

Adoptees In Search (A.I.S.) *National network. Founded 1976.* Organization & support group composed of adult adoptees, adoptive parents & birth parents, to assist adult adoptees in finding birth relatives. Legislative activities to end closed adoption records. Bi-monthly newsletter, phone network. Membership $50. Write: P.O. Box 41016, Bethesda, MD 20824. Call 301/656-8555.

Adoptive Families of America, Inc. *National. 275+ groups. Founded 1967.* Problem-solving assistance & information for adoptive & prospective adoptive families. Creates opportunities for successful adoptive placement. Bimonthly magazine, group development guidelines, $24/yr. membership. Pen pals, phone network, conferences. Write: 3333 Highway 100 N., Minneapolis, MN 55422. Call 612/535-4829.

A.L.M.A. Society (Adoptee's Liberty Movement Association) *Int'l. 65 chapters. Founded 1971.* Search & support for all persons separated from their original families by adoption. Int'l reunion registry. Newsletter. Registration: $60; Renewal: $40. Write: P.O. Box 727 Radio City Sta., NY, NY 10101-0727. Call 212/581-1568.

Committee for Single Adoptive Parents *Int'l. Founded 1973.* Information to assist prospective & actual single adoptive parents to locate sources of adoptable children & support groups. Information & referrals, list of support groups, networking for individuals. Write: P.O. Box 15084, Chevy Chase, MD 20825.

C.U.B. (Concerned United Birthparents, Inc.) *National. 15 branches. Founded 1976.* Support for adoption-affected people. Search assistance for locating family members. Prevention of unnecessary separations. Monthly newsletter. Dues $50/new members, $35/renewals. Pen pals, telephone network. Write: 2000 Walker St., Des Moines, IA 50317. Call 800-822-2777

Latin America Parents Association *National. 5 chapters. Founded 1975.* Helps those seeking to adopt children from Latin America as an alternative to the adoption crisis in the U.S. Information, support, reassurance & guidance through the procedures. Newsletter, chapter development manual. $55 for membership packet. Write: P.O. Box 339, Brooklyn, NY 11234. Call 718/236-8689 (message only). or 515/263-9558.

NOBAR (Nat'l Org. for Birthfathers & Adoption Reform) *National. Founded 1987.* Support & advocacy for fathers who have surrendered children for adoption or who are in jeopardy of being separated from their children by adoption. Newsletter, information & referrals, phone support. Write: Jon R. Ryan, Pres., P.O. Box 1993, Baltimore, MD 21203. Call 301/243-3986.

North American Council on Adoptable Children *Int'l. Umbrella organization. Founded 1978.* Maintains current listing of adoptive parent support groups which conduct a wide range of activities (socials, support, educational workshops, advocacy). Activities vary widely from group to group. Qtrly. newsletter, information & referrals, conferences, help in starting groups. Ind. membership $30. Parent Group Manual ($15). Write: 1821 University Ave. #N498, St. Paul, MN 55104. Call 612-644-3036 (day).

Orphan Voyage *National. 6 groups. Founded 1953.* Information & networking for those searching for natural relatives separated by adoption. Referral to individuals & groups for peer counseling; search assistance. Educational materials. Funded by voluntary contributions. Encourages publication of authentic materials on adoption. Write: 2141 Road 2300, Cedaredge, Co 81413. Include self-addressed stamped envelope.

Yesterday's Children *National. Founded 1974.* Self-help & advocacy for persons who have been separated from their biological families through foster care, adoption, divorce, or death of parents. Assists adults seeking their historical roots. Monthly meetings. National adoption registry. Dues $50. Write: P.O. Box 1554, Evanston, IL 60204.

(Model) **International Families Adoptive Information Service** *Founded 1977.* Information & peer support for those wishing to pursue foreign adoption. Friendship for those who have accomplished this. Newsletter, information & referrals, phone support, meetings. Write: P.O. Box 1352, St. Charles, MO 63302. Call 314/423-6788 (to leave message. Out of area calls will be returned collect).

(Model) **Operation Identity** *Founded 1979.* Self-help organization embracing all facets of the adoption triad. Emotional support & information for adult adoptees searching for birth parents. Newsletter, info & referrals, phone support. Group development guidelines - $20. Write: 13101 Blackstone Rd., NE, Albuquerque, NM 87111. Call 505/293-3144.

CHILDBIRTH / CESAREAN BIRTH
(see also: Parenting, General)

A.S.P.O./Lamaze (Amer. Soc. for Psychoprophylaxis in Obstetrics) *National. 20 chapters. Founded 1960.* Dedicated to Lamaze childbirth & prepared parenthood. Includes 3 sub-groups: professional, provider & family members. Newsletter, publications. Write: 1101 Connecticut Ave., N.W., #700, Washington, DC 20036-4303. Call 800-368-4404 (national referral service) or 202/857-1128.

Cesarean Support Education & Concern *National. Founded 1972.* Support, information & referral re: cesarean birth, cesarean prevention, & vaginal delivery after cesarean. Listing of cesarean support groups nationwide. Quarterly newsletter. Guidelines for starting groups $2.25. Write: 22 Forest Rd., Framingham, MA 01701. Call 508/877-8266.

Int'l Cesarean Awareness Network, Inc. *National. 75 chapters. Founded 1982.* Support for women healing from cesarean birth. Encouragement & information for those wanting vaginal birth after previous cesarean. Education toward goal of lowering the high cesarean rate. Newsletter. Chapter development guidebook. Book & video catalogue. Write: P.O. Box 152, Syracuse, NY 13210. Call 315/424-1942.

International Childbirth Education Association, Inc. *Int'l. 250 groups. Founded 1960.* Individuals & groups committed to family centered maternity care & the philosophy of freedom of choice based on knowledge of alternatives. ICEA network locates classes & birthing options. Journal, books & pamphlets. Write: P.O. Box 20048, Minneapolis, MN 55420-0048. Call 612/854-8660.

La Leche League *Int'l. 2800 chapters. Founded 1956.* Support & education for breastfeeding mothers. Group discussions, personal help, classes & conferences. Publishes literature on breastfeeding & parenting. Bi-monthly newsletter, quarterly abstracts. Telephone support network. Write: Box 1209, Franklin Park, IL 60131. Call 800-LA-LECHE (day) or 708/455-7730.

MELD (Minnesota Early Learning Design) *National. 70+ affiliated groups. Founded 1975.* Discussion groups for parents from last trimester of pregnancy through child's second year. Programs include groups for new parents, young moms, growing families, Hispanic families, parents of special needs kids, deaf parents, Hmong parents, & young dads. Write: c/o Ann Ellwood, 123 N. Third St., #507, Minneapolis, MN 55401. Call 612/332-7563.

National Association of Mother's Centers *National. 80 sites. Founded 1981.* Helps women start mother's centers. Networks the centers together. Research, advocacy, support system for those involved in parenting, pregnancy, childbirth & child-rearing. Non-hierarchal & non-judgmental. Free networking & consultation. Literature, manual $15. Yearly newsletter. Annual conference. Write: 336 Fulton Ave., Hempstead, NY 11550. Call 800-645-3828. or 516/486-6614 (in NY).

NAPSAC (Nat'l Assn. of Parents & Professionals for Safe Alternatives in Childbirth) *National. 25 affiliated groups.* Info. & support re: homebirth, family centered maternity care & midwifery. Directory of alternative birth practitioners. Childbirth activist handbook. How-to's for organizing groups. Newsletter. Write: Rt. 1, Box 646, Marble Hill, MO 63764. Call 314/238-2010.

Sidelines National Support Network *National network. 25 groups. Founded 1992.* Former high risk moms provide support to current high risk patients & their families with both community information & emotional support. Provides newsletter, information & referrals, phone support. Assistance in starting groups. Write: 2805 Park Pl., Laguna Beach, CA 92651. Call 714/497-2265 (7:30-5pm PST).

(Model) **Confinement Line, The** *Founded 1984.* Telephone support network for women confined to bed for high risk pregnancy. Newsletter, information & referrals, guidelines & assistance available for starting networks. Write: P.O. Box 1609, Springfield, VA 22151. Call 703/941-7183.

(Model) **High Risk Moms, Inc.** *Founded 1980.* Provides peer support for women experiencing a high risk or problem pregnancy. Offers telephone contact for bed rest mothers or hospitalized mothers. Also provides monthly meetings, guest speakers, newsletter, networking with other groups nationally. Assistance in starting new groups. Write: P.O. Box 4013, Naperville, IL 60567-4013. Call 708/515-5453.

FOSTER PARENTS / CHILDREN

National Foster Parent Association, Inc. *National. 100 affiliated groups.* Support, education & advocacy for foster parents & their children. Resource center for foster care information. Bi-monthly newsletter. Annual national conference. Chapter development guidelines. Write: 226 Kilts Dr., Houston, TX 77024. Call 713/467-1850; 713/827-0919 (FAX).

MARRIAGE / FAMILY

ASSIST (Answers for Spouses by Spouses, Through ...) *National. 30 groups. Founded 1983.* Mutual aid for spouses of workers in emergency & fire services. Help in coping with their partners' job stress as it affects the entire family. Provides information & referrals, phone support, conferences, assistance in starting groups. Write: JoAnne Hildebrand, ASSIST, 2446 Azalea Rd., Port Republic, MD 20676. Call 410/586-1712.

Association of Couples for Marriage Enrichment *National network. Founded 1973.* Network of couples who want to enhance their own relationship as well as help strengthen marriages of other couples. Support groups, retreats, workshops. Bimonthly newsletter. Leadership training, conferences. Group development guidelines. Write: ACME, P.O. Box 10596, Winston-Salem, NC 27108. Call 919/724-1526.

No Kidding! *Int'l. 150+ Chapters. Founded 1984.* Mutual support & social activities for married & single people who either have decided not to have children, are postponing parenthood, are undecided, or are unable to have children. Newsletter. Group development guidelines. Write: Box 76982, Station "S", Vancouver, BC, Canada V5R 5S7. Call 604/538-7736 (24 hours).

W.E.S.O.M. (We Saved Our Marriage) *National. 10 affiliated groups. Founded 1986.* Self-help for spouses whose marriage is affected by infidelity. Helps couples deal with adultery & save their marriage. Assistance available for starting groups. Write: P.O. Box 46312, Chicago, IL 60646. Call 312/792-7034.

W.O.O.M. (Wives of Older Men) *Int'l network. Founded 1988.* Mutual support to give members the opportunity to feel comfortable socially & familially with their decision to marry someone 8 or more years their senior. Help with step-children, generation gap, rejection, etc. Newsletter, individual development guidelines. Write: c/o Beliza Ann Furman, 1029 Sycamore Ave., Tinton Falls, NJ 07724. Call 908/747-5586.

(Model) Interace *Founded 1983.* Support & advocacy for inter-racial couples, their children, bi-racial adults, & interracial adoptive families. Sharing of concerns such as raising interracial children, family rejection, & housing discrimination. Phone & mail network. Newsletter. NY & NJ regional meetings. Write: P.O. Box 582, Forest Hills, NY 11375-9998. Call Holly & Floyd Sheeger 718/657-2271 (eve).

PARENTING (GENERAL)
(see also: Childbirth)

Family Resource Coalition *National. 2000 affiliated groups. Founded 1981.* Builds support & resources within communities which will strengthen & empower families. Newsletter, information & referrals, conferences, assistance in starting support groups. Write: 200 S. Michigan Ave., #1520, Chicago, IL 60604-2404. Call 312/341-0900.

FEMALE (Formerly Employed Mothers At the Leading Edge) *National. 50 affiliated groups. Founded 1987.* Information, support & encouragement for women who have chosen to interrupt their careers in favor of raising their children. Newsletter, chapter development guidelines. Write: P.O. Box 31, Elmhurst, IL 60126. Call 708/941-3553.

G.A.P. (Grandparents As Parents) *National. 200+ groups. Founded 1987.* Support network & sharing of experiences & feelings between grandparents who are raising their grandchildren for various reasons. Information & referrals, phone support network, group member listings. Assistance in starting groups. Newsletter. Write: 1150 E. 4th St. #221, Long Beach, CA 90802. Call 310/983-6555.

Home By Choice *Int'l. 43 affiliated groups. Founded 1987.* Christian network of mothers who have chosen to stay home to care for their families. Provides referrals to local support groups & homebased business resources. Newsletter, brochures & other publications. Packet on how-to start a support group ($10). Write: P.O. Box 103, Vienna, VA 22183.

M.A.D. D.A.D.S., Inc. (Men Against Destruction Defending Against Drugs) *National. 9 affiliated groups. Founded 1989.* Grassroots organization of fathers aimed at fighting gang- & drug-related violence. Provides family activities, community education, speaking engagements & "surrogate fathers" who listen to & care about the street teens. Assistance in starting groups. Also groups for kids, mothers & grandparents. Write: 2221 N. 24th St., Omaha, NE 68110. Call 402/451-3580.

MELD (Minnesota Early Learning Design) *National. 70+ Affiliated groups. Founded 1975.* Discussion groups for parents from last trimester of pregnancy through child's second year. Programs include adolescent mothers, hearing impaired parents, Hispanic families, parents of handicapped, parents of older children. Write: 123 N. Third St., #507, Minneapolis, MN 55401. Call 612/332-7563.

MOMS Club *National. 60 affiliated groups. Founded 1983.* Mutual support for mothers-at-home. Groups provide emotional & moral support to mothers of children of all ages. Offers a wide variety of activities. Annual dues vary. Newsletter. Assistance in starting groups. Write: 814 Moffatt Circle, Simi Valley, CA 93065. Call 805/526-2725.

MOPS, Int'l (Mothers of Pre-Schoolers) *Int'l. 585 affiliated groups. Founded 1973.* Fellowship of mothers of preschoolers (birth to first grade) offering a nurturing, caring environment with a spiritual focus. Activities available for the children. MOPS groups are sponsored by local churches. Newsletter, area conferences, networking, help in starting local chapters. Write: 4175 Harlan St., #105, Wheat Ridge, CO 80003. Call 303/420-6100.

National Association of Mother's Centers *National. 80 sites. Founded 1981.* Research, advocacy, support system for those involved in parenting, pregnancy, childbirth & child-rearing. Non-hierarchal & non-judgmental. Free networking & consultation. Free packets, manual $15. Yearly newsletter. Annual conference. Write: 336 Fulton Ave., Hempstead, NY 11550. Call 800-645-3828. or 516/486-6614 (in NY).

National Committee for Citizens in Education *National. 400 groups. Founded 1973.* (Bi-lingual) Assists parents & citizens who want to become involved in local public schools. National network of local parent groups working actively for better schools. Assists new groups in organizing techniques & strategies. Information & referrals. Newsletter. Write 900 2nd St. NE #8, Washington, DC 20002-3557. Call 800-NET-WORK (10am-4pm); 202/408-0447; or 800-LE-AYUDA (Hispanic).

National Parent Center, The *National. 7 regions. Founded 1976.* Helps parents become actively involved in all aspects of their children's education. Provides training & technical assistance on a local or regional basis. Newsletter. Write: c/o Edmond School Building, 9th & D Streets, NE #201, Washington, DC 20002. Call 202/547-9286.

ROCKING (Raising Our Children's Kids: An Intergenerational Network of Grandparenting) *Nat'l. 10 groups. Founded 1992.* Confederation of grandparents who are committed to providing a safe haven for their grandchildren (when not living w/their biological parents) & who have become the main financial & emotional caregivers to their grandchildren. Newsletter, phone help, info. & referrals. Help in starting groups. Dues $35/yr. Write: P.O. Box 96, Niles, MI 49120. Call 616/683-9038.

(Model) **Fathers' Network, The** Aims to increase involvement of father in parenting; to encourage mutually fulfilling relationships between fathers & their children; & to challenge traditional "provider" role regardless of marital/custodial status. Opportunity for men to share with others in similar situation. Assistance in starting other fathers' support groups. NOT A DIVORCE RESOURCE. $10 one-time fee. Call 415/453-2839.

(Model) **Full-Time Dads** *Founded 1991.* Provides networking & support for fathers (married or single) who are the primary caregivers for their children. Provides a forum for sharing information, resources & experiences through bi-monthly journal. In process of developing local chapters throughout U.S. Write: P.O. Box 12773, St. Paul, MN 55112-0773.

(Model) **Grandparents Raising Grandchildren in California** *Founded 1986.* Sharing of problems, information & support, for grandparents or relatives raising a child, or concerned about a child's abusive environment. Monthly newsletter. Guidelines on starting groups. Write: 3851 Centraloma Dr., San Diego, CA 92107. Call 619/223-0344.

(Model) **Grandparents Raising Grandchildren, Inc. in Texas** *12 affiliated groups. Founded 1988.* To provide emotional & political support to grandparents who for various reasons find themselves the primary caregivers of their children's children. Meetings twice a month. Newsletter, group development guidelines. Write: Barbara Kirkland, P.O. Box 104, Colleyville, TX 76034. Call 817/577-0435.

(Model) **MOM: An Alliance of Entrepreneurial Mothers.** *Founded 1989.* Support for persons who own their own business, have children & are striving to meet the challenges of both. Provides emotional support, information & resources. Offers networking opportunities. Newsletter, phone support, conferences. Assistance in starting groups. Write: P.O. Box 64033, Tucson, AZ 85728. Call 602/628-2598 (day/eve).

(Model) **Mother's Connection, The** *Founded 1976.* Networking of mothers of pre-schoolers for mutual support & sharing of resources to reduce feelings of isolation. Opportunity to form mothers' groups, childrens' play groups or babysitting co-ops. Pamphlets for starting new groups. Write: 50 Pintard Ave., New Rochelle, NY 10801. Call 914/235-9474.

(Model) **PEP (Post Partum Education for Parents)** *Founded 1977.* Emotional support to parents by parent volunteers. Helps parents adjust to changes in their lives that a baby brings.

Telephone help. Education on basic infant care & parent adjustment. "Guide for Establishing a Parent Support Program in Your Community" $10. Monthly newsletter. Group development guidelines. Write: P.O. Box 6154, Santa Barbara, CA 93160. Call 805/564-3888.

(Model) **Teen Fathers Project (John Dewey H.S.)** *Founded 1988.* Support group for teen parents to provide structured topics on infant care, age appropriate toys, communicating with teen mother & the parents. Literature & assistance in starting groups. Write: Len Mednick, 50 Ave. X, Brooklyn, NY 11223. Call Len Mednick 718/373-6400 ext. 319 (day).

PARENTS OF ADOLESCENTS/ADULT CHILDREN
(see also: Addictions - Alcohol/Drug Abuse)

Tough Love International *Int'l. 650 groups. Founded 1979.* Self-help program for parents, kids & communities in dealing with the out-of-control behavior of a family member. Parent support groups help parents take a firm stand to help kids take responsibility for their behavior. Quarterly newsletter. Group development guidelines. Write: Box 1069, Doylestown, PA 18901. Call 800-333-1069 (M-F, 9-5 EST - leave message other times).

(Model) **Abused Parents of America** *Founded 1990.* Mutual support & comfort for parents who are abused by their adult children. Assistance available for starting similar groups. Write: c/o Beulah Warner, 2873 Roosevelt Ave., Kalamazoo, MI 49004. Call 616/349-6920.

(Model) **Because I Love You: The Parent Support Group** *11 groups. Founded 1982.* Support for parents who have children of all ages with behavioral problems such as truancy, substance abuse, or other forms of defiance of authority. Focus is on parents getting back their self-esteem & control of their home. Write: P.O. Box 35175, Los Angeles, CA 90035-9998. Call 310/ 659-5289.

PARENTS OF PREMATURE / HIGH RISK INFANTS
(see also Disabilities: Parents of Disabled)

National Council of Guilds for Infant Survival *National. 15 chapters. Founded 1962.* Support & education for parents who experience Sudden Infant Death Syndrome (SIDS) & for families using in-home monitors for high risk infants. Quarterly newsletter, group development guidelines, correspondence. Write: P.O. Box 3586, Davenport, Iowa 52808.

Parent Care *National. 500 groups. Founded 1982.* Partnership of parents & professionals dedicated to improving the newborn intensive care experience & future for babies, families & caregivers. Supports development of support groups. Newsletter, phone support, conferences, information & referral. Dues $25-100. Group development guidelines ($2). Write: 9041 Colgate St., Indianapolis, IN 46268-1210. Call 317/872-9913.

(Model) **Intensive Caring Unlimited** *Founded 1978.* For parents who have experienced the birth of a premature or sick baby, baby on medication, developmental problems, high risk pregnancy or the death of a baby. Offers emotional & educational support. Peer counseling, resources, information & referrals. Newsletter. Write: 910 Bent Lane, Philadelphia, PA 19118. Call Lynette 215/233-4723 (PA) or Carol Randolph 609/848-1945 (NJ).

PARENTS OF TWINS & TRIPLETS

National Organization of Mothers of Twins Clubs *National. 400+ clubs. Founded 1960.* Mothers of multiple births share information, concerns, & advice on dealing with their unique problems. Literature, quarterly newspaper $15/yr., group development guidelines, bereavement support, pen pal program. Membership through local clubs. Write: P.O. Box 23188, Albuquerque, NM 87192-1188. Call 505/275-0955.

Triplet Connection *Int'l network. Founded 1982.* Support for families with triplets (or more). Information re: pregnancy & delivery, networking with other families, support for expectant parents as well as parents of older triplets. Pre-term birth prevention info., newsletter. Write: P.O. Box 99571, Stockton, CA 95209. Call 209/474-0885.

SEPARATION / DIVORCE
(see also: Single Parenting)

ACES (Association for Children for Enforcement of Support) *National. 254 affiliated groups. Founded 1984.* Information & support for parents who have custody of their children & have difficulty collecting child support payments. Location service on non-payers. Newsletter, information & referrals, assistance in starting local support groups. Write: c/o Geraldine Jensen, 723 Philips Ave., Suite J, Toledo, OH 43612. Call 800-537-7072 or 419/476-2511.

Banana Splits *Int'l. 100+. Founded 1978.* Peer support for kids to help each other deal with changes in their lives due to parental death, divorce or separation. Also groups for the parents. Children's group are usually school-facilitated. How-to information ($25). Write: c/o Interact Publishers, Box 997, Lakeside, CA 92040. Call 800-359-0961.

Children's Rights Council (Nat'l Council for Children's Rights) *National. 22 groups in 17 states. Founded 1985.* Concerned parents provide education & advocacy for reform of the legal system regarding child custody. Newsletter, information & referrals, directory of parenting organizations, catalog of resources, conferences, group development guidelines. Write: Attn: David L. Levy, 220 I St., NE, #230, Washington, NJ 20002. Call 202/547-6227.

Committee for Mother & Child Rights, Inc. *National.* Provides emotional support, information & networking for mothers with custody problems related to divorce. Write: Route 1 Box 256A, Clear Brook, VA 22624. Call 703/722-3652.

Divorce Anonymous *National. 7 groups. Founded 1987.* Support group for those undergoing divorce, separation, or a relationship break-up. Based on the 12 Step Program of Alcoholics Anonymous. Information & referrals, phone support. Write: Christine Archambault, 2600 Colorado Ave., Suite 270, Santa Monica, CA 90404. Call 310/998-6538.

E.X.P.O.S.E. (Ex-Partners of Servicemen for Equality) *National. 35 chapters. Founded 1981.* Lobbies for changes in military divorce laws. Disseminates information re: rights & legal assistance. Bi-monthly newsletter. Publishes "Guide for Military Wives Facing Separation & Divorce." Write: P.O. Box 11191, Alexandria, VA 22312. Call 703/941-5844 or hotline 703/255-2917.

F.A.C.E. (Father's And Children's Equality) *National. 30 groups. Founded 1978.* Mutual support & information to father's & extended families in divorce situations. Concerned with gaining equal rights for fathers. Advocacy for equal access to children with support obligations. Restores children's rights to equal access to parents. Newsletter. Dues $50/initial; $25 renewal. Write: P.O. Box 117, Drexel Hill, PA 19086. Call 215/688-4748.

Grandparents'-Children's Rights, Inc. *National. Founded 1981.* Info & advocacy for grandparents being denied visitation rights w/grandchildren. Urges grandparents to organize independent contact groups in their area so that they can meet to discuss problems, exchange info. & work together to change legislation.

Write: c/o Lucile Sumpter, 5728 Bayonne Ave., Haslett, MI 48840-4759. Call 517/339-8663.

Grandparents Rights Organization *National. Founded 1984.* Advocates & educates on behalf of grandparent-grandchild relationships primarily with respect to grandparent visits. Assists in the formation of local support groups dealing with the denial of grandparent visitation by custodial parent or guardian. Newsletter, information & referrals, conferences. Dues $35/yr. Write: 555 S. Woodward #600, Birmingham, MI 48009. Call 313/646-7191 (day).

Joint Custody Association *Int'l. 250 affiliated groups. Founded 1979.* Assists divorcing parents & their families to achieve joint custody. Disseminates information concerning family law research & judicial decisions. Advocates for legislative improvement of family law in state capitols. Write: James A. Cook, President, Joint Custody Association, 10606 Wilkins Ave., Los Angeles, CA 90024. Call 310/475-5352.

Mothers Without Custody *National. Founded 1981.* Support network that enhances the quality of life for children by strengthening the role of non-custodial mother through the sharing of information & experiences. Bi-monthly newsletter. Group coordinator's kit available. Write: P.O. Box 27418, Houston, TX 77227-7418. Call 713/840-1622.

NCSAC (National Child Support Advocacy Coalition) *National. 25 affiliated groups. Founded 1987.* Advocates for child support enforcement & collection. Serves as umbrella for independent support groups across the country. Provides networking & assistance for developing groups. Quarterly newsletter. Annual conference. Write: Beth McMinney, P.O. Box 420, Hendersonville, TN 37077-0420. Call 615-264-0151 or Betty Murphy 703-799-5659.

National Congress for Men & Children, Inc. *National. 54 affiliated groups. Founded 1980.* Purpose is to reduce discrimination against men in general & in family courts in particular. Newsletter, information & referrals to local chapters. Write: P.O. Box A, Glenside, PA 19038, Attn: Dr. Ken Lewis. Call 215/576-0177.

National Organization For Men *National. 21 chapters. Founded 1983.* Seeks equal rights for men, uniform national divorce, custody, property & visitation law. Educational seminars. Lawyer referral. Quarterly newsletter. Write: 11 Park Pl., New York, NY 10007-2801. Call 212/686-MALE.

North American Conference of Separated & Divorced Catholics
Int'l. 3000+ groups. Founded 1972. Religious, educational & emotional aspects of divorce & remarriage are addressed through self-help groups, conferences & training programs. Families of all faiths are welcome. Group development guidelines. Newsletter. Membership dues $25 (includes coupons, discounts & resources). Write: NACSDC, 80 St. Mary's Dr., Cranston, RI 02920. Call Dorothy Lezesque 401/943-7903.

Rainbows for All God's Children *Int'l. 4000 affiliated groups. Founded 1983.* Establishes peer support groups in churches, schools or social agencies for children & adults who are grieving a death, divorce or other painful transition in their family. Groups are led by trained adults. Newsletter, information & referrals. Write: 1111 Tower Rd., Schaumburg, IL 60173. Call 708-310-1880.

(Model) **New Beginnings, Inc.** *Founded 1979.* Support group for separated & divorced men & women in the DC Metro area. Discussion meetings, speakers, social events, workshops. Newsletter. Assistance available for starting groups. Dues $40/yr. $30/renewal. Write: 13129 Clifton Rd., Silver Spring, MD 20904. Call 301/384-0111.

SINGLE PARENTING
(see also Separation/Divorce)

Parents Without Partners *National. 700+ chapters. Founded 1957.* Educational non-profit organization of single parents. While most members are divorced, some chapters do have special discussion groups for widowed persons. Newsletter. Single parent magazine, chapter development guidelines. Membership dues. Write: 8807 Colesville Rd., Silver Spring, MD 20910. Call 800-637-7974 or 301/588-9354.

Single Mothers By Choice *National. 10 chapters. Founded 1981.* Non-profit organization that provides support & information to single women who have chosen, or who are considering, single motherhood. Services include "Thinkers" workshops, quarterly newsletter, & membership. For a brochure & list of back issues of newsletter write: SMC, P.O. Box 1642 Gracie Sq. St., New York, NY 10028. Call 212/988-0993.

Single Parent Resource Center *Int'l. Founded 1975.* Network of single parent self-help groups. Information & referral, seminars, consultation, resource library. Working on groups for homeless single parents & mothers coming out of prison. Newsletter. Guidelines & materials for starting parenting & teen groups. Write: 141 W. 28th St., #302, New York, NY 10001. Call 212/947-0221.

(Model) **Solo Parent Empowerment Circles/Peer Support Groups** *Founded 1990.* Opportunity for solo parents to collectively problem-solve challenges & celebrate joys of solo parenting. Issues include: financial independence, parenting skills, finishing school. Home sharing, newsletter, information & referrals. Meetings, socials. Assistance in starting groups. Write: 1202 E. Pike St. #774, Seattle, WA 98122. Call 206/720-1655 (Tues - Fri).

(Model) **Unwed Parents Anonymous** *Founded 1979.* Support to those affected by an out-of-wedlock pregnancy & parenting. 12-Step program. Encourages sexual abstinence outside of marriage. Weekly meetings. Newsletter, group development guidelines $19.95. Write: P.O. Box 44556, Phoenix, AZ 85064. Call 602/952-1463.

STEPFAMILIES

Stepfamily Association of America, Inc. *Founded 1979. 65+ chapters.* Information & advocacy for step-families. Self-help programs through local chapters. Educational resources. Quarterly bulletin. Annual national conference. Chapter start-up information available ($4). Other literature free of charge. Write: 215 Centennial Mall, #212, Lincoln, NE 68508-1813. Call 402/477-7837.

"As long as you can be around others who have been through the same experience you have, you can send messages and know they are received. Giving the message back and forth tells you that you're still alive."

- Mohin Pat...Cambodian refugee
(per Gail Sheehy in <u>Spirt of Survival</u>)

PHYSICAL / EMOTIONAL ABUSE

BATTERING

Batterers Anonymous *National. 30+ chapters. Founded 1979.* Self-help program for men who wish to control their anger & eliminate their abusive behavior toward women. Buddy system. Group development manual $9.95. Write: c/o Batterers Anonymous, B.A. Press, 1269 N. "E" St., San Bernardino, CA 92405. Call Dr. Jerry Goffman 714/355-1100.

For **Battered Women's Self-Help Groups.** Since there are no national mutual aid self-help groups that we know of at this time, you can contact a local helpline, battered women's shelter, or self-help clearinghouse, or call the National Coalition Against Domestic Violence at 800-333-SAFE.

(Guide) **Talking It Out: A Guide to Groups for Abused Women**. While we know of no national group to help with the development of a group for battered women, this book discusses how to start a group, how to lead it (to include co-leadership), group issues, group exercises, groups for specifc populations, and how to prevent burnout. Authored by Ginny Ni Carthy, Karen Merriam, and Sandra Coffman. Available for $10.95 plus $1.50 postage from Seal Press, 3131 Western Ave., Seattle, WA 98121-1028.

CHILD ABUSE
(see also Sexual Abuse)

Believe the Children *National. 3 chapters. Founded 1986.* For parents of children who have been victimized by people outside of the family. Parents & professionals address the issues of sexual & ritualistic exploitation of small children. Newsletter. Chapter development guidelines ($5). Write: P.O. Box 77, Hermosa Beach, CA 90254. Call 310/379-3514.

Parents Anonymous *National. 1200 groups. Founded 1970.* Peer led, professionally-facilitated group for parents who are having difficulty & would like to learn more effective ways of raising their children. Group leaders manual, chapter development manual & other materials to assist in formation of groups. Many chapters also have children's groups. Write: 520 S. Lafayette Park Pl., #316, Los Angeles, CA 90057. Cail 800-421-0353 or 213/388-6685.

V.O.C.A.L. (Victims Of Child Abuse Laws) *National. 41 chapters. Founded 1984.* To protect the rights of persons falsely & wrongly accused of child abuse, & to obtain more protection for children against abusers within the childrens' services system. Referral to psychologists & attorneys. Newsletter. Chapter development guidelines. Write: 7485 E. Kenyon Ave., Denver, CO 80237. Call 303/233-5321.

(Model) **Parental Stress Services** *Founded 1975.* Children & parents from stressful family environments meet in separate groups led by trained volunteers, to talk about feelings, gain understanding & acceptance. Parenting classes, parent groups. Bi-monthly newsletter. Group development guidelines. Films & videotapes. Speakers bureau. Write: 600 S. Federal, #205, Chicago, IL 60605. Call 312/427-1161 or 312/427-6644 (24 hr. hotline).

(Model) **SPEAKS (Survivors of Physical & Emotional Abuse as Kids)** *3 groups in CA.* Modified self-help groups which enable adults who were physically and/or emotionally abused as children to meet with others in a safe & supportive environment to share & understand. Professionals assist at meetings. Assistance in starting new groups. Write: c/o PA of CA, 7520 S. Lafayette Park Pl. #316, Los Angeles, CA 90057. Call 213-649-5212; 213-388-6685; 800-352-0386 (in CA).

SEXUAL ABUSE / INCEST / RAPE

Believe The Children *National. 3 chapters. Founded 1986.* For parents of children who have been victimized by people outside of the family. Parents & professionals address the issues of sexual & ritualistic exploitation of small children. Newsletter. Chapter development guidelines ($5). Write: P.O. Box 77, Hermosa Beach, CA 90254. Call 213/379-3514.

Forbidden Zone Recovery *National. 3 affiliated groups. Founded 1990.* Recovery for women sexually exploited by professional men (lawyers, doctors, clergy, therapists, etc.). Provides education, information & political reform. Information & referrals, newsletter, phone support. Write: 1580 Valencia St. #601, San Francisco, CA 94110. Call 415/572-0571.

Incest Resources, Inc. *Int'l. Founded 1980.* Provides educational & resource materials for female & male survivors & for professionals working with survivors. International listing of survivor self-help groups. Manual for starting survivor self-help group. For information send self-addressed envelope with (2) 1st class stamps to: 46 Pleasant St., Cambridge, MA 02139. (NO CALLS PLEASE).

Incest Survivors Anonymous *Int'l. 300+ affiliated groups. Founded 1980.* Based on the 12 Steps & 12 Traditions of A.A. Men, women & teens meet to share their experience, strength & hope, so that they may recover from their incest experiences & break free to a new peace of mind. Assistance in starting groups. Send a self-addressed stamped envelope to: P.O. Box 5613, Long Beach, CA 90805-1632. Call 310/428-5599.

Multiple Personality Dignity/LOOM (Loved Ones of Multiples) *Int'l. Founded 1989.* For persons with multiple personality or dissociative disorder. Also, Loved Ones of Multiples network. Pen/phone pals, newsletter, support groups. Non-religious 12-practices approach. Must obtain Guidebook ($15 sugg. donation) & sign confidentiality agreement before joining network. Due to curiosity seekers, reporters & abusers, only participants are given meeting info. Write: P.O. Box 4367, Boulder, CO 80306.

S.A.R.A. (Sexual Assault Recovery Anonymous) Society *National. 35 groups. Founded 1983.* Education & self-help for adults & teens who were sexually abused as children. Group development guidelines & assistance provided for starting groups. Literature for behavioral modification available. Newsletter. Dues $10/year. Write: P.O. Box 16, Surrey, BC V3T 4W4 Canada. Call 604/584-2626.

S.A.S.A. (Sexual Abuse Survivors Anonymous) *National. 10 groups. Founded 1991.* 12-step group for survivors of abuse (including incest, rape or any overt or covert abuse). Separate groups for men & women, women only, & partners. All groups are closed (no perpetrators or non-victims). Conference. Assistance in starting groups. Write: P.O. Box 241046, Detroit, MI 48224. Call 313/882-9646.

Stop Abuse by Counselors *National. Founded 1981.* Consumer organization that aims to prevent the exploitation of clients by mental health practitioners. Encourages research. Promotes remedial legislation. Pen pal program. Program development guidelines ($10), 48-page bibliography ($8), other publications. For info. send self-addressed stamped envelope to: P.O. Box 68292, Seattle, WA 98168. Call 206/243-2723.

Survivors of Incest Anonymous *Int'l. 800 groups. Founded 1982.* Self-help 12-step program for men & women 18 yrs or older who have been victims of child sexual abuse & want to survive. Newsletter ($12.50/yr), literature ($23.50 for set), pen pals, assistance in starting groups, volunteer information & referral line, speakers bureau. Send self-addressed stamped envelope to P.O. Box 21817, Baltimore, MD 21222-6817. Call 410/433-2365.

VOICES In Action, Inc. *National network. Founded 1980.* Support for adult victims of childhood sexual abuse, to provide emotional support for victims, generate public awareness & to work toward prevention of incest. Newsletter ($20). Guidelines on starting self-help groups. Special interest correspondence groups. Conferences, publications. Write: P.O. Box 148309, Chicago, IL 60614. Call 312/327-1500 or 800-7-VOICE-8.

(Resource) **Parents United International, Inc.** While sometimes thought of as self-help groups, Parents United actually sponsor over 100 professionally-run therapy groups for parents whose children have been sexually abused. They also offer groups for adults molested as children. Chapter development guidelines & training available for professionals wishing to start groups. Newsletter. Write: 232 E. Gish Rd., San Jose, CA 95112. Call 408/453-7616 ext. 124.

(Model) **Adult Children of Sexual Abuse** *Founded 1986.* Anonymous support & growth group for adults who were victims of sexual abuse as children. Sharing of experiences & solutions to help each other heal. Follows the 12-step program of A.A. Phone support. Assistance in starting new groups. Write: 3110 Merita Dr., Holiday, FL 34691. Call 813/938-7836.

(Model) **Families of Sex Offenders Anonymous** *Founded 1989.* 12-Step group for families & friends of persons afflicted with a destructive sexual addiction, to help each member work through the shock, denial, shame & grief of a behavior associated with deviance & criminality. Newsletter. Meets monthly. Write: 208 W. Walk, W. Haven, CT 06516. Call Carol S. 203/931-0015.

(Model) **It's P.O.S.S.I.B.L.E. (Partners of Survivors Stopping Incest by Learning & Eduction)** *Founded 1989.* Mutual support for non-offending partners & family members of incested persons. Group open to any significant other. Phone support, conferences, information & referrals, on-going meetings. Newsletter being developed. Assistance in starting new groups. Write: RFD #3, Box 505, Augusta, ME 04330. Call Rebecca or Alan 207/547-3532.

(Model) **M.A.L.E. (Male Assisting Leading Educating)** Support network (via newsletter) dedicated to the recovery & assistance of non-offending male survivors of childhood sexual incest. Provides forum for male survivors to discuss issues, share experiences & exchange ideas. Newsletter published 6 times per year ($15/survivor, $25/others). Other support services planned for the future. Write: P.O. Box 380181, Denver, CO 80238-1181. Call 303-320-4365.

(Model) **Molesters Anonymous** *10 groups. Founded 1985.* Provides support with anonymity & confidentiality for men who molest children. Use of "thought stoppage" technique & buddy system. Groups are initiated by a professional but become member-run. Group development manual $12.95. Write: c/o Batterers Anonymous, 8485 Tamarind Ave. #D, Fontana, CA 92335. Call Dr. Jerry Goffman 714/355-1100.

(Model) **MOMS (Mothers Opposed to Molest Situations)** *Regional. Founded 1986.* Mutual support, information & referrals for non-offending mothers of molested children (of any age). Provides newsletter, pen pal program, phone support, & classes. Assistance in starting new groups. Dues $15 individual/$25 family. Professionals assist at weekly meetings. Write: P.O. Box 70665, Eugene, OR 97401. Call 503/484-7252.

(Model) **National Survivors of Child Abuse & Addictions Program** *Founded 1990.* Mutual support for survivors of child abuse, recovering alcoholics/addicts & recovering parents. Various groups offered for the different concerns. Provides information & referrals, phone support, support group meetings, assistance in starting local chapters. Write: Childhelp USA/IOF Foresters, Nat'l Child Abuse Hotline, P.O. Box 630, Hollywood, CA 90028. Call 213/465-4016 (day).

(Model) **Parents Against Molesters, Inc.** *Founded 1983.* Self-help for parents of children who were victims of sexual abuse. Awareness program & education to community. Advocacy for changes in legislation. Bi-monthly newsletter. Phone support network. Group development guidelines: "The Don't List." Write: P.O. Box 3557, Portsmouth, VA 23701. Call Barbara Barker 804/363-2549.

(Model) **Survivor Network, The** *Regional. Founded 1989.* Promotes healing from the effects of childhood sexual abuse. Provides education & advocacy, with a special focus on the arts. Produces news magazine, literary magazine, annual art show & an annual performance. Write: P.O. Box 80058, Albuquerque, NM 87198. Call 505/873-1083.

(Model) **TELL (Therapy Exploitation Link Line)** *Founded 1989.* Support for women who have experienced sexual abuse by psychotherapists & other health care professionals. Resource network to help women file complaints & lawsuits, share referrals & network with others. Offers group meetings, information, phone support, help in starting similar groups. Write: P.O. Box 115, Waban, MA 02168. Call 617/964-8355.

(Model) **W.I.N.G.S. Foundation (Women Incested Needing Group Support)** *Regional. 20 groups. Founded 1982.* Promotes healing through support groups to reduce the trauma of incest. Addresses issue of isolation.   Newsletter, info. & referrals, conferences, referrals to therapists, support groups. Assistance in starting new groups. Write: 8007 W. Colfax, CS27, Box 129, Lakewood, CO 80215. Call 303/238-8660 (day).

For **Rape Victim Self-Help Groups** that may exist, contact your local helpline, self-help clearinghouse, rape crisis service, or women's center. We know of no national self-help mutual aid group for rape victims at this time.

MISCELLANEOUS ISSUES

AGING / OLDER PERSONS
(see also: Caregivers, Women)

AARP (American Association of Retired Persons) *National. 4000 chapters. Founded 1958.* Non-profit membership organization dedicated to addressing the needs & interests of persons 50 & older. Seeks through education, advocacy & service to enhance the quality of life for all by promoting independence, dignity & purpose. Write: 601 E St., NW, Washington, DC 20049. Call 202/434-2277.

Gray Panthers *National. 70 chapters. Founded 1970.* Multi-generational education & advocacy movement/organization which works to bring about fundamental social changes including a national health care system; elimination of all forms of discrimination; economic justice. Qtrly. newsletter, chapter development guidelines. Write: 1424 16th St., N.W., #602, Washington, DC 20036. Call 202/387-3111.

Older Women's League *Nat'l. 200+ chapters. Founded 1980.* Membership organization that advocates on behalf of various economic & social issues for midlife & older women (social security, pension rights, health insurance, employment, caregiver support, etc.). Offers newsletter, chapter development guidelines. Dues $15/yr. Write: 666 11th St., NW, Washington, DC 20001. Call 202/783-6686.

Phenix Society *Int'l. Founded 1973.* Holistic & spiritually-oriented fellowship seeking to explore meaning, wisdom & potential of later years of life. Phoenix Clubs aim to develop spiritually & improve quality of life through reading, weekly meetings & discussions. "Mind Expander" newsletter $6/yr. Club handbook. Group development guidelines. Write: Box 351, Cheshire, CT 06410. Call 203/387-6913.

ARTISTIC CREATIVITY

A.R.T.S. Anonymous (Artists Recovering through Twelve Steps) *Int'l. 83 affiliated groups. Founded 1984.* Spiritual program based on the 12-steps/12-traditions of A.A. The only requirement for membership is a desire to fulfill creative potential. Bimonthly newsletter. Group development guidelines. Send self-addressed stamped envelope to: P.O. Box 175 Ansonia Station, NY, NY 10023-0175. Call 212/969-0144 (will call back collect).

CAREGIVERS
(see also: Health: Alzheimer's; Disabilities: Parents of Disabled)

CAPS (Children of Aging Parents) *National. 12 chapters. Founded 1977.* Provides support & guidance for all caregivers of the aged. Assists in formation of support groups. Programs to educate public re: needs of elderly & caregivers. Educational programs, bi-monthly newsletter, group starter packet & manual $25 + postage. Write: 1609 Woodbourne Rd. #302A, Levittown, PA 19057. Call 215/945-6900; 215/945-2289 (FAX).

Concerned Relatives of Nursing Home Patients *National network. Founded 1976.* Information for families of the elderly about nursing homes, Medicaid, Medicare, patients' rights & complaints. Bi-monthly newsletter "Insight." Group development guidelines. Write: P.O. Box 18820, Cleveland, Ohio 44118-0820. Call 216/321-0403.

Well Spouse Foundation *Int'l. 60 chapters. Founded 1988.* Emotional support for people married to a chronically ill spouse. Works on advocacy for long-term care. Quarterly newsletter, pen pals, conferences. Guidelines & assistance available for starting groups. Write: P.O. Box 28876, San Diego, CA 92198-0876. Call 619/673-9043.

(Model) **DEBUT (Daughters of Elderly Bridging the Unknown Together)** *Founded 1981.* Support group designed by, & for, women struggling with the responsibilities, emotions, & decisions involved in the care of aging parents. Educational programs, phone network, weekly meetings. Group development guidelines. Write: c/o Area 10 Agency Aging, 2129 Yost Ave., Bloomington, IN 47401. Call Pat Meier 812/876-5319.

(Model) **FRIA (Friends & Relatives of Institutionalized Aged, Inc.)** *Founded 1976.* Information & guidance on quality care regulations for New York State nursing homes, allowing persons to better monitor the conditions of their loved one's nursing or adult home. Publishes newsletter & Eldercare in the '90's: A Guide for NY Relatives & Friends (home health care, placement, etc) $27.50. Write: 11 John St., #601, New York, NY. Call Jennifer Ott or Randy Blom 212/732-4455.

CRIME VICTIMS / OFFENDERS

Convicts Anonymous *National. 3 chapters. Founded 1990.* 12-step program for people desiring to stop criminal behavior. Fellowship to talk things out before acting things out. Brochure;

information & referrals; phone support; pen pals; conferences; group development guidelines. Write: P.O. Box 5175, Everett, WA 98206. Call 206/252-4472.

COPS (Concerns of Police Survivors, Inc.) *National. 13 chapters.* Peer support for spouses & families of law enforcement officers who died in the line of duty. Quarterly newsletter, group development guidelines, peer support, conferences. Write: c/o Suzie Sawyer, 9423A Marlboro Pike, Upper Marlboro, MD 20772. Call 301/599-0445.

Forensic Committee of Nat'l Alliance of the Mentally Ill *National. Coordinators in 38 states. Founded 1984.* Support for families of mentally ill persons in prison or going through the criminal justice system. Advocacy for mentally ill in prison, education for criminal justice system. Quarterly newsletter. Write: c/o NAMI, 2101 Wilson Blvd., #302, Arlington, VA 22201. Call 703/524-7600.

M.A.D.D. (Mothers Against Drunk Driving) *National. 400 chapters. Founded 1980.* The mission of MADD is to stop drunk driving & support victims of this violent crime. Newsletter, chapter development guidelines. Write: 511 E. John Carpenter Freeway, Suite 700, Irving, TX 75062. Call 214/744-6233.

National Organization for Victim Assistance *National. 2500 organizations & members. Founded 1975.* Support & advocacy for crime victims. Newsletter, information & referrals, phone help, conferences, group development guidelines. Dues $30/individuals; $100/organization. Write: 1757 Park Rd., NW, Washington, DC 20010. Call 202/232-6682; 202/462-2255 (FAX).

National Victim Center *National. Founded 1985.* Provides crime victims with information & resources. Promotes development of self-help groups. Referrals to existing groups; consultation & guidelines for starting groups. Links up victims one-to-one for mutual support. Quarterly newsletter. Conferences. Write: Linda Lowrance, Nat'l Victim Ctr., 309 W. 7th St., #705, Fort Worth, TX 76102. Call 817/877-3355.

Parents of Murdered Children *National. 325 chapters & contact persons throughout the U.S. & Canada. Founded 1978.* Provides self-help groups to support persons who survive the violent death of someone close, as they seek to recover. Newsletter; court accompaniment also provided in many areas. Write: 100 E. 8th St., B-41, Cincinnati, OH 45202. Call 513/721-5683 (office); 513/721-5685 (FAX).

Parents of Murdered Children of NY State, Inc. *NY Statewide.*
Founded 1982. Support through advocacy for parents of
murdered children & concerned families & friends. Assists families
through criminal proceedings. Provides medium for exchange of
information & ideas re: rights & services for victims & survivors.
Newsletter. Write: POMCONYS, 26 W. 84th St., New York, NY
10024. Call 212/873-3361 or 718/834-7698.

R.I.D. (Remove Intoxicated Drivers) *National. 160 chapters in
40 states. Founded 1978.* Citizens' project organized to advocate
against drunk driving, educate the public, reform legislation & aid
victims of drunk driving. Quarterly newsletter. Chapter information
kit $20. For descriptive pamphlet send self-addressed stamped
envelope to: Doris Aiken, P.O. Box 520, Schenectady, NY 12301.
Call 518/372-0034; 518/370-4917 (FAX).

(Model) **Fortune Society** *Founded 1967.* Support & education
for ex-offenders. Tutoring, employment assistance, AIDS/HIV
education & services, counseling & court advocacy. Counselors
are ex-offenders themselves. Assistance for starting similar groups.
Write: 39 W. 19th St., New York, NY 10011. Call 212/206-7070.

(Model) **Kleptomaniacs/Shoplifters Anonymous** Self-help
group for people who have the problem of compulsive stealing.
Members share ideas & strategies for controlling behavior.
Meetings in New York City. Write: Michele G., 114 West 70th
St., Apt. 3C, New York, NY 10023. Call Michele G. 212/724-4067.

(Model) **Repeat Offenders Anonymous** *10 affiliated groups.
Founded 1989.* 12-step fellowship whose common problem is an
inability to remain crime free. Sharing of experience, strength &
hope in order to solve common problems & help each other to
recover. Write: P.O. Box 56713, Phoenix, AZ 85079-6713. Call
602/938-8255.

(Model) **Shoplifters Anonymous** *Founded 1980.* Mutual support
for shoplifters using the 12-steps of A.A. Members look to each
other for ways to stop shoplifting & find role models from others
who have succeeded in quitting. Assistance available for starting
new groups. Write: P.O. Box 24515, Minneapolis, MN 55424. Call
Lois 612/925-4860.

(Model) **S.O.S.A.D. (Save Our Sons & Daughters)** *Founded
1987.* Support & advocacy for parents of slain children. Weekly
bereavement groups, counseling, training, education on peace
movement to youth, advocacy, education, monthly newsletter,
conferences, rallies & assistance in starting groups. Write: 2441
W. Grand Blvd., Detroit, MI 48208-1210. Call 313/361-5200.

CULTS

Cult Awareness Network *National. 22 affiliates. Founded 1978.* Public education about destructive mind-control cults. Support & assistance for friends & families of cult members & help for former cult members. Works with professionals in human services & attorneys on cult issues. Newsletter, group guidelines. Write: 2421 W. Pratt Ave. #1173, Chicago, IL 60645. Call 312/267-7777.

LaRouche Victims' Support Group *National network.* Offers support to victims & former members of the LaRouche political organization. Helps victims to put their lives back together. Provides information & referrals. Tries to combat illegal activities of cult leaders. Write: c/o Cult Awareness Network, 2421 W. Pratt Blvd. #1173, Chicago, IL 60645. Call 708/382-9128.

DONOR'S OFFSPRING (ARTIFICIAL INSEMINATION)

Donors' Offspring, Inc. *Int'l. Founded 1981.* Information, support & reunion registry forms for donors & offspring. Provides newsletter ($20 for 2 years); quarterly national phone conference ($15). Assistance in starting new groups. Write: P.O. Box 37, Sarcoxie, MO 64862. Call 417/548-3679.

DREAMSHARING

(Model) **Dreamsharing Grassroots Clubs** *Founded 1987.* Information on dream-related activities in the Northern U.S. area. Helps community dream groups to recruit members & network. Participants in dream groups are often people seeking internal self-guidance in their passage through a difficult life transition. Networking newsletter $5/4 issues. Send $1 & a self-addressed stamped envelope for sample to: P.O. Box 8032, Hicksville, NY 11802-8032. Call 516/796-9455.

EMPLOYMENT

40 Plus of New York *National. 16 clubs. Founded 1939.* Mutual aid for unemployed managers, executives & professionals over age 40. Members must have earned at least $35,000 yearly. Career counseling, resume preparation, interviewing skills. $399 initial membership entrance fee; $75 monthly dues (for office expenses). Write: 15 Park Row, New York, NY 10038. Call 212/233-6086.

9 to 5, National Association of Working Women *National. 26 chapters. Founded 1973.* Support, advocacy & legislative assistance on issues that affect women who work. Job problem counselors advise women on making changes in their jobs. Dues $25/yr. Phone support, conferences, newsletters. Group development guidelines. Write: 614 Superior Ave., N.W., Cleveland, OH 44113. Call Hotline 800-522-0925 (day) or 216/566-9308.

Women Employed *Founded 1973.* Promotes economic equity for women through education & advocacy. Career development services, networking, conferences to link women. Quarterly newsletter, publications list. Dues $25-$45. Write: 22 W. Monroe St., #1400, Chicago, IL 60603-2505. Call 312/782-3902.

(Model) **Employment Support Center** *12 groups. Founded 1984.* Develops self-help support groups for the unemployed & underemployed. Trains leadership for groups; provides technical assistance. Newsletter. Network of group leaders & employment professionals. Helps replicate the program in other cities "Self-Help Bridge To Employment" manual ($22.50). Write: 900 Massachusetts Ave., NW #444, Washington, DC 20001. Call 202/783-4747.

(Model) **Energy for Employment** *4 groups. Founded 1983.* Provides support & materials to a network of support groups for the unemployed & those seeking career changes. Groups meet weekly with trained leaders & group alumni. Uses job search curriculum as well as round table discussion. Not an employment search. Literature. Write: P.O. Box 58002, Philadelphia, PA 19102. Call 215/561-1660 (recorded message only).

(Model) **Forty Plus of Philadelphia** *14 affiliated groups. Founded 1939.* Non-profit self-help association of managers, executives & professionals who are temporarily unemployed & who use their skills in a cooperative effort to find jobs. Members must be 40 or older & have earned $25,000 or more per year. Write: 1218 Chestnut St., Philadelphia, PA 19107. Call 215/923-2074.

(Model) **Job Transition Support Group** Support & encouragement for people laid off from their jobs, or seeking a change. Weekly meetings include speakers' presentations & small group discussions. Facilitated by volunteers who have experienced job termination or transition. Group development guidelines. Write: c/o Colonial Church of Edina, 6200 Colonial Way, Edina, MN 55436. Call 612/925-2711.

(Model) **MATCH (Mother's Access To Careers at Home)** *Founded 1990.* Provides networking, emotional support & advocacy for mothers who wish to pursue careers from home. Provides newsletter, information & referrals, phone support, special interest groups. Assistance in starting new groups. Write: P.O. Box 1461, Manassas, VA 22110. Call 703/791-6264 or 703/764-2320.

(Model) **Philadelphia Unemployment Project** *Founded 1975.* Membership organization of unemployed workers. Provides information, support & advocacy. Assistance with mortgages, food vouchers & referrals to job-training programs. Works to provide health care for the uninsured. Write: 116 South Seventh St., #610, Philadelphia, PA 19106. Call 215/592-0935.

(Model) **Shoulder to Shoulder** *Founded 1991.* Support for female partners of the unemployed/underemployed. Provides emotional support, networking, phone pals, networking & referrals. Deals with stress & coping skills. Assistance in starting similar groups. Write: Donna Montelle-Pedonti, 53 Copperfield Dr., Madison, CT 06443. Call 203/421-5799 or Maryann Grimaldi, 14 Franks Way, Madison, CT 06443. Call 203/245-3920.

(Model) **W.A.J.E. (Women's Alliance for Job Equity)** *Founded 1979.* Organization of Delaware Valley working women to improve job conditions. Peer counseling & advocacy concerning unfair or illegal job practices, programs on sexual harassment prevention & pay equity, workshops on career development & equal rights. Newsletter. Write: 1422 Chestnut St., Suite 1100, Philadelphia, PA 19102. Call 215/561-1873.

FAMILY DAY CARE PROVIDERS

(Model) **Family Day Care Provider Support Group** *Founded 1987.* Help, information, & friendship for people providing child care services in their home. Monthly meetings, discussions, workshops. Assistance available for starting groups. Write: Tammie Brown, 1307 Airport Rd., Endicott, NY 13760. Call 607/785-4413.

FOOD BANK

World S.H.A.R.E. (Self-Help And Resource Exchange) *National. 23 affiliates. Founded 1983.* Dedicated to community development & providing a monthly supplemental $30 food package to those willing to help themselves & others. Members sign up with a host organization, contribute $13/package, & pledge 2 hours of community service. Newsletter. Group development guidelines. Write: 3350 E St., San Diego, CA 92102-3332. Call 619/525-2200.

FUNDAMENTALISTS

Fundamentalists Anonymous *National. 50 chapters. Founded 1985*. Provides support & guidance for dissatisfied fundamentalists who want to get out of fundamentalism. Public education on dangers posed by fundamentalism. Bi-monthly newsletter, chapter development guidelines. Write: P.O. Box 20324, Greely Square Station, New York, New York 10001.

HAZARDOUS WASTE

Citizen's Clearinghouse for Hazardous Wastes, Inc. *National. 7,000 groups. Founded 1981*. Grassroots environmental crisis center, providing information & networking for people affected by toxic waste. Assists in organizing self-help groups; provides them with scientific & technical backup. Conferences, information & referrals. Newsletters. Write: P.O. Box 6806, Falls Church, VA 22040. Call 703/237-2249.

HOLOCAUST SURVIVORS

Child Survivors of the Holocaust *National. 10 groups. Founded 1983*. Support group for Jewish child survivors of the holocaust (those who were in Europe during World War II, up to age 16 at end of War). Newsletter, group meetings, social events, conferences, phone support. Write: c/o Ms. Natalie Gold, 837 W. Knoll Dr., Apt. 111, Los Angeles, CA 90069. Call 310/657-6437.

LIGHTENING/SHOCK

Lightning Strike & Electric Shock Victims Int'l. *Int'l network. Founded 1989*. Mutual support for victims of lightning or electric shock, their families & interested others. Studies the long-term effects. Provides information & referrals, phone support, annual conferences, assistance in starting groups & newsletter. Write: 214 Canterbury Rd., Jacksonville, NC 28540. Call Steve Marshburn, Sr. at 919/346-4708.

MALPRACTICE

(Model) **Litigation Stress Support Group** *Founded 1986*. Peer support for doctors, dentists & their families going through malpractice suits. Telephone support network. Group development guidelines will be available. Write: 2 Princess Rd., Lawrenceville, NJ 08648. Call 609/896-1766 (day).

MEN

Bald-Headed Men of America *Nat'l. 6 affiliated groups. Founded 1973.* Self-help group instilling pride in being bald. Exchanging feelings & experiences through group discussions have led to acceptance of being bald. "We believe the best cure for baldness is to promote a positive mental attitude...with humor." Annual conference, newsletter. Write: 102 Bald Dr., Morehead City, NC 28557. Call 919/726-1855; 919/726-6061 (FAX).

National Men's Resource Center *National. Founded 1982.* National resource center on men's issues including support groups, organizations, publications, research, conferences, books, special events, & organizations. Assists in developing local men's resource calendars. Write: P.O. Box 800-SH, San Anselmo, CA 94979-0800. Call 415/453-2839.

National Organization for Men *National. 21 chapters. Founded 1983.* Seeks equal rights for men, uniform national divorce, custody, property & visitation law. Lawyer referral. Educational seminars. Quarterly newsletter. Write: 11 Park Place, New York, NY 10007. Call 212/686-MALE.

RECAP (RE-Cover A Penis) *Nat'l. 2 affiliated groups. Founded 1989.* (MEN ONLY) Provides a safe environment in which men can, without fear of being ridiculed, share their concerns for a desire to be intact & whole again. Confidential discussions of goals & methods of restoration. Info. & referrals, phone support, assistance in starting new groups. Write: 3205 Northwood Dr. #209, Concord, CA 94520-4506. Call 510/827-4077 (eve).

(Model) **Men's Support Groups** *4 groups. Founded 1978.* Small, informal rap groups meet in members' homes which create a comfortable environment for discussion, friendship & support for each other's life goals. Informal telephone support network. Write: c/o Tom Landsberg, 21 G Andover Circle, Princeton, NJ 08540. Call 609/683-0968.

(Guide) **Men's Friends: How to Organize and Run Your Own Men's Support Group.** Since, to our knowledge, there is no national association of men's self-help groups, we are providing information on this helpful how-to guide. Written by Bill Kauth, the manual has 27 chapters (you need only read the first five to start the group). Copies are available for $17.50 postpaid from: Men's Awareness, 8120 S. 68th St., Franklin, WI 53132.

MESSINESS

Messies Anonymous *National. 45 Groups. Founded 1981.* Aims to improve the quality of life of disorganized homemakers by providing motivation & a program for change to help members improve self-image as control of house & life is obtained. Quarterly newsletter $5. Optional dues. Write: 5025 SW 114th Ave., Miami, FL 33165. Call 305/271-8404.

(Model) **Clutterers Anonymous** *10 affiliated groups. Founded 1989.* Helps people who have problems with clutter, compulsive saving, poor organization & procrastination, to bring order into their lives & have more control over the state of their possessions. Open to families & friends. Assistance in starting groups. Write: Craig J., 908 S. Marguerita #1, Alhambra, CA 91803 Call 818/570-8079.

NEAR DEATH EXPERIENCE

IANDS (Int'l Assn. for Near-Death Studies) *Int'l. 15+ affiliated groups. Founded 1981.* Support for persons who've had a near-death experience, their families & professionals. Info. & education, research. Newsletter, referrals, group development guidelines. Write: 638 Prospect Ave., Hartford, CT 06105-4298. Call 203/232-4825.

PEOPLE OF COLOR

(Model) **BEBASHI (Blacks Educating Blacks About Sexual Health Issues)** Founded 1985. Information & education among the African American & Latino communities about sexual health issues, especially AIDS. Peer-counseling, guest speakers, workshops, phone help. Write: 1528 Walnut St., Suite #200, Philadelphia, PA 19102. Call 215/546-4140.

(Model) **Black Focus on the West Side, Inc.** *Founded 1973.* Responds to the specific needs of Black families, including referrals to supportive services, outreach programs, domestic violence prevention, drug awareness activities, advocacy. Assistance in starting new groups. Write: 4115 Bridge Ave., #309, Cleveland, OH 44113. Call Sherry Dunn 216/631-7660. Crisis intervention hotline 216/631-7475.

(Model) **Concerned Black Parents Assn. of Kentwood.** To preserve & promote an understanding of African & African American culture & history through educational programs. Advocacy, trips, newsletter. Assistance in starting new groups. Write: 4765 Brooklyn SW, Kentwood, MI 49508. Call 616-532-0304.

145

PREJUDICE

(Model) **Racism & Bigotry Anonymous** *2 groups. Founded 1990.* 12-step program designed to heal the hurt/pain experienced as a result of racism & bigotry. For anyone willing to come out of denial of how they have been hurt/shamed by the effects of racism/bigotry. Phone support, information & referrals. Assistance in starting groups. Write: 256 Farallones, San Francisco, CA 94112-2939. Call 415/239-4398.

PROSTITUTION / SEX INDUSTRY

Prostitutes Anonymous World Service Office *Int'l. Founded 1988.* 12-step group for men & women who have desire to leave some part of the sex industry (prostitution, phone sex, nude dancing or pornography), or want to recover from its effects. Phone help, waiting list (if no group exists in your area). Starter manual $8. Other publications available. Send self-addressed stamped envelope to: 11225 Magnolia Blvd. #181, N. Hollywood, CA 91601. Call 818/905-2188.

(Model) **PRIDE** *Founded 1978.* Self-help groups for women & teenagers who want to get out or stay out of prostitution. Write: c/o Family & Children Service, 414 S. 8th St., Minneapolis, MN 55404. Call 612/340-7444 or 612/340-7469.

PUBLIC SPEAKING

Toastmasters International *Int'l. 7000 chapters. Founded 1924.* Mutual help for people to improve speaking skills, express themselves more effectively & to gain confidence. For those who are hesitant to speak before an audience. Leadership training. Monthly magazine. Write: P.O. Box 9052, Mission Viejo, CA 92690-7052. Call 714/858-8255.

RURAL COMMUNITIES

(Model) **FACTS (Farmers' Assistance Counseling and Training Service** *Statewide. Founded 1985.* Provides assistance to rural families, businesses & communities, including community resource development, employment/retraining, direct services, educational outreach, legal assistance, etc. Information & referrals. Assistance in starting similar programs. Write: 9 Leisure Hall, Kansas State Univ., Manhattan, KS 66506. Call 913/532-6532 or 800-321-3276.

SEXUALITY / GAY & LESBIAN

Dignity *National. 85 chapters. Founded 1969.* Organization of lesbian & gay Catholics & their friends. Concerned with spiritual development, education & advocacy. Newsletter. Chapter development guidelines. Write: 1500 Massachusetts Ave., NW #11, Washington, DC 20005. Call 202/861-0017 or 800-877-8797.

Finding Our Own Ways *National. Founded 1987.* Support network for persons with intersex conditions (variously known as ambiguous genitalia, hermaphroditism, pseudohermaphroditism, gonadal agenesis or dysgenesis) & for persons of any gender who are asexual (w/o interest in sexual relationships). For information send self-addressed stamped envelope to: P.O. Box 1545, Lawrence, KS 66044.

Homosexuals Anonymous *National. 55 chapters. Founded 1980.* A Christian fellowship of men & women who have chosen to help each other to live free from homosexuality. Group support through weekly meetings. Newsletter, chapter manual. Write: P.O. Box 7881, Reading, PA 19603. Call 215/376-1146 or 800-253-3000.

International Foundation for Gender Education *Int'l. 100 affiliates. Founded 1986.* Mutual support for cross-dressers & transsexuals & their families, through education, information & cooperative action. Provides telephone crisis line, research library, information & referrals, peer counseling, conferences, newsletter & literature. Write: P.O. Box 367, Wayland, MA 01778. Call 617/899-2212 or 617/894-8340; 617/899-5703 (FAX).

National Gay & Lesbian Task Force *National. Founded 1973.* Advocacy & lobbying for the rights of lesbians & gay men. Technical assistance for local gay groups. Information & referral to gay & lesbian organizations nationwide. Education to raise public awareness. Newsletter. Write: 1734 14th St., NW, Washington, DC 20009-4309. Call 202/332-6483.

P-F.L.A.G. (Parents & Friends of Lesbians & Gays Federation) *Int'l. 300 chapters. Founded 1981.* Helps families understand & accept gay family members. Offers help in strengthening families, parent support groups, educational outreach, newsletter, chapter development guidelines, family AIDS groups, advocacy, info. & referrals. Write: P.O. Box 27605, Washington, DC 20038-7605. Call 800-4-FAMILY or 202/638-4200; 202/638-0243 (FAX).

Presbyterians for Lesbian & Gay Concerns *National. 25 chapters. Founded 1974.* Support for lesbians & gays in the Presbyterian Church. Advocacy of ministry with gays & lesbians.

Peer counseling, newsletter. Write: P.O. Box 38, New Brunswick, NJ 08903. Call 908/932-7501 (day) or 908/846-1510 (eve).

Society for the Second Self *National. 26 chapters. Founded 1976.* Organization offering support & companionship for heterosexual transvestites & their wives & girlfriends. Emphasizes privacy & confidentiality of membership. Pen pal program, newsletter. Annual convention, chapter development guidelines. Write: Box 194, Tulare, CA 93275. Call 209/688-9246 (eve).

(Model) **Bi-Sexual Gay & Lesbian Youth of New York, Inc.** *Founded 1969.* Youth-run & youth-organized mutual support group for gay & lesbian young people. Weekly rap groups, outreach program, advocacy & social activities. Newsletter, group development guidelines. Call 212/777-1800 or 212/242-1212.

(Model) **Survivors of Transexuality Anonymous** Fellowship of men & women who share their experience, strength & hope with each other, that they may solve their common problems & help others heal from the effect of gender identity conflict. Assistance in starting new groups. Write: Katherine Miller, 246-13 Madison Gardens, Old Bridge, NJ 08857. Call Katherine 908-721-7469.

(Model) **Your Turf** *Founded 1987.* Rap group for teenage gays & lesbians. Provides safe area for teens to deal with same-sex orientation. Peer-counseling, social activities. Group development guidelines. Write: c/o Committee for Sexual Minorities, Capital Region Conference of Churches, 30 Arbor St., Hartford, CT 06106. Call Bill Mann 203/278-2455.

SHORT / TALL

Human Growth Foundation *National. 48 chapters. Founded 1965.* Local chapters provide members the opportunity to meet other parents of short-statured children, for mutual sharing of problems, research & public education. Monthly newsletter. Chapter development guidelines. Write: P.O. Box 3090, Falls Church, VA 22043. Call 703/883-1773 or 800-451-6434.

Little People of America *National. 40 chapters. Founded 1957.* Dedicated to helping people of short stature. Provides fellowship, moral support, & information for people whose height is 4 feet 10 inches or under. Teenagers program, parent support groups, newsletter. Write: P.O. Box 4897, Washington, DC 20016. Call 301/589-0730 or 800-24-DWARF.

Tall Clubs International *Int'l. 55 groups. Founded 1938.* Social support for tall persons, men at least 6'2", women at least 5'10". Also advocacy for clothing & other special needs of tall people. Group development guidelines, information & referrals, conferences, newsletters. Write: P.O. Box 4301, Huntington Beach, CA 92605. Call 800-521-2512 (leave name & they will send information to you).

STUTTERING

International Foundation for Stutterers, Inc. *Int'l. 6 chapters. Founded 1980.* Aims to eliminate stuttering through speech therapy in conjunction with self-help groups. Education for public & professionals about stuttering & self-help. Newsletter, speakers, phone help system, guidelines on forming self-help groups. Write: P.O. Box 462, Belle Mead, NJ 08502. Call Elliot Dennis 609/275-3806 (eve).

National Center for Stuttering *National. 12 chapters. Founded 1974.* Mutual support for stutterers who have learned a special therapeutic technique, to get together to practice. Phone support, information & referrals, newsletter, pen pal programs, annual banquets. Write: 200 E. 33rd St., #17C, New York, NY 10016. Call 800-221-2483.

National Stuttering Project *Nat'l. 75 groups. Founded 1977.* Information about stuttering. Self-help chapter meetings provide supportive environment where people who stutter can learn to communicate more effectively. Network of groups. Referrals, advocacy, monthly newsletter, group development guidelines. Dues $30/year. Write: 2151 Irving St. #208, San Francisco, CA 94122-1609. Call 415/566-5324.

Speak Easy International Foundation, Inc. *Int'l. 8 chapters. Founded 1981.* Self-help group for adult & adolescent stutterers. Must have speech dysfunction or phobia. Phone network, peer counseling, newsletter. Annual national symposium. Dues $50/yr. Write: Antoinette & Bob Gathman, 233 Concord Dr., Paramus, NJ 07652. Call Antoinette or Bob 201/262-0895.

(Model) **Compulsive Stutterers Anonymous** *Founded 1988.* Fellowship of men & women who share their experience, strength & hope with each other that they may find freedom from compulsive stuttering. Practices the principles of the 12-steps. Supportive of professional speech therapy in conjunction with self-help. Group development guidelines available. Write: P.O. Box 1406, Park Ridge, IL 60068. Call 815/895-9848.

TELEVISION ADDICTION

(Model) **Society for the Eradication of Television (S.E.T.)** *(Bay Area Chapter) 3 groups. Founded 1983.* Discussion for people concerned with our national obsession with television & how it impacts our lives. For those wishing to curb their reliance on TV. Newsletter ($5), phone support, information & referrals, assistance in starting new groups. Write: Steve Wagner, Box 10491, Oakland, CA 94610-0491. Call 510/848-2625.

TRAUMA

(Model) **Trauma Recovery, Inc.** *2 affiliated groups. Founded 1979.* Mutual support for people recovering from serious injuries & their families. Emotional support, friendship & practical help with day-to-day problems. Write: c/o Linda Wolfe, 1992 Gooseneck Rd., Pasadena, MD 21222. Call Linda Wolfe 301/255-3074.

VETERANS / MILITARY

Adult Children of Military Personnel, Inc. *Int'l network. Founded 1991.* Support for persons experiencing problems resulting from growing up in a military family. International registry for locating childhood friends ($15). Newsletter, information & referrals, conferences. Assistance in starting new groups. Write: P.O. Box 82282, Lincoln, NE 68423.

Blinded Veterans Association *National. 38 groups. Founded 1945.* Information, support & outreach to blinded veterans. Help in finding jobs, information on benefits & rehabilitation programs. Bi-monthly newsletter. Chapter development guidelines. Regional meetings. Write: 477 H St., NW, Washington, DC 20001. Call 202/371-8880 or 800-669-7079.

Concerned Americans for Military Improvements (CAMI) *National. 35 chapters. Founded 1982.* Guidance, advice, support & referrals for military personnel (veterans or active) & their families who are victims of military malpractice, preventable accidents & other injustices. Newsletter, phone support, conferences, help in starting groups. Write: c/o Mary Day, 293 Webster Ave., Cranston, RI 02909. Call 401/943-5165.

Disabled American Veterans *National. 2760 chapters. Founded 1920.* Assists veterans in gaining benefits earned in military service. Sponsors self-help groups for all disabled veterans & their families. Supports legislation benefiting disabled vets. Monthly magazine. Guidelines for developing chapters. Write: P.O. Box 14301, Cincinnati, OH 45250-0301. Call 606/441-7300.

In Touch (Friends of the Vietnam Veterans Memorial) *Nat'l. Founded 1990.* Offers locator & networking services for families, children, friends & fellow veterans of those who died in Vietnam. Provides newsletter, name rubbings from the Vietnam Veterans Memorial, phone support & referrals. Write: In Touch, c/o FVVM, 2030 Clarendon Blvd. #412, Arlington, CA 22201. Call 703/525-1107.

Society of Military Widows *National. 29 chapters. Founded 1968.* Support & assistance for widows/widowers of members of all U.S. uniformed services. Help in coping with adjustment to life on their own. Promotes public awareness. Newsletter. Dues $12. Chapter development guidelines. Write: 5535 Hemstead Way, Springfield, VA 22151. Call 703/750-1342.

Vietnam Veterans of America, Inc. *National. 587 chapters. Founded 1978.* Devoted to the needs & concerns of Vietnam Era Veterans & their families. Provides leadership & advocacy in all areas that have an impact on veterans, with an emphasis on Agent Orange related problems & post traumatic stress disorder. Monthly newspaper, group development guidelines. Write: 1224 M St., NW, Washington, DC 20005-5183. Call 202/628-2700.

(Model) **Eastern Paralyzed Veterans Association** *33 chapters. Founded 1946.* To promote independence for paralyzed veterans, enhance their health & medical care & protect the civil rights of the disabled. Monthly newsletter. Covers NY, NJ, PA & CT. Write: 75-20 Astoria Blvd., Jackson Heights, NY 11370-1178. Call 718/803-3782.

WOMEN

Business & Professional Women/USA *National. 3000 chapters. Founded 1919.* Oldest & largest organization of working women, to elevate their status & provide networking opportunities. Lobbying efforts, quarterly magazine, periodic publications, resource center. Annual national convention. Write: 2012 Massachusetts Ave., NW, Washington, DC 20036. Call 202/293-1100.

F.E.M.A.L.E. (Formerly Employed Mothers At the Leading Edge) *National. 50 groups. Founded 1987.* Information, support & encouragement for women who have chosen to interrupt their careers in favor of raising their children. Newsletter, chapter development guidelines. Write: P.O. Box 31, Elmhurst, IL 60126. Call 708/941-3553.

Love-N-Addiction *Int'l. 31 chapters. Founded 1986.* Explores how loving can become an addiction. Builds a healthy support system to aid in recovery from addictive love into healthy love. Uses ideas from book "Women Who Love Too Much" by Robin Norwood. Chapter development guidelines ($10). Write: P.O. Box 759, Willimantic, CT 06226. Call Carolyn Meister 203/423-2344 (will return call collect return or leave mailing address).

N.O.W. (National Organization for Women) *National. 600+ chapters. Founded 1966.* Women & men committed to equal rights. Advocacy, educational meetings & national newsletter. Chapter development guidelines. Write: 1000 16th St., N.W. #700, Washington, DC 20036. Call 202/331-0066.

Women Employed *National. Founded 1973.* Promotes economic equity for women through education & advocacy. Career development services, networking, conferences to link women. Quarterly newsletter, publications list. Dues $25-$45. Write: 22 W. Monroe St., Suite 1400, Chicago, IL 60603. Call 312/782-3902.

(Model) **D.A.W.N. (Dis-Abled Women's Network)** *10+ chapters. Founded 1985.* Feminist organization controlled by & comprised of women with disabilities. Support & advocacy to assist women with disabilities to become self-determined. Bridge between the disabled consumer movement & the women's movement. Write: Maria Barile, 7785 Louis Hebert, Montreal, Canada 82E 2Y1; phone 514/725-4123 or Pat Israel, 4 Warner Ave., Toronto, Ontario, Canada M4A 1Z3, 406/288-8147.

(Model) **F.I.F. (Facial Inferiority Forum)** *Founded 1992.* Mutual support & problem-solving for women who feel inferior because of the appearance of their faces. For women who are having trouble coping because they were teased as children. Support group meetings, phone support. Assistance in starting new groups. Write: 51 Upper Montclair Plaza, #24, Upper Montclair, NJ 07043. Call Fran Mann 201/744-6429.

(Model) **S.O.W.N. (Supportive Older Women's Network), The** *Regional. 34 groups in Philadelphia area. Founded 1982.* Helps women (60+) cope with their specialized aging concerns. Provides support groups, leadership training, consultation, outreach & networking. Newsletter: "The Sounding Board." Group development guidelines. Write: 2805 N. 47th St., Philadelphia, PA 19131. Call 215/477-6000.

Remember: Model groups are not national organizations. They should be contacted primarily by those individuals who are interested in starting similar groups.

(Model) **Women - Midlife & Menopause (WMM)** *Founded 1989.* Mutual support & sharing of experiences for women going through midlife changes & menopause. Discussion of solutions. Offers feedback, warmth, understanding mutual respect & humor. Provides information & referrals, phone support, meetings. Assistance in starting local groups. Group materials packet $5. Write: Clara Wood Anthony, 7337 Morrison Dr., Greenbelt, MD 20770.

WORKAHOLICS

Workaholics Anonymous *Int'l. 60 groups. Founded 1983.* For men & women who feel their work lives have gotten out of control. Also for affected family members & friends. Mutual support in solving problems of compulsive over-working. Weekly meetings. Groups development guidelines. Follows the 12-step program. Send self-addressed stamped envelope to: P.O. Box 661501, Los Angeles, CA 90066. Call 310/859-5804.

YOUTH / STUDENTS

International Youth Council *Int'l. 30 chapters. Founded 1972.* Brings teens from single parent homes together to share ideas & problems, develop leadership skills, & plan fun activities. Networking & guidelines available for starting groups. Sponsored by local chapters of Parents Without Partners. Write: 8807 Colesville Rd., Silver Spring, MD 20910. Call 800-637-7974 or 301/588-9354.

Just Say No Int'l *Int'l. 13,000 clubs. Founded 1985.* Helps communities form "Just Say No Clubs" - groups of children (ages 7-14) who are committed to not using drugs, tobacco or alcohol. Offers educational, social, community service, & outreach activities. Newsletter, group development guidelines. Provides technical assistance, materials & training. Write: 2101 Webster St., #1300, Oakland, CA 94612-3027. Call 800-258-2766 or 510-451-6666.

S.A.D.D. (Students Against Driving Drunk) *National. 25,500 groups. Founded 1982.* To help eliminate drunk driving, end underage drinking & drug abuse, alert students to dangers of drinking driving, & to organize peer counseling programs for students concerned about alcohol & drugs. Newsletter, group development guidelines. Special programs: "Student Athletes Detest Drugs". Write: P.O. Box 800, Marlboro, MA 01752. Call 508/481-3568.

SELF-HELP CLEARINGHOUSES

To find a local mutual aid self-help group for your concern, review the list of self-help clearinghouses below to see if there is a one that serves your area. Self-help clearinghouses can provide you with information on local support groups, especially the one-of-a-kind groups that are not affiliated with any national self-help organization. In addition, many of the clearinghouses listed below provide consultation to new & existing groups, training workshops, how-to material, & other services of interest to self-help groups.

UNITED STATES

CALIFORNIA

California Self-Help Center *(Statewide)* Referrals to other self-help clearinghouses in Calif. Write: c/o UCLA, Psych. Dept., 405 Hilgard Ave., Los Angeles, CA 90024-1563. (Fran Jammott Dory, Exec. Dir.) Call 800-222-LINK (in CA); 310- 825-1799 (outside CA).

Bay Area Self-Help Center Write: c/o Mental Health Assn., 2398 Pine St., San Francisco, CA 94115. (Duff Axsom, Coordinator) Call 415-921-4044; 415-921-1911 (FAX).

Central Region Self-Help Center Write: c/o Merced County Dept. of Mental Health, 650 W. 19th St., Merced, CA 95340. (Mary Jo Burns, Coordinator) Call 209-725-3752.

Northern Region Self-Help Center (Eastern Div.) Write: c/o Mental Health Assn., 8912 Volunteer Lane, #210, Sacramento, CA 95826-3221. (Pat Camper, Coordinator) Call 916-368-3100.

Northern Self-Help Center (Western Div.) Write: c/o Mental Health Assn. of Yolo County, P.O. Box 447, Davis, CA 95617. (Elaine Talley, Coordinator) Call 916-756-8181.

SHINE of the Inland Empire Write: c/o Riverside Mental Health Assn., 3763 Arlington Ave., #103, Riverside, CA 92508. (Karen Banker, Secretary) Call 714/684-6051.

Southern Region Self-Help Center Write: c/o Mental Health Assn. of San Diego, 3958 Third Ave., San Diego, CA 92103. (Joe Horton, Coordinator) Call 619-298-3152.

Southern Tri-Country Regional Self-Help Center Write: 5839 Green Valley Circle, #100, Culver City, CA 90230. (Al Jenkins, Coordinator) Call 310/645-9890.

CONNECTICUT

Connecticut Self-Help/Mutual Support Network *(Statewide)* Write: 389 Whitney Ave., New Haven, CT 06511. (Carol Shaff, Coordinator) Call 203-789-7645.

ILLINOIS

Illinois Self-Help Center *(Statewide)* Write: 1600 Dodge Ave. #S-122, Evanston, IL 60201. (Daryl Isenberg, Exec. Director) Call 708/328-0470 (I&R); 708/328-0471 (admin); 708/328-0754 (FAX).

Macon County Support Group Network Write: c/o Macon County Health Dept., 1221 E. Condit, Decatur, IL 62521. Call 217-429-HELP.

Self-Help Center Write: c/o Family Service of Champaign County, 405 S. State St., Champaign, IL 61820-5196. (Mellen Kennedy, Coordinator) Call 217-352-0099; 217-352-9512 (FAX).

IOWA

Iowa Self-Help Clearinghouse *(Statewide)* Write: c/o Iowa Pilot Parents, Inc., 33 N. 12th St., P.O. Box 1151, Fort Dodge, IA 50501. (Carla Reed, Dir.) Call 515-576-5870; 800-383-4777 (Iowa only).

KANSAS

Self-Help Network *(Statewide)* Write: Campus Box 34, Wichita State Univ., Wichita, KS 67208-1595. (Greg Meissen, Director) Call 800-445-0116 (in KS) or 316/689-3843.

MASSACHUSETTS

Massachusetts Clearinghouse of Mutual Help Groups *(Statewide)* Write: c/o Massachusetts Cooperative Extension, 113 Skinner Hall, Univ. of Mass., Amherst, MA 01003. (Warren Schumacher, Director) Call 413-545-2313.

MICHIGAN

Michigan Self-Help Clearinghouse *(Statewide)* Write: c/o Michigan Protection & Advocacy Svc., Inc., 106 W. Allegan #210, Lansing, MI 48933-1706. (Toni Young, Director) Call 517-484-7373 or 800-752-5858 (in MI only). (Specify Self-Help Clearinghouse)

Center For Self-Help *(Berrian County area)* Write: c/o Riverwood Center, P.O. Box 547, Benton Harbor, MI 49022- 0547. (Pat Friend, Coordinator) Call 800-336-0341 (in MI only); 616-925-0594.

MINNESOTA

First Call For Help *(Referrals to local self-help groups only)* Write: 166 E. 4th St. #310, St. Paul, MN 55101. (Diane Faulds, Coordinator) Call 612/224-1133 (I&R); 612/291-8427 (Admin).

MISSOURI

St. Louis Self-Help Clearinghouse Write: c/o Greater St. Louis Mental Health Assn., 1905 S. Grand Blvd., St. Louis, MO 63104. (Peggy Corski, Coordinator) Call 314/773-1399.

Support Group Clearinghouse Write: c/o K.C. Assn. for Mental Health, 1009 Baltimore Ave. #5-FL, Kansas City, MO 64105-1810. (Julie Broyle, Coordinator) Call 816/472-HELP.

NEBRASKA

Self-Help Information Services *(Statewide)* Write: 1601 Euclid Ave., Lincoln, NB 68502. (Barbara Fox, Director) Call 402-476-9668.

NEW JERSEY

New Jersey Self-Help Clearinghouse *(Statewide)* Write: c/o St. Clares-Riverside Med. Ctr., 25 Pocono Rd., Denville, NJ 07834. (Edward Madara, Director) Call 800-367-6274 (in NJ) or 201/625-9565, TDD: 201/625-9053.

NEW YORK

Brooklyn Self-Help Clearinghouse Write: 20 Third Ave., Brooklyn, NY 11217. (Rose Langfelder, Dir.) Call 718/875-1420.

Westchester Self-Help Clearinghouse Write: 456 North St., White Plains, NY 10605. (Leslie Borck Jameson, Dir.) Call 914-949-6301.

Upstate New York: Some counties in upstate New York have self-help clearinghouses. For information contact the Westchester Self-Help Clearinghouse above.

NORTH CAROLINA

SupportWorks *(Meklenberg County area)* Write: 1012 Kings Dr., #923, Charlotte, NC 28283. (Joal Fischer, Director) Call 704-331-9500.

OHIO

Greater Dayton Self-Help Clearinghouse *(Dayton area)* Write: c/o Family Services Assn., 184 Salem Ave., Dayton, OH 45406. (Shari Peace, Coordinator) Call 513/225-3004.

OREGON

Northwest Regional Self-Help Clearinghouse (Includes Seattle, WA area) Write: 718 W. Burnside, Portland, OR 97209. (Jean Hadley, Coord.) Call 503/222-5555 (I&R); 503/226-9360 (admin).

PENNSYLVANIA

Self-Help Group Network of the Pittsburgh Area Write: 1323 Forbes Ave., #200, Pittsburgh, PA 15219. (Betty Hepner, Coordinator) Call 412/261-5363; 412/471-2722 (FAX).

Self-Help Info. & Networking Exchange (SHINE) *(Scranton area)* Write: c/o VAC of Northeastern PA, 225 N. Washington Ave., Park Plaza (lower level), Scranton, PA 18503. (Gail Bauer, Director) Call 717/961-1234.

Self-Help Institute *(Philadelphia area)* Write: 462 Monastery Ave., Philadelphia, PA 19128. (Gwen Olitsky, Contact Person) Call 215/482-4316.

SOUTH CAROLINA

Midland Area Support Group Network Write: c/o Lexington Med. Ctr, 2720 Sunset Blvd., W. Columbia, SC 29169. (Nancy Farrar, Director) Call 803/791-9227 (I&R); 803/791-2049 (Admin).

TENNESSEE

Self-Help Clearinghouse *(Memphis & Shelby Counties)* Write: c/o Mental Health Assn., 2400 Poplar Ave., Memphis, TN 38112. (Carol Barnett, Coord.) Call 901/323-8485; 901/323-0858 (FAX).

Support Group Clearinghouse *(Knox County)* Write: c/o Mental Health Assn. of Knox County, 6712 Kingston Pike, #203, Knoxville, TN 37919. (Judy Balloff, Prog. Coord.) Call 615/584-6736.

TEXAS

Texas Self-Help Clearinghouse *(Statewide)* Write: c/o Mental Health Assn. in Texas, 8401 Shoal Creek Blvd., Austin, TX 78758-7544. (Christine Devall, Coord.) Call 512/454-3706.

Dallas Self-Help Clearinghouse Write: c/o Mental Health Assn. of Dallas County, 2929 Carlisle, #350, Dallas, TX 75204. (Carol Madison, Director) Call 214/871-2420.

Greater San Antonio Self-Help Clearinghouse Write: c/o Mental Health in Greater San Antonio, 901 N.E. Loop 410, #500, San Antonio, TX 78209. Call 512/826-2288.

Self-Help Clearinghouse *(Houston area)* Write: c/o Mental Health Assn. in Houston & Harris County, 2211 Norfolk, #810, Houston, TX 77098. (Dianne Long, Coord.) Call 713/523-8963.

Tarrant County Self-Help Clearinghouse Write: c/o Mental Health Assn. of Tarrant County, 3136 W. 4th St., Fort Worth, TX 76107-2113. (Roxanne Rudy, Coord.) Call 817/335-5405.

WASHINGTON, DC

Self-Help Clearinghouse of Greater Washington (DC, N. VA, S. MD) Write: c/o Mental Health Assn. of VA, 7630 Little River Turnpike #206, Annandale, VA 22003. (Lisa Saisselin, Director) Call 703/941-5465.

NATIONAL INFORMATION - U.S.

American Self-Help Clearinghouse Write: c/o St. Clares-Riverside Med. Ctr., 25 Pocono Rd., Denville, NJ 07834. (Edward Madara, Director) Call 201/625-7101; 201/625-8848 (FAX); 201/625-9053 (TDD).

National Self-Help Clearinghouse Write: CUNY, Graduate School & University Ctr., 25 W. 43rd St., Rm. 620, New York, NY 10036. (Frank Reissman, Director) Call 212/642-2944.

CANADA

Canadian Council on Social Development Write: Self-Help Initiatives Newsletter, Conseil Canadien de Developpment Social, P.O. Box 3505, Station C Ottawa, Ontario, KIY 4GI, Canada. Call 613/728-1865; FAX 728-9387.

Family Life Education Council Write: 33 12th Avenue S.W. Calgary, Alberta T2R OG9, Canada. (Sonia Eisler, Exec. Director) Call 403/262-1117.

Self-Help Clearinghouse of Metropolitan Toronto. Write: 40 Orchard View Blvd., Suite 215, Toronto, Ontario M4R 1B9, Canada. (Janet McCloud, Director; Randi Fine, Seniors Prog. Coord.) Call 416/487-4355

Self-Help Collaboration Project Write: c/o United Way of the Lower Mainland, 1625 West 8th Ave., Vancouver, B.C. V6J IT9 Canada (Rae Folster, Contact Person) Call 604/731-7781.

Self-Help Connection, The Write: c/o Mental Health Association 63 King Street, Halifax, Nova Scotia, B3J 2R7, Canada. (Margot Clarke, Director) Call 902/466-2011

Self-Help Development Unit (temporarily closed). For now direct mail to: c/o Sharon Miller, 10 Porteouf Crescent, Saskatoon, Sasketchewan S7J 2S8, Canada. Call 306/966-5580 (admin. only, ask for Sharon)

Winnipeg Self-Help Resource Clearinghouse Write: c/o NorWest Coop & Health Center, 103-61 Tyndall Ave., Winnipeg, Manitoba Canada R2X 2T4. (Bernice Marmel, Director) Call 204/589-5500 or 633-5955.

INTERNATIONAL

Int'l Information Centre on Self-Help & Health. Write: E. Van Evenstraat 2 C, B-3000 Leuven, Belgium. (Peter Gielen, Coord.) Call 30-891-4019.

AUSTRALIA

Collective of Self-Help Groups, The Write: 247-251 - Flinders Lane, Melbourne 3000 Australia. Call (03) 650 1455/1488

Western Institute of Self-Help Write: 80 Railway St., Cottesloe, 6011 Western Australia. (Cheryl A. Dimmack, Contact Person) Call (09) 383-3188.

AUSTRIA

Servicestelle Fur Selbsthilfegruppen Write: Schottenring 1 - 24/3/31, A-1010 Vienna, Austria. (Ilse Forster, Director) Call 222-66-14405.

BELGIUM

Trefpunt Zelf Hulp   Write: E. Van Evenstraat 2 C, 3000 Leuven Belgium. (Linda Verwimp, Director)

CROATIA (formerly the YUGOSLAVIAN contact)

College of Nursing, University of Zagreb, Mlinarska 38 Y-41000 Zagreb, Yugoslavia. (Arpad Barath, Contact Person)   Call (050) 28-666

DENMARK

Laikos - National   Write: Tordenjkjoldsvei 20, 3000 Helsinor Denmark. (Ulla-Britta Buch, Coordinator)

Selvhaelps-Grupper Centre In Kolding   Write: Vesterskovog 19, 6091 Bjest, Denmark. (Bonde Petersen, Lisbeth, Director)

SR - BISTAND   Write: Social Radgivning og Bistand, Sortedam Dosseringen 3, st. th., 2200 Kobenhavn N, Denmark.   (Birthe Gamst, Director; Ann Gamst, Coordinator)   Call 31-31-71-97.

ENGLAND

National Self-Help Support Centre   Write: c/o National Council for Voluntary Organizations, 26 Bedford Square; London WC1B 3HU; England.   (Ms. Katrina McCormick, Director)   Call 01-636-4066.

Help for Health Project   Write: Wessex Regional Library Unit South Academic Bloc, Southampton General Hospital, UK-Southampton S09 4XY England.   Call 703-77-90-91

Self-Help Alliance, The   Write: Lower King's Rd. 29; Berkhamstead, UK-Herbs HP 4 2AB; England

Self-Help Group Project, The   Write: c/o Leisester Council for Voluntary Services, DeMontfort St. 32, UK-Leisester LEI 7GD England.   Call 0533-55-56

Self-Help Team, The   Write: 20 Pelham Road; UK-Nottingham NG5 1AP; England. (Judy Wilson, Team Leader)   Call 44-0602 691212.

GERMANY (has over 100 clearinghouses; a sample of a few are given after national)

Nationale Kontakt-Und Informationsstelle Zur Anregung Und Unterstutzung Von Selbsthilfegruppen (NAKOS) Write: Albrecht-Achilles-Strasse 65, D-1000 Berlin 31, Germany. (Klaus Balke, Director) Call 30-891-4019.

Deutsche Arsseitsgemeinschaft Selbsthilfegruppen e.v (DAG SHG) Write: c/o Friedrichstrasse 28, D-6300 Giessen, Germany. (Jurgen Matzat, Contact Person) Call 641-702-2478.

Kontakt-und Informationsstelle Fur Selbsthilfegruppen (KISS) Write: Gaubstrasse 21, D-2000 Hamburg 50 Germany. Call 40-390-57-67 or 40-390-99-98

Landesarbeitgeminschaft Write: Jurgen Dudeck, Regiertungsprasidium Chemnitz, PF-848, Swickaub St. 38, 9001 Chemnitz, Germany.

Munich Self-Help Resource Center Write: Bayerstrasse 77A Write: D-8000 Munchen 2, Germany. (Wolfgang Stark, Director)

HUNGARY

National Committee of Mental Health Promotion Write: P.O. Box 39, H-1525 Budapest, Hungary. (Bela Buda, Coordinator)

ISRAEL

National Self-Help Clearinghouse Write: 37 King George St., P.0. Box 23223, Tel-Aviv 61231, Israel. (Martha Ramon, Director) Call 03-299389.

JAPAN

Society for the Study of Self-Help Groups Write: c/o Department of Social Welfare, Faculty of Humanities, Sophia University, 7-1, Kioicho, Chiyoda-ku, Tokyo, 102, Japan. (Tomofumi Oka, Director) Call office 011-81-03-3238-3645; FAX/voice line 011-81-297-72-3118.

POLAND

Njational Centre for Health System Management Write: Dluga 38/40, 00-238 Warszawa, Poland. (Elzbieta Bobiatynska, Coordinator)

SPAIN

Institut Municipal de la Salut Write: Pa. Lesseps, 1, 08023 Barcelona, Spain. (Francina Roca, Coordinator)

Programme' Cronicat' Write: Facultad de Medicina (Despacho 15), Hospital de San Pablo, Padre Claret 167, E-Barcelona 08026, Spain. (Elvira Mendez, Director) Call 93-256-3612.

SWEDEN

Dis-Triktlakare Write: Villavagan 14, S-9390 Arjeplog Sweden. (Bo Henricson, M.D., Contact Person) Call 961-11230.

SWITZERLAND

Selbsthilfezentrum Hinderhuus Write: Verena Vogelsanger Feldbergstrasse 55, 4057 Basel, Switzerland

Team Selbsthillfe Zurich, Wilfiedstrabe 7 CH-8032 Zurich, Switzerland. (Midi Muheim, Contact Person) Call 01-252-3036.

STATE ABBREVIATIONS

AL	Alabama	MT	Montana
AK	Alaska	NE	Nebraska
AZ	Arizona	NV	Nevada
AR	Arkansas	NH	New Hampshire
CA	California	NJ	New Jersey
CO	Colorado	NM	New Mexico
CT	Connecticut	NY	New York
DE	Delaware	NC	North Carolina
DC	District of Columbia	ND	North Dakota
FL	Florida	OH	Ohio
GA	Georgia	OK	Oklahoma
HI	Hawaii	OR	Oregon
ID	Idaho	PA	Pennsylvania
IL	Illinois	RI	Rhode Island
IN	Indiana	SC	South Carolina
IA	Iowa	SD	South Dakota
KS	Kansas	TN	Tennessee
KY	Kentucky	TX	Texas
LA	Louisiana	UT	Utah
ME	Maine	VT	Vermont
MD	Maryland	VI	Virgin Islands
MA	Massachusetts	WA	Washington
MI	Michigan	WV	West Virginia
MN	Minnesota	WI	Wisconsin
MS	Mississippi	WY	Wyoming
MO	Missouri		

TOLL-FREE SPECIALTY NUMBERS

The following toll-free numbers might be a helpful, cost-free source for individuals and groups. Many of these agencies provide information & referrals, literature & other services regarding a specific topic.

ADOPTION Nat'l Adoption Ctr 800-TO-ADOPT (day) I&R re adoption agencies, support groups.

AIDS Nat'l AIDS Hotline 800-342-AIDS; 800-344-SIDA (Spanish); 800-AIDS-TTY (TDD) I&R, literature ♦ Nat'l AIDS Hotline 800-458-5231 (day) Resources, support groups, publications, research ♦ Project Inform 800-822-7422 (day) Info re: experimental drugs, treatment, journal, mail service, newsletter ♦ Teens TAP 800-234-TEEN (aft/eve) Education, prevention, testing.

ALCOHOL 800-ALCOHOL (24 hrs) I&R re: alcohol/drugs ♦ Federal Drug, Alcohol & Crime Clrnghs 800-729-6686 (24 hrs) Info on alcohol & drug abuse, prevention, crime, treatment, research, groups, AIDS, criminal justice ♦ Nat'l Council on Alcohol & Drugs 800-475-HOPE (24 hrs) Info on local treatment centers; literature

ATTORNEY Referral Network 800-624-8846 (24 hrs) Computerized legal service that recommends attorneys in callers' area.

BEREAVEMENT Nat'l Grief Recovery 800-445-4808 (day) Helps people move beyond loss; lists national grief seminars

BLIND & VISUALLY IMPAIRED Amer Fdn 800-AF-BLIND; TDD: 212/620-2158 (day) I&R for agencies, products & publications; travel ID# ♦ Nat'l Library Service 800-424-9100 (day) Reading material, tapes, braille, large print materials ♦ Recording For The Blind 800-221-4792 (day) Info on free cassettes, recorded textbooks, publications ♦ Nat'l Ctr for Sight 800-331-2020 (day) Eye health/safety; educational materials ♦ Blind Children's Ctr 800-222-3566 (day) I&R for parents of visually impaired children

BREAST IMPLANTS FDA Nat'l Hotline 800-532-4440 Info on key symptoms of problems, how to report problems; answers specific questions regarding breast implants; consumer package

CANCER AMC Cancer Research 800-525-3777 (day) Info & counseling ♦ Cancer Info Svc 800-4-CANCER (Bi-lingual) Causes, symptoms/treatment; I&R ♦ Amer Cancer Soc 800-227-2345 I&R

CAREERS Nat'l Job Corps 800-733-5627 (day) Referrals to job corps training (persons 16-21) (English/Spanish)

CHILD ABUSE Child Help USA 800-422-4453 (24 hrs) Info, referrals to local agencies; crisis counseling ♦ Nat'l Council on Child Abuse & Family Violence 800-222-2000 (24 hrs) I&R on child abuse & other types of family violence

CIVIL INFO Civitex 800-223-6004 (day) Info on a broad range of problems (alcoholism, homelessness, family problems)

CIVIL RIGHTS Office on Civil Rights 800-368-1019 (day) I&R for people discriminated against by a federally-funded facility.

CONSUMER U.S. Consumer Product Safety 800-638-2772 (24 hrs) Product safety, literature ♦ People's Med Soc 800-624-8773 (day) Helps medical consumers become aware of their rights; literature

CREDIT Consumer Credit Counseling 800-388-CCCS Info on local credit counseling services

CYSTIC FIBROSIS Cystic Fibrosis Fdn 800-FIGHT-CF (day) I&R re insurance, pharmaceutical services, research; brochures

DEAF/HEARING IMPAIRED ASHA Hearing & Speech Helpline 800-638-TALK (Voice/TDD) (day) Speech, hearing & language disabilities; referrals to clinics; devices; special packets for military families & others ♦ Captioned Films for the Deaf 800-237-6213 Voice/TDD (day) Captioned films for deaf & hearing impaired ♦ Grapevine 800-352-8888 (Voice/TDD) (day) Info re: childhood deafness ♦ Hearing Aid 800-521-5247 (day) Hearing aids & hearing loss ♦ Hearing Screening Test 800-222-EARS (day) Referrals to local phone hearing tests ♦ Ear Well 800-327-9355 (day) Info & literature on hearing; lists doctors, audiologists, speech therapists, hearing aids ♦ Hearing Helpline 800-424-8576 (day) Literature on hearing loss; lists of certified professionals; sources of possible financial aid ♦ HEAR Now 800-648-HEAR Helps financially needy hearing aids/cochlear implants; newsletter, I&R, hearing aid bank

DISABILITIES HEATH Resource Ctr. 800-54-HEATH Voice/TDD (day) I&R on post-secondary education & adult training programs ♦ Job Accommodation Network 800-526-7234 (Voice/TDD) (day) Info on accommodations for people with job-related disability ♦ Ctr for Spec Ed Tech 800-873-8255 (24 hrs) I&R ♦ Handicapped Media, Inc. 800-321-8708 (Voice/TDD) (day) I&R on services & manufacturers; advocacy ♦ Nat'l Info Clearinghouse 800-922-9234 (voice/TDD) (day) I&R for persons (0-21) with developmental disabilities, chronic-illnesses or life-threatening diseases. Also info.

for high-risk, ill, or multiply disabled infants (0-3). Info. on medical centers, residential facilities. Networks parents ♦ Nat'l Org. on Disability 800-248-2253 (24 hrs) I&R via mail ♦ IBM Nat'l Support Ctr for Persons w/Disabilities 800-426-2133 I&R re computer-related products to assist with learning, visual, speech, mobility & hearing impairments, via mail ♦ Nat'l Center for Youth With Disabilities 800-33-6293 (day) I&R, literature, technical consultation, newsletters ♦ NICHCY 800-999-5599 (day) Info on education for persons with disabilities from birth to age 22; info. on products, libraries. ♦ Abledata 800-346-2742 (day) Info on products for handicapped & disabled persons ♦ Northeast Disability & Business Tech Asst Ctr 800-487-2805; 800-676-2831 (TDD) Info & assistance in the implementation of the Americans with Disabilities Act.

DOMESTIC VIOLENCE Nat'l Hotline 800-333-SAFE (24 hrs) (Bi-lingual) I&R for women who are abused verbally, mentally or physically.

DOWN SYNDROME Hotline 800-221-4602 (day) I&R; packets to new parents, info on education, support groups, medical research, newsletter, phone support, information on conferences.

DRUG ABUSE 800-COCAINE (24 hrs) I&R for drug & alcohol addiction & treatment ♦ Drug Abuse Ref Helpline 800-662-HELP; 800-66AYUDA (Spanish) (day) Info on drug abuse, referrals to treatment & counseling centers, literature ♦ Federal Drug, Alcohol & Crime Clearinghouse 800-729-6686 (24 hrs) Info on alcohol & drug abuse, prevention, crime, treatment centers, research, groups, community programs, AIDS, crime ♦ Drug Info. & Strategy Clearinghouse 800-955-2232 (day) Info & assistance to the public & assisted housing community on drug-related crime control

DYSLEXIA HEATH Resource Ctr 800-54-HEATH (Voice/TDD) (day) I&R on post-secondary education & adult training programs ♦ Orton Dyslexia Soc 800-ABCD-123 (day) I&R

EATING DISORDERS Grace Sq. Hosp. Eating Disorder Hotline 800-382-2832 (24 hrs) I&R

EPILEPSY I&R Dept Epilepsy Fdn of Amer 800-332-1000 (day) I&R & materials

EYE CARE Nat'l Eye Care Prog 800-222-3937 (day) Assists financially disadvantaged persons (65+) in obtaining eye care.

FACIAL SURGERY Facial-Plastic Surgeons Soc 800-332-FACE (24 hrs) Referrals to facial surgeons; brochures about operations.

GAYS & LESBIANS Nat'l Gay & Lesbian Hotline 800-347-TEEN (Thurs-Sun, 7pm-11:45pm EST) Support & counseling for gay & lesbian teenagers.

HEALTH NORD 800-999-6673 (day) Info & networking for persons with rare disorders; literature ◆ NIS 800-922-9234 (Voice/TDD) (day) I&R for parents of infants with disabilities/life-threatening illnesses; support groups, education, treatments, community services, financial aid, advocacy, adoption services ◆ Nat'l Health Info Ctr 800-336-4797 I&R to support groups, prof. societies, government agencies, publications ◆ Nat'l Info. Ctr. for Orphan Drugs & Rare Diseases 800-456-3505 (day) Referrals to support groups, health centers; services for orphan drugs

HEADACHE Nat'l Headache Fdn 800-843-2256 (day) I&R re chronic, recurrent headaches, seminars, research, newsletter, info on diets, biofeedback; brochures

HOSPITAL Shriner's Hosp 800-237-5055 (day) Info on free hospital care available to children under the age of 18 needing orthopedic care or burn treatment ◆ Hill Burton Hotline 800-638-0742 (24 hrs) Info re: free hospital care for low income; medical centers

HOSPICE Hospice Link 800-331-1620 (day) I&R re hospice programs & care ◆ Children's Hospice Int'l 800-24-CHILD (day) Refers to hospices & specialists, literature

KIDNEY Amer Kidney Fund 800-638-8299 (day) Info, brochures & financial assistance for persons with kidney disease.

LITERACY Nat'l Literacy Hotline 800-228-8813 (mornings) I&R to literacy programs for both volunteers & people needing services.

LUPUS T Gotthelf Lupus Research Inst 800-82-LUPUS (day) Info on lupus research; provides lists of treatment centers.

MARROW TRANSPLANTS Nat'l Marrow Donor Program 800-654-1247 (day) I&R re becoming a marrow donor, data bank of available tissue-typed marrow donors nationwide.

MENTAL HEALTH Nat'l Clrnghs Family Support/Children's Mental Health 800-628-1696 (24 hrs) I&R

MILITARY Nat'l Info. System for Vietnam Vets & Their Children 800-922-9234 ext. 401 (day) I&R for vet's children w/special needs & their families; Agent Orange, outreach services

MISSING CHILDREN Vanished Children 800-VANISHED (24 hrs) Helps victims; conducts investigations; training & materials, registry; counselors; listening ♦ Child Find 800-426-5678 (day) Helps locate children; helps lost children ♦ 800-A WAY OUT (24 hours) Info for parents who have abducted their children in violation of a court order ♦ Nat'l Ctr. for Missing & Exploited Children 800-843-5678 Info re: missing/exploited youth; helps locate missing children

MULTIPLE SCLEROSIS Fnd 800-441-7055 (day) Support; grants for research, I&R on traditional/alternative treatments; phone support, newsletter

ORGAN DONATION Living Bank 800-528-2971 (24 hrs) Nat'l organ registry & referral service ♦ Organ Donor Hotline 800-24-DONOR (24 hrs) Waiting lists of transfer recipients, info on organ donations.

PARKINSON'S Nat'l Parkinson's Fdn. 800-327-4545 (day) Professional will answer any question

PRE-MENSTRUAL SYNDROME PMS Access 800-222-4PMS; 800-558-7046 (day) I&R

PREGNANCY Hotline 800-238-4269 (24 hrs) Info & counseling to pregnant women, referrals to free pregnancy test facilities, foster & adoption centers.

PRIMARY IMMUNE DEFICIENCY J. Modell Fd 800-JEFF-844 I&R to major medical centers, psychiatric & social support services; info on insurance reimbursement.

PROSTATE Info 800-543-9632 (day) Info & treatment alternatives

REHABILITATION Nat'l Rehab Info. Ctr. 800-34-NARIC (day) Resource/research center for rehab; I&R

RESPIRATORY Nat'l Jewish Lung Line 800-222-LUNG (day) I&R. Info on lung diseases (asthma, allergies) & immune disorders (lupus); referrals to doctors, literature. ♦ Asthma & Allergy Ref Line 800-822-2762 (24 hrs) Pamphlets on asthma/allergies; doctors

RUNAWAYS Runaway Hotline 800-231-6946 (24 hrs) I&R, message relay ♦ Nat'l Runaway & Suicide Hotline 800-621-4000 (24 hrs) I&R re: shelter, counseling, food, transportation, suicide/crisis counseling ♦ Nat'l Runaway Hotline 800-HIT-HOME (24 hrs) Crisis counseling, I&R for runaways/youth w/other problems

SENIOR CITIZENS Eldercare Locator 800-677-1116 (day) Info for families & friends; re insurance, medicaid, taxes, respite care, etc.

SEXUALLY TRANSMITTED DISEASE Nat'l STD Hotline 800-227-8922 (day/eve) Education, research; info on yeast, chancroid, herpes, genital warts, syphilis, gonorrhea; free pamphlets.

SOCIAL SECURITY 800-772-1213 I&R

SPINAL CORD INJURY APA Hotline 800-526-3456 (24 hrs) I&R & support for patients/families ♦ Nat'l Coord. Council on Spinal Cord Injury 800-424-8200 (day) I&R, advocacy for disabled vets.

STUTTERING Stuttering Fnd of Amer 800-992-9392 I&R, phone support, conferences, referrals to speech pathologists.

SUDDEN INFANT DEATH SYNDROME Nat'l SIDS Fnd 800-638-7437 (24 hrs) I&R, research, comm. services, education ♦ Amer SIDS Inst 800-232-SIDS; (day) Education, support, clinical svc.

SUICIDE Nat'l Runaway & Suicide Hotline 800-621-4000 (24 hrs) I&R for runaways re: shelter, counseling; food pantries; transportation; suicide & crisis counseling.

TAX Federal Tax Info 800-829-1040 (day) Answers questions

TRAUMA Amer. Trauma Soc. 800-556-7890 (day) Referrals & educational materials on the prevention of traumas.

UROLOGIC DISEASE Amer Fdn for Urologic Disease Booklets: 800-242-2383; Info: 800-828-7866 (day)

YOUTH NineLine 800-999-9999 (24 hrs) Referrals for youth or parents re: drugs, homelessness, runaways, etc. Message relays, reports of abuse. Helps parents with problems with their kids. If all counselors are busy, stay on line & one will be with you as soon as possible.

RESOURCES FOR RARE DISORDERS

One of the most important organization that can be counted upon to be most helpful in providing information on what agencies, networks, and resources already exist for rare disorders is called **N.O.R.D. - National Organization for Rare Disorders, Inc.** Begun as an informal coalition of national voluntary health agencies, NORD now provides information (including computer-accessible database through CompuServe), referral, and advocacy for orphan illness research. Most importantly, NORD provides a "networking program" service, linking together persons or families with the same disorder. Write: P. 0. Box 8923, New Fairfield, CT 06812. Call 800-999-NORD or 203/746-6518,

National Information Center for Orphan Drugs and Rare Diseases of the National Health Information Clearinghouse, is another resource that responds to questions on rare disorders using the NHIC's computer database and library. Call 800-456-3505 (toll-free in U.S.). Or write: NICODARD, P.O. Box 1133, Washington, DC 20013-1133.

There are few times when the need for a mutual help group is felt more strongly than when you or your loved one is suddenly diagnosed with a rare illness or syndrome. Self-help groups or networks can help. The seeds for the development of many of today's health foundations and agencies dealing with rare illness historically have first taken the form of mutual aid self-help groups, as victims or their families first came together to share their common experiences and needs. With improved medical technology, research, and increased survival rates for previously terminal illnesses, this cycle continues today as we see more genetic, chronic or "orphan illnesses" being identified.

To meet the needs of an increasing portion of the population suffering from a rare condition or illness for which no self-help groups exist anywhere else, the American Self-Help Clearinghouse helps individuals who want to start new, first-of-their-kind, mutual aid networks. If you are interested in starting a mutual aid group or network for a particular problem for which no group currently exists, our Clearinghouse will help you explore the possibilities of mutual aid correspondence, telephone and/or home computer networks. If interested, write: **American Self-Help Clearinghouse**, St. Clares-Riverside Medical Center, 25 Pocono Rd., Denville, NJ 07834; or call 201/625-7101.

RESOURCES FOR GENETIC DISORDERS

Alliance of Genetic Support Groups is a partnership of self-help groups and professionals addressing communication, service delivery, and advocacy issues for member support groups that are composed of individuals and families affected by genetic disorders. The Alliance seeks to sponsor special projects and publishes a newsletter. Write: 1001 22nd St., Suite 800, NW, Washington, D.C. 20037, phone 800-336-GENE or 202/331-0942.

National Center for Education In Maternal & Child Health was formerly the National Clearinghouse for Human Genetic Diseases. They continue to provide information on genetic disorders and resources, and among the publications available from them is one focused upon how to start a self-help group for a genetic illness, Learning Together: A Guide for Families with Genetic Disorders. Write: 38th & R Streets, N.W., Washington, D.C. 20057, phone 202/625-8400.

March of Dimes Birth Defects Foundation provides information, and publications that deal with all types of birth defects, to include many genetic disorders. One of their publications is a Guide for Organizing Parent Support Group (limited supply). Write: 1275 Mamaroneck Ave., White Plains, NY 10605, phone 914/428-7100.

National Easter Seal Society publishes information on all types of physical disabilities, to include genetic disorders. Consider contacting them for a copy of their publication list. Write: 2023 West Ogden Avenue, Chicago, IL 60612, phone 312/243-8400.

"I believe in self-help as an effective way of dealing with problems, stress, hardship, and pain...Mending people, curing them is no longer enough; it is only part of the total care that most people require."

- former Surgeon General C. Everett Koop at his national Workshop on Self-Help and Public Health, 9/20/87

HOUSING AND NEIGHBORHOOD RESOURCES

ACORN is a non-profit network of 23 neighborhood development and housing organizations across the country run by and for low and moderate income people. Write: 739 8th Street, Washington, D.C. 20003, or call 202/547-9292 for information.

Community Information Exchange provides help to neighborhood groups in the form of housing and community development technical assistance. Newsletter. Computer Bulletin Board. Membership $50 for community organizations. Write: 1029 Vermont Avenue, N.W., Suite 710, Washington, D.C. 20005 or call 202/628-2981.

RESOURCES FOR THE HOMELESS

National Resource Center on Homelessness and Mental Health, Policy Research Associates - The Center provides a free packet on "Self-Help Programs for Persons Who Are Homeless & Mentally Ill" and other information. Write: 262 Delaware Ave., Delmar, N.Y. 12054. Call 800-444-7415 or 518/439-7415.

Homelessness Information Exchange - National non-profit service with information on model programs, research, funding sources, and technical advisors. Write: 1830 Connecticut Ave., N.W., Washington, D.C. 20009. Call 202/462-7551.

For families of the homeless or missing who are mentally ill, see Homeless and Missing Network in Families of the Mentally Ill category on page 106.

OTHER SELF-HELP RESOURCES

National Council on Self-Help & Public Health - The Council works to implement recommendations for the Surgeon General's Workshop on Self-Help and Public Health, which was held in 1987. The Council has developed a national network of researchers examining and working with self-help groups (see following entry). Write: 310 Maple Ave. W., #182, Vienna, VA 22180. Betsy Wilson, Chairperson.

Interest Group on Self-Help and Mutual Support. Part of the Society for Community Research and Action (Division 27), American Psychological Association. A network of different professionals who share information on research work/interest and action projects. For more information, write: Greg Meissen, Dept. of Psychology, Wichita State University, Wichita, KS 67208.

National Network for Mutual Help Centers (an association of self-help clearinghouses in the U.S.) Contact Toni Young, President, at Michigan Self-Help Clearinghouse, c/o Michigan Protection & Advocacy Svc., Inc., 106 W. Allegan #210, Lansing, MI 48933-1706.

International Network for Mutual Help Centers (an association of self-help clearinghouses in the U.S. and Canada). Contact Lori Dessau, Chairperson, 2 Mount Royal Ave., Hamilton, Ontario, Canada L8P 4H6; call 416/529-3480.

SHALL - The Self-Help ALLiance. The Self-Help Alliance is a developing national coalition of self-help groups with purposes of mutual support, education, and empowerment for self-help groups. For example, in coordination with the National Network for Mutual Help Centers, the Alliance is initially planning to use a portion of the Network's newsletter for self-help groups to share news, ideas, problems and insights. To aid in Alliance efforts, or for information, write to: Ms. Lee Miller, Apt. C-41, 68-37 Yellowstone Blvd, Forest Hills, NY 11375.

IDEAS AND CONSIDERATIONS
FOR STARTING A SELF-HELP MUTUAL AID GROUP

- Edward J. Madara

Self-help groups offer people who face a common problem the opportunity to meet with others and share their experiences, knowledge, strengths and hopes. Run by and for their members, self-help groups can better be described as "mutual help" groups.

Hundreds of these groups are started each week across the nation by ordinary people with a little bit of courage, a fair sense of commitment, and a heavy amount of caring. The following guidelines are based on our experience at the Self-Help Clearinghouse helping hundreds of individuals to start groups. While there is no one recipe for starting a group (different national groups offer different model approaches), we have listed below a few general considerations and strategies that you may find helpful.

1. Don't Re-invent the Wheel. If you are interested in starting a group around a particular concern or problem, learn from those who have done it before. Check with your local self-help clearinghouse or the helplines serving your area to find out about existing local groups. Use the Sourcebook to find any national offices or model groups that address your concern. Contact these existing groups by phone or mail. Ask for any "how-to" starter packet information they may have, or sample materials they have used, e.g. flyers, press releases, etc. If you do have a local self-help clearinghouse in your area, determine how they can help you in starting a group, e.g. materials, workshops, listing your interest in their newsletter, etc. Especially if you're trailblazing and developing a completely new type of self-help group, consider contacting or attending a few meetings of other self-help groups to get a feel for how they operate--then borrow or adapt what you consider their best techniques to use in your own group.

2. Think "Mutual-Help" From the Start. Find a few others who share your interest in starting (not simply joining) a self-help group. To do this, first distribute some flyers or letters that specifically cite your interest in hearing from those who would be interested in "joining with others to help start" such a group. Consider including your first name and phone number. Xerox copies and post them at places you feel most appropriate, e.g., library, community center, or post office. Mail copies to key people whom you think would know others like yourself. You can also have a notice published in your local newspaper or

church bulletin. When, hopefully, you receive a response, discuss with the caller what their interests are, share your vision of what you would like to see the group do, and finally ask if they would be willing to share the work with you for a specific period of time (e.g., eight months or so) to try to get the group off the ground. Suggest that the work could be greeting people at the door and introducing new members, bringing refreshments, making coffee, co-chairing or helping to run the meeting, etc. Once a couple of people have said yes, you have a "core group" or "steering committee" - and you won't have to do it alone. It's much easier to start a group if the work is shared. But most importantly, if several people are involved in the initial work at that first meeting (refreshments, publicity, name tags, greeting new people, etc.), they will model for newcomers what your self-help mutual aid group is all about--not one person doing it all, but truly a group effort shared by many members. If you don't involve others in leadership and work from the very beginning, you won't get them later. As one self-help group leader put it, "If you serve people breakfast in bed, they'll never learn to cook for themselves." Lastly, consider obtaining the help of any professionals who may be sensitive to your needs and willing to assist you in your efforts. They may be helpful in various ways, from providing needed referrals and information, to locating resources and providing suggestions.

3. Find a Suitable Meeting Place and Time. Try to obtain free meeting space at a local church, synagogue, library, community center, hospital or social service agency. If you anticipate a small group and feel comfortable with the idea, consider initial meetings in members' homes. Would evening or day meetings be better for members? Most prefer weeknights. It is also easier for people to remember the meeting time if it's a regular day of the week or month, like the second Thursday of the month, etc.

4. Publicize and Run Your First Public Meeting. Reaching potential members is usually not easy. Depending upon the problem area, consider where potential members go. Would they be seen by particular doctors or agencies? Contacting physicians, clergy or other professionals can be one approach to try. Flyers in post offices, community centers, hospitals, libraries is another. Free announcements in the community calendar sections of local newspapers can be especially fruitful. Consider simply calling the paper and asking to speak with an editor to suggest an article on the group and the issue. Editors are often grateful for the idea. The first meeting should be arranged so that there will be ample time for you to describe

your interest and work, while allowing others the opportunity to share their feelings and concerns. Do those attending agree that such a group is needed? Will they attend another meeting, helping out as needed? What needs do they have in common that the group could address? Based on group consensus, make plans for your next meeting.

5. Identify and Respond to the Felt Needs of Your Members. If your group is new and doesn't follow a set program for helping members help one another, always remember to plan your group's activities and goals based upon the expressed needs of your members. Share your vision. At the very first meeting, go "round-robin" permitting each member an opportunity to say what they would like to see the group do. Then discuss these needs and come to a consensus as to which ones you will address first. Don't make the same mistake that some professionals make in professionally run groups - of thinking that you know the members' needs without ever asking them. Remember to regularly ask your new members about their needs, and what they think the group might do to meet those needs. Similarly, be sure to avoid the pitfall of the core group members possibly becoming a clique. The welcoming of new people into the group is a process that continues well beyond welcoming them at the door.

6. Future Meetings. Other considerations for future meetings:

   A. Defining the purpose(s) of the group. Are they clear? You may want to add them to any flyer or brochure that you develop for the group. Some groups also include any guidelines that they have for their meetings right on their flyer or brochure.

   B. Membership. Who can attend meetings and who cannot? Do you want membership limited to those with the problem? An associate membership for spouses and family?

   C. Meeting format. What choice or combination of discussion time, education, business meeting, service planning, socializing, etc. best suits your group? What guidelines might you use to assure that discussions be non-judgmental, confidential and informative? Topics can be selected or guest speakers invited. A good discussion group size may be about 7 to 15. As your meeting grows larger, consider breaking down into smaller groups for discussion.

D. <u>Phone network</u>. Self-help groups should provide an atmosphere of caring, sharing and support for their members. Many groups encourage the exchange of telephone numbers or a telephone list to provide members with help over the phone when it is needed between meetings.

E. <u>Use of professionals</u>. Consider using professionals as speakers, advisors, consultants to your group, and as sources of continued referrals.

F. <u>Projects</u>. Begin with small projects, e.g. developing a flyer, obtaining newspaper coverage by calling editors, issuing a newsletter, etc. Rejoice and pat yourselves on the back when you succeed with these first projects. Then, if the group desires, work your way up to more difficult tasks and projects, e.g. planning a conference, advocating the introduction of specific legislation, etc.

G. <u>Sharing responsibilities and nurturing new leaders</u>. You will want to look for all the different, additional roles that people can play in helping other members and making the group work, e.g., group librarian, arranging for speakers, greeter of new members, group liaison with an agency, etc. In asking for volunteers, it's sometimes easier to first ask the group what specific tasks they think would be helpful. You'll come to know the special satisfaction and benefits of helping others. Remember to give all your members that same opportunity to help. By sharing responsibilities you help create opportunities for others to become key members and leaders in the group.

H. Expect your group to experience regular "ups and downs" in terms of attendance and enthusiasm. It's natural and to be expected. You may want to consider joining or forming a coalition or an association of leaders from the same or similar types of self-help groups, for your own periodic mutual support and for sharing program ideas and successes.

SOME SUGGESTIONS FOR LOCATING A MEETING SPACE

The most obvious place to have a small meeting, especially a first meeting of your core group, is in someone's home. If you expect more people than such a space can hold, or if you personally prefer not to open your home to people who are (initially) strangers, consider the possibilities listed below:

- Churches are the most common public meeting place for self-help groups. They seem the most cooperative. You and members of your core group can contact your local pastor, rabbi or priest to request a room for your meeting. The personal connection is the best, and could mean no charge initially. More and more churches have been requiring a minimal charge or donation to go towards heating and utilities.

- Community organizations or agencies such as Community Mental Health Centers, Red Cross, Salvation Army, Rotary, Lions, Kiwanis, or Senior Citizens centers will sometimes provide space free of charge for self-help group meetings. Again, does anyone in your group personally know a staff member or officer? Your local library or daycare centers and schools, bank, municipal town hall or community college are other facilities where self-help groups hold meetings.

- Hospitals are another option, especially if your group is health related. Contact the community relations department or the social services department to request a meeting space.

- Your local YMCA/YWCA also can provide meeting space for your group. Contact the community relations person at the "Y".

Availability of a kitchen or at least a sink with running water is desirable for making coffee or other refreshments. It is helpful to place chairs in a circle or around a table, or several tables pushed together. In this way, members may face each other and the atmosphere is friendlier and more supportive. A table can serve to display books, pamphlets, articles, announcements and other printed materials. A small amount of storage space can also be helpful for storing supplies, etc., if it could be made available.

When inquiring about a meeting place, be sure to communicate the fact that your group is a voluntary, non-profit organization that intends to provide a service to the public free of charge. Be clear on the specific nights that you would like your meetings to take place, how long they will be, and who will be responsible for opening and closing the facility. Such attention to detail will serve you and your group well!

SOME IDEAS FOR STRUCTURING YOUR GROUP MEETING

Meeting formats for self-help groups range from loosely structured discussion groups to more formally structured meetings. If you are not following the specific program of an established national group, the following may be helpful. These activities are common to some self-help group meetings and can be used as an initial guide for structuring your meeting. It is not necessary to incorporate every activity mentioned here in each meeting agenda.

1. Welcoming New Members: It is a practice of many self-help groups that a volunteer member greets and welcomes new members at the door when they arrive, introducing them to other members, especially those who have a similar situation.

2. Formal Opening of Meeting: At the agreed upon time, the meeting should be called to order by the host or chairperson. Some groups open their meetings with a welcoming statement, a formal statement of the group's purpose, and possibly more, e.g., a serenity prayer.

3. Introduction of Members: Going around the room, each member can introduce himself/herself and may state their reason for coming to the group. This is especially appropriate for new groups forming to help members get to know one another and learn about common concerns.

4. Discussion, Education, and Information Sharing: For newly formed groups, it is helpful to regularly ask members for suggestions on discussion topics that are of interest to them. Groups can also invite guest speakers to address issues. Tapes, books or articles can be reviewed and discussed. Time is allotted for sharing of personal experiences and helping each other.

5. Business/Planning Section: If included, this time could be set aside for any business the group wishes to take up, such as planning projects or activities, arranging for future meetings (choosing discussion topics/guest, speakers, etc.), making announcements, collection of dues or voluntary contributions.

6. Formal Closing: It is important that some signal be given to indicate that the meeting is formally closed, e.g., a closing statement or other ritual at the end of each meeting. Members are reminded of time and place of next meeting.

7. Refreshments are often served after some meetings, providing an important time for informal meeting and conversation.

SOME GUIDELINES FOR GROUP DISCUSSION

Self-help groups can be as formal or informal as their members wish. But some groups find discussion easier if there are some general guidelines to follow. Here are some examples to choose from. Guidelines can be included in the group's brochure, so that new members know from the outset what the ground rules are.

- We know what we share about our personal lives is confidential - what is said in the group stays in the group.

- We encourage members to share their strengths, skills, insights, successes, and their hopes.

- We encourage "I" statements, so that everyone speaks in the first person.

- It is important that we actively listen when someone is talking and avoid having side conversations.

- We try not to discuss persons who are not present.

- Each person has the right to take part in any discussion or not.

- We each share the responsibility for making the group work.

- Each member's right to anonymity is respected.

- The primary responsibility of the leader/facilitator, if there is one, is to ensure that the group is a "safe place" for its members to disclose their personal stories, fears, etc.

- It is recognized that the leader/facilitator, if there is one, is not the "expert".

- We, having benefitted from the help of others, recognize the need for offering our help to others in the group.

MORE IDEAS FOR RECRUITING GROUP MEMBERS

Here are some possible techniques for recruiting group members. Simply sit down with several group members to review and discuss these ideas. Select which ones will be tried and those persons who will be in charge of carrying each out.

- Draw-up and distribute a one page flyer on your group.

- Place notices in key posting areas: post offices churches, community centers, clubs, organizations, shops, hospitals, nursing homes, libraries, or doctors' offices.

- Publicize your group in a local newspaper by calling the editor and asking if they would be interested in doing a story on your group.

- Phone clergymen, doctors, agency directors, social workers, media, nurses, (i.e. anyone who might be sympathetic to your need), and ask them if they would make referrals.

- Talk to persons from similar self-help groups and ask what methods they found most helpful in recruiting group members.

- Contact local agencies, associations and foundations that address your concern. Ask if they would help.

- Call your local information and referral helpline/hotlines - make sure they have your group in their listings.

- Identify organizations that print community or social service directories, contact them and request your group be included.

- Write a brief notice to be placed in a church bulletin/newsletter. Consider other newsletters, YMCA, office on aging, etc.

- Write a "letter-to-the-editor" explaining the group's purpose.

- Write two sentences explaining how group is starting and where to call for information, and send it to local radio stations, requesting they air it as a community service announcement.

- Consider forming a professional advisory committee and enlist their help in publicizing your group.

- Establish a Speakers Bureau and offer to make presentations before community service organizations, agency staff meetings, church groups, and others.

POSSIBLE DISCUSSION QUESTIONS

While well established groups usually have developed structured exercises to help members share their experiences, strengths, hopes, coping skills, and practical information, other groups simply plan initial group discussions on the basis of their members' common needs and interests. Consider just surveying the members and have them select those <u>discussion topics</u> that interest them the most. Then members can take turns on different days to simply introduce a chosen topic by giving a brief summary of the issue and then introducing discussion questions. If they need to prepare, they can read up on the topic or ask other members about their experiences or perspectives. Topics could range from education to advocacy issues, but the most important point is that the topic be based on the needs of your members.

Discussion can also be based on <u>discussion questions</u>, determined by members beforehand. Here some suggested questions that can be used for a particular health problem or disability. They would need to be revised for other types of issues. Members may want to review them and select those they would like to schedule for a particular day. On the day or night of the discussion, individuals could go "round-robin." taking turns answering.

Remember that the purpose of asking these questions is to help individuals share, think about, and learn from each others' experiences and insights. There are no right or wrong answers, only answers reflecting the different personal experiences and views that people have in coping with the stresses and challenges. It's important that the group shouldn't be too large, to be sure to allow each person the opportunity to talk. If it is too large, consider breaking into smaller groups.

1. Who has been most supportive to me in helping me deal with this condition? What have they done or said that has helped me the most?

2. Who has been lease supportive? What have they done or said that has not helped?

3. What did I used to think about people who had this problem before I knew I had it? What's the most important point that the public should know about this that they don't know now? How can or should they best be taught?

4. How did I feel and react when I was first told that I (or another family member) had _____? How has my attitude changed with time and experience?

5. What was my family and friend's reaction to the news that I had
   _____? How did it differ from what I expected? From what
   I wanted?

6. How do people react to me when they learn that I have _____?
   Have I been able to shape people's reactions to me? How?

7. What would I say in a note or a letter to someone (or their
   spouse/family) who was facing what I have faced?

8. What is the worst problem that I must face as a result of this?

9. Who is the easiest person to talk to about this? Why? Who is
   the hardest person to talk to about this? Why?

10. If I am seeing a doctor, what could I tell him/her to better help
    me?

11. How do I deal with any stigma or discrimination that I have
    suffered, at work or elsewhere due to my condition.

12. What problems related specifically to _____ have I faced and
    overcome? What problems have I not succeeded in dealing
    with and why not?

13. Generally, how has my life changed? What new values and
    priorities do I have now that I did not have before?

14. In what ways does the life event or illness control my life? In
    what ways have I learned ways to regain control of my life?

15. For what in my life am I most grateful? What do I now like
    most about my life?

16. What long term goals have I set for my life? What is the major
    one and how do I plan to reach it?

17. If I have learned anything special about life or human nature
    as a result of my situation, what is it?

Other questions:

SOME HELP FOR THE HELPER:
A GUIDE FOR THE SELF-HELP GROUP CONTACT PERSON

by Barbara White and Pat de la Fuente

As a contact person, you are the essential link between someone in need and your self-help group. When a prospective member finally gets the courage to call, your response can make determine whether or not that person will come to a meeting. You will also be a crucial link to the public at large; your name and phone number will appear on your group's media announcements and flyers. Your responsibilities can seem overwhelming unless your have support--that's where this Guide comes in. Designed primarily for the new contact person, we hope this Guide will be useful to experienced contact people as well.

Some contact people with experience in self-help groups have already given us some good advice, which can be summed up as: "Know yourself." One group leader described the ideal contact person as "patient, compassionate, understanding." Another advised contacts to be "sensitive to other people's needs, but not so overly sensitive that you take their problems home with you." Other groups look for "a good listener - willing to listen to a 40-minute phone conversation;" "someone who knows when to share the load with others in the group;" "someone able to give full attention to a person in crisis." Chances are, if you and your group want you to be a contact person, you already have many of these qualities.

Most groups have found that callers are most comfortable talking with a contact person who shares their problem and is involved in the group. This is especially true of groups that deal with very sensitive issues such as incest, AIDS, child abuse, etc. In some instances it is much more comfortable for the caller to be offered the option of talking with someone of the same sex, age group, or with the same condition or experience, etc. It is advisable that contact people be veterans, which means they have had a good deal of experience dealing with their own situation, which places them in a much better position to be of help to others.

A few groups prefer a professional as the contact person, to determine whether the caller can be helped by the group or requires an alternative such as individual therapy. However, a new person often prefers to talk to someone who has "been there." If, after doing some soul-searching, you feel that you know yourself and the needs of your group, this guide may be able to help you.

SETTING UP A TELEPHONE SYSTEM

As always, the best advice is: Don't try to do it alone! Is there a way to rotate coverage of the phones? Can your flyers list two or more phone numbers? The phone company has a "call forwarding" service which, although expensive, may make it possible for several members to act as telephone contact people.

Answering Machines: Pros and Cons

Answering machines are great for taking messages when you are away. They can also give you the opportunity to return calls at your convenience, when you are not busy with personal matters and you have the emotional energy to respond to someone who needs support. If you do use an answering machine, the message should include:

- Your name and the name of your group.
- Date, time and place of the next meeting (updated regularly).
- Best time for you to return the call.
- Name & phone number of another contact person, if available.

Try not to crowd the message tape with too much information; it can confuse the caller. And make sure you call back promptly.

But answering machines do have their drawbacks. Some callers are not comfortable leaving messages on machines, especially when talking about personal matters. Picking up the phone to make the call may have taken tremendous courage, and callers may become frustrated and discouraged when they hear a recorded message. Nothing can replace a caring human voice and a listening ear.

Answering Service

Some groups, particularly large organizations with many chapters, employ an answering service or local hotline to be used as the main number for callers seeking information about their group. Although answering services can be efficient, and sometimes offer their services around the clock, they tend to be less personalized than contact people. They lack the firsthand experience with the group and the problem which helps people make the decision of whether or not they want to attend a meeting. Services can, however, offer the names and phone numbers of local members should someone want to talk. Answering services can be costly and they have limitations; however, they are an alternative for groups who receive a lot of calls.

RESPONSIBILITIES OF A CONTACT PERSON

One experienced contact person described responsibility as "the ability to respond." Your response to callers can include: listening to them; educating them about your group; encouraging them to come to group meetings; referring them to other resources.

Listening

Being a good listener is probably the most important quality of a contact person. Here are some ways to brush up on your skills:

1. **Compliment the courage of the caller.** As a self-help group contact person you are often the first person the caller has reached out to and asked for help. Many people find it exceedingly difficult to admit they need help with a problem. To go one step further and ask a stranger for help is clearly a courageous act. To support a caller who may be extremely anxious during this initial contact, it is helpful to compliment the person on having the courage to call.

2. **Use the caller's name frequently.** If the caller has given you a first name, remember it and use it frequently during the phone conversation. This helps communicate a sense of caring about the caller and gives the conversation a friendly tone.

3. **Be an active listener.** Most of us need a little time before we feel comfortable enough to talk about sensitive issues. Encourage callers to tell their story and express their concerns and feelings without interrupting or pressuring them to get to the point. Bear in mind that sometimes a caller's true concerns will come up later in the conversation.

4. **Clarify the person's problem or need.** During the course of the conversation, clarify the caller's problem and expectations. If your group is not likely to meet the caller's expectations let the person know and, if possible, refer them to a more appropriate resource.

5. **Be clear about your limitations.** Rather than present yourself as an "authority" on the issue, be yourself, another person who shares the caller's problem, and focus on sharing what has worked for you.

6. **Share some of your experience.** While sharing experiences is fundamental to self-help, during this initial contact, talk about your own situation only as it relates to the caller's experiences. Refrain from overwhelming callers with your problems.

7. **Follow through on promises.** The credibility of your group is at stake. If you make any promises (e.g. returning the call, sending literature, etc.), try to follow through as soon as possible. If you do not have the time, ask for some back-up from other group members.

Educating Callers About Your Group

You need to tell callers the purpose of your group and what it does and does not offer. Try to be as accurate as possible. Although you may be very enthusiastic about your group, too much enthusiasm during this initial contact, particularly regarding your group's philosophy or beliefs, can turn people away. Beware of overwhelming your caller.

Try to offer "cautious optimism." Often a caller believes that you and your group can "make it all better." You need to remind the person that recovery is an ongoing process which won't happen overnight (or ever), but you can also offer something positive, such as "Now you know that a support group exists, and we are here for you."

Callers will need factual information, such as the date, time and meeting place of your group. They may also have some basic questions such as:

1. What is the purpose of your group? - (e.g. Is the main focus educational; mutual support, social, advocacy)

2. What are the group members like? - (e.g. How many people attend meetings; number of males versus females; average age of members; how long do most members stay with the group)

3. Are the members' problems the same or similar to the caller's concerns? (e.g. How broad is the focus; has anyone experienced the same loss, medical treatment, illness, problem?)

4. How does the group work? (e.g. Does it follow a 12-step program; is it facilitated by a professional; how is it structured; does everyone have to talk; are there guest speakers?)

Encouraging Callers to Attend Group Meetings

Since people often get nervous at the prospect of attending a meeting with a group of strangers, your job as contact person is to lessen some of that anxiety and make it possible for them to take that next step. Some useful strategies include:

1. **Acknowledging the caller's concerns**. Letting a person know that most people feel nervous about coming to a first meeting can be reassuring to a caller. Offer to meet prospective members at the door of the meeting place a few minutes before the meeting begins to help them get acquainted. Just knowing that you will be greeted by a somewhat familiar person can help a person feel more comfortable.

2. **Describe a typical group meeting**. People tend to be more willing to approach new situations if they know what to expect. In describing a typical meeting, include general information and a description of how a meeting works. Reassure the caller that the group respects a person's decision not to participate in group discussions. This is particularly important for people who are anxious about talking in front of groups.

3. **Respect a caller's decision not to attend a meeting**. Let callers decide if and when they are ready to come to a meeting, and respect that decision. People who are initially hesitant sometimes need to give their situation a little more thought before they're ready to take that next step.

4. **Set limits on your availability to listen.** Since a group helps in ways that extend far beyond a phone call, keep in mind that your job is to help people take their next step toward helping themselves ... joining a mutual help group.

Handling Difficult Calls
and Helping Callers Through Difficult Situations

Experienced self-helpers understand that "difficult people" are actually just "people experiencing difficulty." These difficulties can be expressed in a variety of ways which may try your patience. Below are some suggestions for dealing with some of these other situations.

1. **Unwilling or "unready" to attend a meeting**. People dealing with a difficult situation may need to vent their anger and frustration during a contact call. After you have provided a caller with the opportunity to express feelings, the person may be ready to listen to suggestions and information about your group. But sometimes, after a lengthy talk or several phone calls, a person still may not wish to attend a meeting. At that point, you can say that you cannot provide any more help; emphasize that the group can offer more information and support than you can give over the phone. Don't be surprised if the person calls back later, relieved that someone finally listened, and is now ready to hear about a self-help group.

2. **Long Phone Calls**. If a caller starts to repeat previous statements or begins bringing up new information not relevant to support group issues, it's time to end the call. A useful technique for this situation is to let the caller know that you think what they are saying is important, so important that it should be saved for the whole group to hear. Another approach is to let the caller know that while you cannot stay on the phone any longer, you will be happy to pick up this discussion at the next group meeting.

3. **Phone Calls at Inconvenient Times.** If you do not use an answering machine, you may be plagued by inquiries at times when you are least able to focus attention on the caller. One way of dealing with this situation is to gently say "I only have a few minutes to talk right now - I'd be happy to call you back at a later time." If the caller sounds upset, the value of a backup contact person is that you can refer them to another resource. Acknowledge the caller's feelings and needs and offer them the alternative (e.g. "You sound upset and I understand your need to talk right now. Unfortunately, I was just leaving but let me give you a number of another person that may be able to talk with you now"). Always let a caller know that you are sorry that you cannot talk with them at the moment, but that you would be very happy to talk with them when you have the time to really listen. Be careful not to sound as if you do not care or won't make the time to listen or you may lose a prospective member. On the other hand, don't berate yourself for not being able to be available all the time.

4. **A Person in Crisis.** For most contact people, veterans and newcomers alike, the most difficult caller you may encounter is the person who is suicidal or experiencing an emotional crisis. The call is difficult for a number of reasons, not the least of which is the contact person's concern for "doing the right thing." Keep in mind that as a contact person, it is not your job to provide crisis intervention. Your major goal is to try to calm the caller down so that you can refer them to an appropriate resource or collect enough information (e.g. name and location) to get a local emergency team to the caller.

If faced with a crisis call here are some pointers:

- **Use a calm, reassuring voice**. A calm voice can help calm a distraught caller. Gently acknowledge their feelings, e.g., "You sound upset. Just take your time and we'll talk when you are ready" or "Why don't you take a couple of deep breaths to make you feel better." Let them know that it's all right that they are upset. Realize that it was probably very hard for them to call a stranger in their time of crisis, and they may even feel a little foolish. Helping the caller to feel more relaxed might enable them to explore with you other support networks they may have, such as family, clergy, mental health centers, or friends. You may ask, "Can you talk to a family member about this?" or "Have you considered professional help to get over this rough time?"

- **Be empathetic**. Let the caller know that you understand and care. Make an occasional "MmHmm" so that they know you are listening. Let them do most of the talking.

- **Make referrals**. If they are still in crisis, refer them to local emergency resources (i.e. mental health center, hospital emergency room, police department, or hotline). If a caller is in imminent danger of committing suicide, it is imperative that you try to find them professional help as quickly as possible.

- **Know your local resources**. This is not the time to go hunting for information. Always keep a current listing of local resources near your phone. It might be a good idea to call the local mental health centers, emergencies rooms and helpines beforehand to find out exactly what kind of services they provide, and how you can use them if you are ever faced with a crisis call.

- **Know your role and accept your limitations.** Many contact people participate in their group because they want to help other people. However, helping people to help themselves is not the same as rescuing. As a contact person, you are probably not trained in crisis intervention. You can listen to the person in crisis, and make referrals, but it is important to acknowledge your limitations to yourself.

- **Referring Callers to Other Resources.** As noted above, it is vital to have a list of local resources when dealing with someone in crisis. In addition, you will probably find it helpful to maintain an updated list of community resources such as physicians, social workers, home health aides, etc.

5. **Dealing with the Media**. If your group is large enough, you may be able to have someone else handle phone calls from the media (newspapers, radio and television), while you attend to prospective members. Keep in mind that publicity of any kind is likely to generate a large number of phone calls, and you

may be overwhelmed. Don't be afraid to ask other group members for help. It is your job to develop rapport with the media, your ability to discuss your issues clearly and enthusiastically will be a great asset to your group.

6. **Obscene Phone Calls.** The best way to handle an obscene phone call is to hang up. Many times the caller's sole purpose is to get a reaction. If you merely hang up instead of responding or listening, the caller may stop calling. If the caller persists, contact the phone company. Making an obscene call is against the law.

PREVENTING BURNOUT

Burnout is a serious problem with no easy solutions. However, you can work to organize your group so that no one is unduly stressed. Suggested strategies to prevent burnout include:

- Have more than one contact person and rotate the name of the first person listed on any publicity material. This will provide a more even distribution of calls among your contact people with no one serving as the "one and only."

- Use one telephone number to give out names of contact persons to call. These names can be changed every month or so. This way, many members share the responsibility throughout the year.

- Limit the contact person's length of service. If your group receives many phone calls, it can help to know that you will be rotated off duty after a certain amount of time. Just anticipating the "foreverness" of the duty can accelerate burnout.

- Develop structured guidelines. Some groups develop specific guidelines on how to handle certain situations or types of calls (e.g. talking with the media, handling inappropriate callers, how long to talk with a caller). This policy can relieve the contact of worrying too much about handling certain situations. Written guidelines also ensure continuity and consistency between contact persons and can serve as a training manual for members new to the job.

- Share with your group. As a final point, please keep in sight the fact that you are a member of a support group... people helping people. If you feel overburdened or if you are concerned about a particular call, share your feelings with the other members of your group. That's what it's all about.♦

SELF-HELP PHILOSOPHY

The goal of a self-help group is to empower its members with the tools necessary to make adjustments needed to continue a life of dignity and independence.

Self-help groups:

... share a common health concern.

... govern themselves and their agenda with success dependent on each member's feelings of ownership.

... may use professionals as resource persons but not as leaders.

... provide non-judgmental emotional support.

... gather and share accurate and specialized information.

... have membership that is fluid - newcomers are helped by veterans and become veterans who may outgrow the need for a group.

... have a cause and actively promote that cause.

... increase public awareness and knowledge by sharing their unique and relevant information.

... charge small or no dues for involvement.

... and typically struggle to survive.

Developed by the **International Polio Network**, 5100 Oakland Ave., #206, St. Louis, MO 63110. Reprinted with permission.

SOME ADDITIONAL "HOW-TO" GUIDES

As we have indicated earlier, the best how-to materials for starting a specific group are usually available from the national self-help group itself. But here are some additional "how-to start" references that may be of interest.

Hill, Karen (with update by Hector Balthazar). Helping You Helps Me: A Guide Book for Self-Help Groups, (for starting and maintaining groups), 1987, 88 pages. Order for $5 per copy from Canadian Council on Social Development, Attn: Publications; P.O. Box 3505, Station C; Ottawa, Ontario; Canada KIY 4GI.

Humm, Andy. How to Organize a Self-Help Group, 1979, 48 pages. Order for $8 from National Self-Help Clearinghouse, CUNY Graduate Center, 25 West 43rd St., New York, N.Y. 10036.

The Stroke Group Leader Manual is one of the best how-to manuals developed. While it is written primarily for starting a stroke group, it does a good job describing some of the basic issues and strategies involved in starting a self-help group for almost any illness. The 76-page manual costs $16.95, plus $3.50 postage/handling. Order from the Courage Stroke Network, 3915 Golden Valley Rd, Golden Valley, MN 55422.

Newman, Minna, Organizing & Maintaining Support Groups for Parents of Children with Chronic Illness & Handicapping Conditions, 102 pgs., 1986. One of the most comprehensive guides for running a group for parents of ill or disabled children, with sample documents. Order for $18.50 post-paid from Assn. for the Care of Children's Health, 7910 Woodmont Ave., #300, Bethesda, MD 20814.

B.& J. Overbeck, Starting & Running Support Groups, 1992, 31 pages (but quite concise). Order for $19.95 plus $2.50 postage/handling from TLC Group (publications for "transition, loss & change"), P.O. Box 28551, Dallas, Texas 75228.

DEVELOPING SELF-HELP GROUPS:
TEN SUGGESTED STEPS FOR PROFESSIONALS

- Edward J. Madara

Among the variety of roles that professionals play in support of self-help groups - which range from providing referrals, to being a guest speaker or serving as a group advisor - no role is more challenging and productive over the long term than that of helping to create a new self-help group. It appears that about one out of every three self-help groups is started with some help from a professional. By the very nature of his or her work and specialty, the professional is often in a favorable position to identify and link persons who have the potential to start a mutual help group.

For most professionals helping to start a self-help group, the task involves their assuming what very well may be a new type of professional role - that of a <u>consultant</u>, a consultant in group organization. The following serves as an overview of ten basic steps that the professional can follow in helping self-help groups organize. These are suggested guidelines that have proven helpful to many professionals. It represents one general approach. Actual group development and the sequence of steps may vary slightly, based upon choice of a particular self-help group model or other special circumstances, preferences or opportunities. The ten steps are to:

1. <u>Acquire a Basic Understanding of Self-Help Group Dynamics and Benefits</u>. The professional who contemplates starting a self-help group is probably already aware of the general needs for such a group (e.g., social support, experiential knowledge, normalization, shared coping skills, helper-therapy, positive role models, etc.) and has recognized the way in which the group could supplement professional services. The professional needs to familiarize him/herself with the basic understanding of self-help group dynamics, and how they differ from professionally-run therapy or support groups. For a better understanding as to how self -help groups operate as mutual help organizations, the professional can refer to readings on mutual help (see bibliographical section). An excellent way to learn is simply to attend a local group that has meetings open to professionals.

2. <u>Assess Current Groups and Models</u>. If you have determined that a need exists for a particular type of self-help group, check as to what national or model self-help groups may already exist for that problem. At the same time, you also want to confirm that there is no local chapter or similar group already existing

in your immediate area. A variety of these national and model self-help groups print development manuals or helpful "How to Start" guideline materials that you should obtain and review. To determine what groups may exist, consult the Sourcebook.

3. Identify Persons Interested in Starting a Group. Identify at least two former/current patients or clients who have experienced the problem, and who express an interest "in starting" a group. Simply having persons interested "in joining" a group is not sufficient. Ideally you will want to include "veterans" who have had greater experience at coping with the problem and are willing to help others. Some opportunities for locating potential group founders include: contacts with other professionals and agencies; announcements at the conclusion of educational programs or conferences on the topic; and registration of your specific group interest in starting a group with your local self-help clearinghouse if there is one. As potential core group members are identified, you will want to be sure they understand what a mutual-help group is, and what roles and strategies they might adopt in developing one. You may want to provide these individuals with a copy of the previous section on "Ideas and Considerations for Starting".

4. Form a Core Group. Once several persons have been identified, the next step is to have a preliminary meeting to organize these persons into a "core group." The professional will want to confirm their interest and emphasize that this is a "mutual help" effort to create a mutual help group. All members of the core group should be expected to contribute in some way to the development of the group by sharing in the work. They should make this commitment to one another, possibly for a specific period of time.

5. Clarify and Negotiate the Relationship. It is important at this preliminary meeting also to clarify the professional's role in relationship to the development of the group. The most appropriate role for the professional to assume at this stage is that of a consultant. A common pitfall for professionals is to continue at this time to play the traditional role of leader, which unfortunately promotes ongoing dependence on the professional, while also stifling the member's own sense of responsibility and ownership that spark the very energy and dynamics of most mutual help groups. The role of the consultant, the types of assistance available, and a time frame for providing consultation, should be explained and agreed upon with members of the core group. The consultation would focus primarily on group organization, but also might include assistance in resource identification, skills building, program

development, and collaboration in problem solving. As in the
case of any consultant, the professional provides advice and
counsel, but does not assume responsibility for actual
leadership, decision making or group tasks, unless the group
itself requests such assistance. Some groups refer to this ideal
professional role as being "on tap, not on top." The importance
of the members themselves taking responsibility for the group,
and the professional serving in an ancillary role, is key.

6. Advise on Planning & Publicizing First Public Meeting. With
the consultative relationship established, members of the core
group should turn their attention to their first project - the first
general meeting of the self-help group. Core group members
should share responsibilities for the meeting. This they can do
by sharing tasks such as serving as co-chairpersons, making
arrangements for the meeting space, serving as greeter, making
refreshments and coffee, etc. Shared responsibilities reduce
the high risk of "one leader burn-out" that is often faced when
only one person assumes the responsibilities.   More
importantly, at that first meeting core members will "model," by
their shared volunteer activities, what mutual help is - not one
person doing it all, but shared responsibilities and contributions
by members.   Core group members can begin work on
publicity, by letters to the editor, notices in church bulletins,
printing and distribution of flyers, etc. The professional can
assist in promoting referrals to this first meeting by contacts
with other key professionals, agencies and associations.

7. Assist at the First Meeting. A professional's participation in the
first meeting may vary from providing moral support to core
group members who are chairing the meeting to addressing
the group as a speaker, or possibly even being a co-leader if
necessary. The role should be minimal in order to allow the
group to exercise and develop its own group competencies.
Time should be allowed for all members to introduce
themselves and describe the needs they feel the group might
address. It will take several meetings of trust-building before
members take more initiative in contributing to group
discussion and work. At the close of the first meeting there
should be general consensus on the needs for a group and
agreement on a suitable site and time for a second meeting.
It is easier for people to remember future meeting times if it is
held on a particular day of the week or month, e. g., the
second Thursday of the month.

8. Advise on Plans for Subsequent Meetings and Continued
Organizational Development. The format for future meetings
should include a portion of time devoted to the "business" of

developing the organization, as well as to continuing discussion. Many groups include guest speakers, films, or special service projects as part of their educational program for members. For example, one service would be the establishment of an audio tape library of guest speaker presentations. Another would be development of a lending library of books and medical articles on the specific problem the group addresses. Future projects may include community education and visitation programs. The organizational structure for the group may be as formal or informal as members prefer, with or without elected officers and written bylaws. But general guidelines for group meetings and discussion, which the professional can help the group develop, are often helpful. The group itself may decide to establish several working committees, e.g., program, publicity, or study committees, to examine needs that were prioritized at the first meeting. Another helpful resource that the group can begin to develop is that of a professional advisory committee.

9. Identify & Address Any Special Problems. With any consultation there often is the need to "trouble-shoot" or address new problems as they arise. The professional, as a consultant, can be very helpful in advising the group of solutions to problems that they may encounter, e. g., handling a member who dominates discussion, or increasing membership through better publicity. Problem solving should usually be a collaborative effort with members. It is also important to note the responsibility for addressing these problems should continue to be focused on group competencies, rather than too quickly providing professional intervention at times critical to group development.

10. Review and Evaluate Role. At the conclusion of the consultation time period, an assessment of the consultation and a reassessment of the professional role should take place jointly between the consultant and consultee. If the group is operating without problems, the consultation may be terminated. At the request of the group, the professional may remain available on an ad hoc basis as a consultant. He or she may also assume a somewhat different role, such as a resource or agency liaison person who may or may not continue to attend meetings to answer questions related more to their expertise rather than group process issues. At other times the professional may be called upon to assume additional temporary roles, such as serving as a trainer in skills-building.

In summary, an important factor in the development of a viable and self-sustaining mutual help group is the need for the professional to assume a consultation role. This permits the group members to assume responsibilities for the operation of the organization, for exercising and developing group competencies, and for directly addressing the felt and unmet needs of its members. The extent to which members perceive the group as "their own" will directly determine the amount of responsibility they take for it and the amount of investment they make in it. The importance of self-help, as ultimately reflected in the members' ability to take responsibility for the group, is crucial to developing and realizing many of the unique benefits that self-help groups have to offer.

"Today, the benefits of mutual aid are experienced by millions of people who turn to others with a similar problem to attempt to deal with their isolation, powerlessness, alienation, and the awful feeling that nobody understands...The future of health care in these troubled times requires cooperation between organized medicine and self-help groups to achieve the best care for the lowest cost."

-Former Surgeon General C. Everett Koop, for the Forward of the book, Self-Help: Concepts and Applications, Charles Press, 1992, p. xviii.

BIBLIOGRAPHY

Most of the more appropriate books and references for better understanding mutual aid self-help groups can be obtained from the self-help group contacts listed in this directory. Their materials can often express the purpose and value of the group better than any textbook can. Here some references which, for the most part, examine self-help groups in general and are written primarily for a professional audience.

Self-Help: Concepts and Applications, edited by Alfred Katz, H.L. Hedrick, D.H. Isenberg, L.M. Thompson, T. Goodrich, & A.H. Kutsche, is an informative collection of over 30 perspectives on self-help group dynamics and professional interface. Several chapters examine the value of groups for conditions like AIDS, hearing loss, cancer, death of a child, lupus, and others. A number of presentations made at the 1989 "Symposium on the Impact of Life-Threatening Conditions: Self-Help Groups and Health Care Providers in Partnership" are included. There are several chapters that look at professional and self-help group relationships, including the first chapter on empowerment that provides an extensive and updated review of policy and partnership developments. For health care providers and others with an interest in the study of self-help groups, there are many insights to be gleaned. The book, published 1992, is available from Charles Press, P.O. Box 15715, Philadelphia, PA 19103 for $24.95 postpaid.

The Self-Help Resource Kit was prepared for professionals by Jani Cardinal and Professor Andy Farquharson of the School of Social Work, University of Victoria, P.O. Box 1700, Victoria, BC, Canada V8W-2Y2. The kit costs $75 for those in the U.S. and less in Canada. This is a collection of materials to guide the implementation of educational programs for "professionals to help their colleagues to become more effective in supporting the work of self-help groups." Using significant input from self-helpers, Cardinal and Farquharson have assembled materials suitable for a variety of educational applications, such as workshops, seminars or short courses to be given by professionals to other professionals. Dr. Farquharson has drawn on his extensive background in adult education to form the material as a coherent experiential program.

The Self-Help Way: Mutual Help and Health, by Jean-Marie Romeder with contributions from Hector Balthazar, Andrew Farquharson, and Francine Lavoie, gives an overview of the growth and development of the self-help groups, while probing the dynamics of "the self-help way." it provides a variety of views and insights that would be of interest to both the general public as well as professionals.), 1990, 158 pages, Canadian Council on Social Development, P.O. Box 3505, Station C; Ottawa, Ontario K14 4Gl, Canada.

The Recovery Resource Book, by Barbara Yoder, describes different self-help groups, agencies, books, and other resources dealing with various addictions & dependencies - providing samples of groups' materials, 1990, New York: Simon and Schuster, 314 pages.

Helping One Another: Self-Help Groups in a Changing World, by Dr. Alfred Katz and Dr. Eugene Bender, includes 22 chapters that provide different perspectives on self-help group approaches (e.g., for elder citizens, occupational stress, and ethnic minorities), on issues (professional relationships, self-help as a social movement, and history), and on countries (Yugoslavia, the Netherlands, and European movements). Printed 1990, 272 pages, costs $23.95 (including shipping) from Third Party Publishing, P.O. Box 13306, Montclair, Station, Oakland, CA 94661.

Working With Self-Help edited by Thomas Powell, includes 17 chapters written primarily for professionals that vary from a look at 12-Step programs to self-help and the Latino communities, from bereavement groups to parents of the mentally ill in Israel. Printed 1990, 338 pages, American Association of Social Workers, 7981 Eastern Avenue, Silver Spring, MD 20910.

The Surgeon General's Workshop on Self-Help and Public Health, printed by the U.S. Department of Health & Human Services, Public Health Service, (summary of presentations & recommendations), printed 1988, 60 pp. (copies available from the American Self-Help Clearinghouse for $1.80 mailing cost).

Self-Help Organizations and Professional Practice, by Thomas Powell, provides his analytical review of self-help organizations and relationships with professionals. Printed 1987, 366 pages, National Association of Social Workers, 7981 Eastern Avenue, Silver Spring, MD 20910.

The Self-Help Revolution, by Alan Gartner and Frank Reissman, (Series of 18 essays that review particular groups, professional interface and evaluation), 1984, 266 pages, Human Sciences Press, 72 Fifth Avenue, New York, N.Y. 10011.

Rediscovering Self-Help: Its Role in Social Care, edited by Diane Pancoast, P. Parker and C. Froland, 1983, SAGE Publications.

Helping People to Help Themselves: Self-Help and Prevention, edited by Leonard Borman, Leslie Borck, Robert Hess and Frank Pasquale, 1982, 129 pages, Haworth Press.

Mutual Help Groups: Organization & Development, by Phyllis R. Silverman (guide to starting groups, with attention to professional relationships and roles), 1980, 143 pages, SAGE Publications, P.O. Box 5024, Beverly Hills, CA 90212.

Self-Help Groups for Coping with Crisis, by Morton A. Lieberman & Leonard D. Borman (review of literature & research on groups), 1979, 462 pp., Jossey Bass Publishers, San Francisco, CA.

Self-Help in the Human Services, by Alan Gartner and Frank Reissman (reviews range, variety and principles of groups), 1977, Jossey Bass Publishers, San Francisco, CA.

Support Systems and Mutual Help: Interdisciplinary Explorations, edited by Gerald Caplan and Marie Killilea, (contains excellent chapter on literature review by Marie Killilea), 1976, 325 pages, Grune and Stratton, Inc.

The Strength in Us: Self-Help Groups in the Modern World, edited by Alfred H. Katz and Eugene I. Bender (history, typology, political aspects), 1976, 258 pages, New York: New Viewpoints Press.

"Clergy and Self-Help Groups: Practical and Promising Relationships" by E. Madara, and B.A. Peterson, The Journal of Pastoral Care, Vol. 41, No. 3, September, 1987, pp. 213-220.

"Hospitals and Self-Help Groups: Opportunity and Challenge" by E. Madara and W. D. Neigher, Health Progress, Vol. 67, No. 3, April, 1986, pp. 42-45.

"Introducing and Tapping Self-Help Mutual Aid Resources," by C.J. Paskert, and E. J. Madara, Health Education, (written for school personnel), Vol. 16, No. 4, Aug/Sept., 1985, pp. 25-29.

"The Self-Help Clearinghouse Operation: Tapping the Resource Development Potential of I & R Services," by E. Madara. Information and Referral: The Journal of the Alliance of Information and Referral Systems, (written primarily for I&R agencies) Vol. 12, No. 1, Summer, 1985, pp. 42-57.

"Self-Help and How We Teach Tomorrow" What's New in Home Economics, (written primarily for teachers), Vol. 17, No. 4, December, 1983, pp. 1 & 4.

MUTUAL HELP VIA YOUR PERSONAL COMPUTER

- Edward J. Madara

Every Wednesday and Sunday night, there is an open Alcoholics Anonymous meeting that people from across the country attend. A diabetes group meets Thursday evenings, and the closed incest survivors group is on Friday. Yet **those participating in these national meetings never leave their homes**. They may never ever see any of the participants. They are among the increasing number of people who are using their home computers to go beyond the bounds of traditional face-to-face communities to share common concerns, practical information, emotional support, and advocacy plans via electronic networks.

While it may at first seem inappropriate to describe a community by the means it uses to communicate, the computer networks are **electronic mutual aid communities** - unique entities with distinct advantages and disadvantages for building and providing community. While they lack some of the aspects of face-to-face groups, they do provide a sense of belonging and participation. The meetings are not cold or impersonal as some may think, i.e., people find friends, exchange home phone numbers, and worry if someone hasn't been heard from in a while.

While very much still in its infancy, computer telecommunication is providing special mutual help opportunities to **an ever increasing number of people - especially those persons who may otherwise have difficulty attending an actual face-to-face meeting**. These include persons with disabilities, as well as those in more rural areas, who can participate in message exchanges and actual "on-line" meetings. Those who are ill and unable to leave their beds have even participated, using laptop computers. Caregivers without respite services have benefited. But even groups like working parents, or lonely widowed persons in the middle of the night, report having found needed help and support.

There are several ways that individuals are creating and accessing these networks. Most of the "on-line" group meetings take place on **national commercial computer information networks**, like CompuServe, Genie or America OnLine. But an increasing amount of mutual help interactions take place by contacting local free Bulletin Board Systems (or BBS's as they are called).

Additional **advantages** of computer telecommunications include the time and expense saved that would otherwise be spent in traveling to either a distant group or even a national conference.

The medium is not as intrusive as a phone call, since one enters the system to receive messages only when desired, and is immediately advised of any waiting messages. There is also a tendency to be brief and to the point when typing responses. The need to type may constitute a major disability for those who do not know how to type. As Georgia Griffith, who happens to be deaf and blind, and runs the Wednesday night CompuServe conference on disability expresses it, "It's the many executives who cannot type who are disabled in this new world."

Some on-line groups envision greatly **increased advocacy potential** through computer telecommunications, e.g., diabetes self-help. "There aren't diabetes recovery groups as such," says Dave Groves, who runs the Diabetes Forum on CompuServe. A diabetic himself, Groves feels his forum provides practical and frank discussions, especially for those who are newly diagnosed. His experience has been that hospital-run group meetings are all too often fairly stern lectures that provide far too little attention to discussions of what it means to be a diabetic. But "if I could ever unite the 12 million diabetics in the U.S., we'd have a voting bloc that could really get things done."

Networking has often led to the early identification of new or growing health or social problems, as people began to recognize their similarities, and come together to form self-help groups. Many of the groups, in turn and with time, took the form of more formal health and social service organizations. Indeed, the seeds of many long-standing health foundations, societies, and agencies dealing with various health and social problems have historically first taken the form of mutual aid self-help groups or networks. These community support services were often created by individuals and/or families as they networked with one another and became aware of both their common needs and their abilities to help one another through group support and action. These small informal networks are often the first to provide support, information, skills sharing, education of professionals, and needed advocacy. The **increased personal use of computer networks will definately accelerate this networking process** and increase the development of new self-help organizations that provide needed support, education, and advocacy.

It is only a matter of time. More affordable computer equipment, and the subsequent integration and availability of home entertainment-information-telephone-TV-computer systems, telecommunications will enable many more people to participate in mutual help activities. It will do this by overcoming some of the traditional problems: lack of an existing local group to attend, lack of transportation or time available for travel, rarity of the condition, and most limitations of physical disability. It has already begun to revolutionize society, increasing the linkage of people, ideas, and concerns on national and international levels. **Better understanding and use of these empowering tools and networks can indeed accelerate the natural cycle of social change** - helping people network, organize, educate, and advocate for their needs more quickly.

Bulletin Board Systems (BBSs)

There are **hundreds of free BBSs** across the country that may be called almost 24 hours a day. Some are available with only a local call. While few BBSs have enough multiple phone lines to offer on-line conferencing with others, they do provide opportunities for message exchanges and access to database and program libraries. Essentially what people do is to leave or post messages, which they usually compose on their computers before they actually phone the BBS. Then others, who call the BBS, read those messages and type replies. So when you call back in a couple of days, you can check on any replies.

Here are just a few examples of the BBSs across the country, that can be checked out with a long distance phone call (preferably later at night or weekends when rates are their lowest): for disabilities, **Project Enable** in West Virginia at (304)766-7842 or the **ADA Net** in Alabama at (205)854-5863; the **Recovery Bulletin Board** in Virginia (703) 821-2925 which has a special focus on ACOA's (adult children of alcoholics), or the **Easy-Does-It Recovery BBS** in New Hampshire at (603) 228-0705; the **AIDS information BBSs** in the San Francisco area at (415)626-1246 and 863-9718; and the **OASIS BBS** for overeaters at (510)444-8246. Personal computer newspapers and magazines sometimes have listings of BBS'S. But by logging on to any of the above, or to any health related BBS, you can often copy or "download" any available file that contains listings of similar BBSs.

At the time of this printing (9/92), a very good **listing of over 300 health-related Bulletin Boards** (BBSs) is available for $5.00 and a legal size self-addressed envelope sent to: Ed Del Grosso, Apt. A-2, 29 Golfview Drive, Newark, Delaware 19702. If you already have your modem and telecommunications software, you can copy or download this listing of BBSs which is usually available on the menu of Ed Del Grosso's "**Black Bag BBS**" by calling his BBS in Delaware at (302) 731-1998.

With BBS's, it is very rare that you would be required to pay any type of registration or user fee, but there are a few that may ask. Almost all BBS's are run out of people's own homes. The person who runs a BBS is called a Systems Operator (or Sysop for short). Primarily what people do on a BBS is to scan, read and/or **post messages**. In order to save time on the phone, you can compose a message on your computer (often using your telecommunications software) before you actually phone the BBS to post it. Then others, who call that BBS, read your message and type replies. The next time that you call back that BBS, you will be advised if there are any replies to your original message.

After reading and posting messages, a second capability of a BBS is its **file or library sections** that can provide you with different text files or computer programs that you can either read or "download" (to download is to have your computer copy a file quickly, as opposed to your reading it). A third capability that is available with **only a few BBSs that have** multiple phone lines is **on-line conferencing**.

When you call a BBS for the first time, you will be asked to register by providing your name, address, a few other details, and selecting a password. You will also be asked a few questions about the type of computer you have and questions related to your computer. When using a BBS, you usually find that it is user friendly, that is, you are often shown a "menu" of possible commands. If you get lost or you're not sure what to do, you can usually type a question mark or the word "Help" and you will be provided with the possible commands or options. To exit off a BBS, you usually type "G" for goodbye or just "Bye".

Please understand that the messages and files of most BBSs are concerned with computer issues. That is why BBSs started, to help "techies" share information, ideas, and programs. While there are many BBS's, only a few at this time deal with health, mental health or recovery issues.

FidoNet BBS's

One of the most interesting types of BBSs are those that they carry **national Fido Net "echoes" or "conferences" focused upon special issues**. Such BBSs have several special issue sections or echoes that are **shared with an international network of other BBSs**. You post your message on one local BBS one day. Then later, in the wee hours of the night, that BBS computer will then send out your message through the Fidonet network to other BBSs that carry that same special issue echo. On the third day, you could be reading replies from anywhere across the country or the world.

Some of the existing national FidoNet specialty echoes or conferences include those for: AIDS, Alcoholism and Drug Abuse, Child Abuse, Diabetes, Disabled Interests, Grand Rounds Medical, Holistic Health, Nurses Network, Psychiatry, Overeaters, Social Services, Spinal Injury, Stroke/CVA, Visually Impaired, Deaf Users, Stress Management, and more. Ed Del Grosso's BBS listing, mentioned earlier, cites many Fidonet BBSs.

National Computer Information Systems

In addition to BBS's, there are the **larger commercial computer networks**, like CompuServe, GEnie, America OnLine, and Prodigy. There are similar systems that address specific social concerns, like PeaceNet and EcoNet. There are national non-profit systems too, like SeniorNet, or WID Net. All usually have a monthly maintenance fee and a prorated hourly charge.

These national systems have the capability for **on-line meetings**, i.e., usually people arrange a set time to meet and talk, e.g., deciding to meet at 9:30 PM Eastern time on a particular day. In actual on-line "meetings" or conferences, there is usually one facilitator who keeps track of the agenda and the discussion. People take turns typing in their comments. The facilitator actually has an easier time of keeping track of people's requests to speak (than he or she would in a non-visual telephone conference). For example, when someone wants to speak, they will first type an exclamation point (!), which is much like raising your hand to be recognized to speak. If they want only to ask a question of the current "speaker", they will type a question mark (?). The facilitator will recognize each person in turn. Depending upon which service you are using, you will learn the different commands that need to be used in conferencing.

While one is missing the nonverbal communication, some make up for that by using expressions, e.g. "<g>" following a sentence or phrase means "said with a grin." The more that you use the computer for telecommunications, the more you will learn about how people use it in different ways to express themselves

To contact our American or New Jersey Self-Help Clearinghouses on CompuServe, direct your mail to 70275, 1003. Clearinghouse staff answer requests for information on self-help groups in the GoodHealth Forum of CompuServe, within the Self-Help/Support section. Through CompuServe, the Clearinghouse has also assisted a number of groups to "meet", from persons with rare illnesses who were able to meet for the first time, to the first national computer meeting for agoraphobics.

Examples of CompuServe Message Sections & Conferences

We have included examples of some of both the message sections and current CompuServe conferences or "group meetings". Please note that sections and conferences are subject to change.

Health & Fitness Forum
Examples of Sections Available: Self-Help/Support, Addiction/Recovery, Mental Health, and Family Health.
On-line Conferences: **Alcoholics Anonymous** open meetings on Sunday and Wednesday evenings at 9:30PM Eastern; **Al-Anon** on Mondays, 9:30PM; **Overeaters Anonymous** on Tuesdays at 9:30PM; **Narcotics Anonymous** on Thursdays at 9:30PM.

Cancer Forum
Informal conferences every Tuesday and Saturday night, starting at 9:00pm EDT.

Human Sexuality Forum
Message sections: Problems of Parents, Online Relating, Shyness Workshop, Living With AIDS, Gay Alliance.
On-line conferences - closed meetings and sections (requiring prior screening): "I Was Abused" section for victims of sexual or emtional abuse, "Yes, I Can" for persons with physical disabilities, Women Only, and Men's Talk.

Issues Forum
Message Sections Available: Parenting, Adoption, Self-Help & Handicap, Native Americans, Masculist Issues, Village Elders, Ethics/Human Rights, and Lesbian/Gay Issues.
On-Line Conferences: Parenting Issues, Mondays at 10 p.m. EDT; Handicapped Issues, Wednesdays at 9:30 p.m. EDT.

Disabilities Forum
Weekly conferences and various disability message sections.

Work at Home Forum
May be especially helpful to some persons with disabilities.

Diabetes Forum
Conference Discussions on Thursday nights at 9:00 PM Eastern.

Military Forum, (was previously restricted just to veterans, started by Vietnam Veterans of America, but now open to all).

NORD Rare Disease Database
Maintained by the National Organization for Rare Disorders, the NORD Database that provides information on specific illnesses

regarding any or all of the following: General Discussion; Symptoms; Causes; Affected Population; Related Disorders; Standard Therapies; Investigational Therapies; Resources & Organizations; and References. While there is no message board sections, there are also newsletters, updates, immediate signup for their Networking Program, and a "feedback to NORD" section.

Information about CompuServe and other computer system subscriptions can be obtained from most retail computer stores.

Examples of Other National Computer Systems

The New Parents Network is a BBS that seeks to provide information on social services, support groups and government agencies that support parents. It also provides interaction among parents. Through its national NP Net, there are fourteen other BBS's across the country that carry the same bulletins, message forums, and files, e.g. (718) 402-1699 in Brooklyn, N.Y., or (510) 836-4717 in Oakland, CA. For more information, send a stamped self-addressed envelope to:

New Parents Network
P.O. Box 44226
Tucson, AZ 85733-4226

or call the main BBS direct via modem at (602) 326-9345.

World Institute on Disability's WID Net is actually an international electronic information service, accessible by local phone calls (e.g., in over 600 cities in the U.S.). Provides communication links between persons with disabilities, communities, and agencies. Has electronic conferencing, forums, file libraries, and searchable databases. Offers three plans, e.g., 20 hours per month for $20.00. For more information, write:

WID Net
World Institute on Disability
510 16th Street, First Floor
Oakland, CA 94612

or call (510)763-4100.

SeniorNet is a non-profit organization whose goal is "to create a community of computer-using older adults." In addition to access to its national online network, SeniorNet provides persons who are

55 or older with computer instruction at local sites in many areas of the U.S. and Canada. Some self-help group discussions are developing on SeniorNet. Registration is $25.00 and unlimited weekend and evening use is $9.95 per month. For more information, phone them at (415)750-5030, or write:

SeniorNet
399 Arguello Boulevard
San Francisco, CA 94118

National Association of People With Aids - NAPWA-Link
NAPWA-Link is a national computerized AIDS information bulletin board, run by this national self-help organization. On-line services include: key-word searchable information database, members' message exchange board, daily news from wire services, local resource listings, newsletters, AIDS and medical terminology glossary, drug interaction database, calendar of events, latest statistics, limited on-line conferencing, information on developing treatments, and confidential physician referrals. Non-membership cost of access is $65.00. NAPWA-Link subscribers must now call their Washington, D.C. modem number. For application, write:

National Association of People With Aids (NAPWA)
Attn: NAPWA-Link
1413 K Street, N.W., 10th Floor
Washington, D.C. 20005-3405

If you are interested in learning more about telecommunications, before purchasing any computer equipment, you should do some personal networking and explore the "electronic mutual help communities" through a friend or a friend-of-a-friend who already has the equipment and some basic knowledge, determining for yourself the benefits and the drawbacks.

There also are hundreds of **computer "user groups"** that meet face-to-face across the country to explore the uses of specific types of computers. A few of these mutual help "user groups" are developing to meet special needs, e.g., groups for parents of children with disabilities started by the PACER Center in Minneapolis, where "The real experts in this area are parents who have tried a variety of new things."'

Know of other national computer systems that do a good job of promoting mutual help or hosting group meetings? Please let us know.

KEYWORD INDEX